Dear Fri

It's a happy fact that more and more people are discovering the great change-of-pace pleasure of cooking and eating outdoors—in the backyard, on the terrace, by the shore, at a campsite, even afloat. Chances are that you're among this group. And why not? Nothing is more appetizing than the sight and aroma of food grilling over glowing coals. And no meal is more fun to prepare.

But from the letters we receive we know that many outdoor-cooking enthusiasts, both beginners and "old pros," face problems. "Why are my steaks always burned on the outside and uncooked in the middle?" "What should I pack for a two-day hike for three?" "Our boat has no galley to speak of, and I'm getting tired of serving sandwiches. Any suggestions?" "Can you help me plan something different for a barbecue party?"

And so we developed this book for those of you who have questions like these—and more. In it you will find helpful information for planning, preparing and presenting all kinds of outdoor meals; a whole section devoted to the ABC's of barbecuing; plus, of course, hundreds of recipes—for meats from the grill, rotisserie and smoker; for delicious vegetables, salads, breads and desserts. And every recipe has been tested on the patio of the Betty Crocker Kitchens and again by families in homes all across the country—your assurance of success.

We hope you'll turn to this book often. We're sure it will spark your imagination and make your hours of outdoor living—at home or away—more enjoyable.

Betty Crocker

Betty Crocker's
NEW OUTDOOR COOKBOOK

Illustrated by Frank Lacano

BANTAM BOOKS
TORONTO · NEW YORK · LONDON

*This low-priced Bantam Book
has been completely reset in a type face
designed for easy reading, and was printed
from new plates. It contains the complete
text of the original hard-cover edition.*
NOT ONE WORD HAS BEEN OMITTED.

BETTY CROCKER'S NEW OUTDOOR COOKBOOK
*A Bantam Book / published by arrangement with
Western Publishing Company, Inc.*

PRINTING HISTORY
Golden Press edition published April 1967
2nd printing . . . . . . April 1971
3rd printing . . . . . . October 1972
4th printing . . . . . . April 1974
Bantam edition / June 1976

ISBN-553-02510-4

Published simultaneously in the United States and Canada

*Bantam Books are published by Bantam Books, Inc. Its trade-
mark, consisting of the words "Bantam Books" and the por-
trayal of a bantam, is registered in the United States Patent
Office and in other countries. Marca Registrada. Bantam
Books, Inc., 666 Fifth Avenue, New York, New York 10019.*

PRINTED IN THE UNITED STATES OF AMERICA

Contents

The Basics of Barbecuing — 1
  All About the Fire — 2
  Barbecue Equipment — 16
  Setting Out the Spread — 31

Barbecue Favorites — 33
  Sizzling from the Grill — 34
  Done to a Turn on the Rotisserie — 75
  Foods with a Smoky Flavor — 93
  Sauces and Marinades — 103
  Barbecue Go-withs — 114
  Patio Parties—with a Cross-country Flair — 169

On-the-go Cooking—Near and Far — 191
  Breakfasts and Brunches — 192
  For Picnic Time — 197
  Cooking Afloat — 207
  Family Camp-outs — 214
  Packtrips — 240

Home Is the Hunter — 247

Index — 263

The
Basics
of
Barbecuing

All About the Fire

There's something irresistibly challenging, especially to men, about cooking a meal outside over the glowing coals of a barbecue fire. But like anything else worth crowing about, that barbecue fire takes some knowledgeable handling.

So, the first and most important rule of outdoor cookery is: Understand your fire. With the right fire, even with equipment as simple as a grid propped on bricks, you can gain local fame as a barbecue chef. With the wrong fire, even with the most elaborate and expensive gear, your efforts at the grill can be a dismal flop.

Working with the fire is a breeze once you know where to build it, how to build it (of the right size and with the right fuel), how to tell when it's ready and how to control it. And it doesn't take long to learn all of this.

Just remember that in many ways the barbecue fire is a fickle creature. The temperature and humidity, the strength and direction of the wind, the amount of fuel and the way you arrange the coals all influence the fire's character and performance. It's no wonder, then, that every fire you kindle will behave differently, even when you use the same kind and amount of fuel in the same location. Only firsthand experience develops that second sense that produces consistent, reliable results.

Here are some basic guidelines for fire building and control that will give you a fast start as a master barbecuer:
• Read any directions or recommendations that come with your grill, and follow them.
• Before you start the fire, have at hand *all* the fuel you expect to use—and then some.

• If you find you have to add fuel to a well-established fire, add it at the edges; then, when it's well kindled, gently rake it into the other coals. (Fresh fuel added to the center of a fire will reduce heat rapidly.) Better yet, if you expect to use additional fuel—for instance, when you're cooking a roast for a long period of time—have a small brazier or hibachi of glowing coals ready and waiting at the side of your barbecue unit.

• Allow plenty of time for the fire to reach its proper cooking temperature. Figure on half an hour to 45 minutes for charcoal briquets.

• Once your fire is well under way, disturb it as little as possible. Constant poking and raking breaks up pockets of heat and lowers the temperature of the fire. Knocking the grey ash off briquets will raise the temperature.

Where to Build the Fire

Flavor the food, not your friends. All fires give off some smoke—in fact, smoke is an inevitable part of cooking outdoors. In the backyard, in the woods or at the shore, locate your fire in a spot where any breeze will blow smoke away from, not toward, the eating area. And always build the fire at a safe distance from shrubs, trees or dry grass.

If you're cooking over a stationary fireplace, set up the tables farther from the grill than you think really necessary and avoid the possibility of sitting down to a meal in smoke-filled air. If you have a movable unit, simply change its location—several times, if necessary.

A Foundation for the Fire

No matter what type of barbecue equipment you have, always read any instructions that come with it. Some manufacturers recommend one method of fire-building over another, and some methods are unique for a particular unit. The manufacturer knows what's best for his product.

For any relatively simple grill, a lining of heavy-duty aluminum foil—shiny side up—protects the firebox and allows for the neat handling of aftermath ashes. The foil also reflects the heat from the coals up to the food on the grid.

Some manufacturers suggest the use of commercial gravel-like material to line the firebox and protect it from the intense heat of the coals, but *dry* pea gravel will serve this purpose just as well. (Like any wet rock, a moisture-soaked piece of gravel can explode when heated.)

This material will also absorb dripping fats and juices to some degree and keep them from running into the hot coals. And when starting a fire in a brazier that has no draft door, the gravel builds up the level of the firebed and allows some air to feed in under the charcoal.

After several grillings, the liner will be full of greasy drippings; replace it.

Fuel for the Fire

Charcoal is far and away the most popular form of outdoor-cooking fuel used today. It comes in compact units, and it's easy to store, transport and use. Furthermore, it produces a bed of bright coals more quickly and reliably than wood—and without the hazard of flying sparks!

Charcoal is sold in lumps and compressed in briquets, briquets being the more popular form. Although charcoal lumps ignite and reach grilling heat faster than the more compact briquets, they also burn out faster. However, they are useful when a fire of brief duration is needed. Briquets maintain a more reliable, consistent heat for a longer period of time. They are excellent for foods of all types and sizes.

But briquets vary in their performance. Some brands kindle more slowly than others. Some, such as those made from fruit pits, produce more heat than do those made from woods. Some impart a flavor to the food.

The most reliable briquets—the type used to test the recipes in this book—are those made from hardwoods. But personal tastes and outdoor cooking plans do differ. Experiment with several brands to find the one that gives you the most dependable results. Then stick with it.

A few trial runs at the grill will almost inevitably teach you that you need less fuel than you imagine. Too many cooks new to open fire techniques cover the entire firebox with briquets heaped three deep, creating a fire that is far too hot. What's more, it will burn on and on, well into the evening. On the other hand, nothing is more defeating than a stingy fire that leaves part of the food underdone. If in doubt, use a few more briquets. You won't be wasting them. After charcoal (in any form) has been doused to extinguish the fire, it can be reused later, when it has had time to dry *thoroughly*. (Store charcoal in a dry place to protect it from the moisture in the air.)

Put safety first. Use charcoal briquets in a well-ventilated spot. They give off carbon monoxide as they burn. Outdoors, there is no danger at all. But if you want to try your hibachi in the fireplace, make *sure* the fireplace has a good draft.

Wood, of course, is the classic fuel of the rugged camper. Even today it is still favored by some for fireplace barbecues, and especially by those lucky enough to have a smoke oven.

Hardwoods, such as oak, hickory, ash, maple, and fruitwoods, are best for grilling. They produce hot, long-burning coals and give off an even heat. Soft woods are strictly for kindling. They burn away too quickly to produce a bed of evenly glowing coals.

Avoid resinous woods. Pine leaves a strong turpentine taste in your food. Cedar, fir and spruce add a biting flavor. And eucalyptus smoke, though it has a lovely aroma, will make your outdoor dinner taste like cough drops.

A wood fire is not made by a random pile of wood. Sticks of kindling are arranged over the tinder (usually crumpled paper) to form a tepee. This shape allows air to get in and feed the fire. Once the sticks are burning, keep adding larger pieces of hardwood until you have a fire of the right size. Always wait until the last pieces are burning well before you add more wood. (See page 216 for some typical wood cooking fires.)

Starting the Fire

Before you begin building your fire consider the fact that all fires need a draft to get under way and to keep burning. If your brazier has a shallow firebowl, the normal flow of light breeze will provide enough draft —though briquets will kindle much more rapidly if there is a draft door you can open in the bottom of the unit. Even the tepee shape used for building a wood fire leaves spaces for the air to enter and feed the flames.

Charcoal fires are especially easy to start. In fact, self-starting briquets are now available; all you do is place a package in the firebox and put a match to it. Fuel packaged in this way is particularly good for picnic and camping grill-outs—it's so easy to pack.

Charcoal lumps or sticks will ignite quickly enough if placed in a tepee shape over a kindling of crumpled balls of paper and a few dry thin sticks. But this method is slow for briquets, so most barbecuers speed up the kindling process by using an electric or commercial fire starter. Whatever method you choose to use, and unless directed otherwise on the instructions accompanying the starter, charcoal is best piled in a pyramid shape for starting.

Liquid Starters—There are many safe liquid starters on the market, and they are particularly effective for briquets. There's really no excuse, then, for resorting to home brews. Kerosene will only leave a lingering flavor in the firebed. And a few unburned drops can add an unpleasant taste to your food. Never, under any circumstances, use gasoline for a starter. It's much too dangerous.

Be sure to follow all directions carefully. A *little* liquid starter usually goes a long way. Drizzle it on the pyramid slowly. You want it to soak into the fuel, not the firebox. Let it stand a few minutes; then light it in several places with a match. (When using any liquid starter, put the cap back on tightly and place the container a safe distance away before lighting the fire.)

Don't expect immediate results. Firmly resist the temptation to add more starter fluid. The coals will just sit there for awhile, cold and stubbornly black except for a few whitish-grey spots. These spots of ash mean the fire is on its way. In 10 or 15 minutes, you can begin to turn the briquets that have a good covering of ash; they will aid the others to catch on. In another 15 to 30 minutes, all the coals will have a red glow and a covering of grey. Only then should you spread them out to cover the cooking area.

Liquid starters offer you a chance to try some double-quick fire-starting tricks:

• Fill a metal container, perhaps a coffee can, with briquets. Cover them with liquid starter and let them soak for an hour or so. One or two will get a fire off to a fast start. Store the other soaked briquets in a tightly sealed can for future use.

• Remove both ends of a large tin can. Cut a few notches at one end to provide a draft. Place the can notched end down in the center of the firebox. Fill the can with briquets, pour on the starter fluid and light. When this "pilot" fire is burning brightly, remove the can carefully (with tongs) and add the rest of the briquets.

Electric Starters—If you have an electric outlet near your grill, this is the starter to use. It's neat and fast. Simply hold the starter by its handle and rest the heating element on or amid the briquets. Electricity brings the element to a high heat, and the heat is rapidly conducted to the fuel. Grey ash will start to build up in minutes. (Some covered rotisserie units come with built-in starter coils.)

Solid and Semisolid Starters—These compact, safe-to-travel fire starters are perfect for picnics and camping trips, too. No dangerous spills to worry about. Canned solid fuel is the most familiar of these starters, but flakes, cubes, sticks, jellies and foams are also available. They're all effective.

Kindling—A few brittle twigs and small hardwood sticks set tepee-fashion over crumpled newspaper or birch bark is the classic beginning for a wood fire. (They can also be used to start a briquet fire.) Simply light the tinder and the fire is off to a good start. Wait until the kindling is burning before adding the larger pieces of wood.

If no kindling is available, "Cape Cod logs" are a good substitute. Stack three sheets of newspaper and roll diagonally from one corner to the opposite one. Tie the resulting tight paper wand in a knot. Pile small pieces of wood (or briquets) over a couple of "logs." Add the remaining fuel when the first pieces are burning well.

See page 240 for more hints about starters for wood fires.

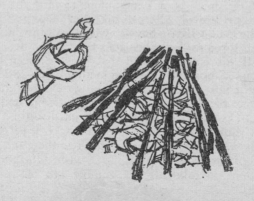

Is the Fire Ready?

No fire is ready until it is reduced to coals that glow with even color and smokeless heat. Leaping flames from a wood fire are not as powerful as they look; their heat dances away in the air. And food cooked over such a flame is scorched on the outside and barely warm inside. Briquets should have a completely ash-grey covering over their glowing, fully ignited hearts before food is placed over them. If some areas of black still show, the briquets are not quite ready for cooking.

Only when the coals are ready should they be arranged for cooking—usually under the cooking area for grilling, to the rear or around the edge of the firebox for rotisserie cooking, but always according to the manufacturer's directions. (See the diagrams at right.)

Even if the coals are right, the cooking temperature may be wrong. Use a grill thermometer on the grid or attached to the turnspit to determine the temperature of coals at food level, where it matters.

No thermometer? Use your hand—it's the gauge campfire cooks have used for years. To get a reading for grilling, hold your hand, palm toward the heat, near the grid level. (Be careful. Don't let your hand touch the grid.) If you have to withdraw your hand in less than three seconds, consider the coals hot (about 400°). If you can keep it at that level between three and four seconds, the coals are medium (about 350°). For low coals (about 300°), you should be able to keep your hand at grid level between four and five seconds. (For a good spit reading, you should be able to hold your hand at *spit* level four to five seconds.) Use the "one-second-one" or "one-thousand-one" method of counting seconds, if you wish. After all, you don't want to take all the gamble out of outdoor cooking.

If the temperature's right, put the food on. If it's too high or too low, simply adjust the heat. (See Controlling the Heat on page 12.) And check from time to time during the cooking period to see that the coals maintain the proper temperature.

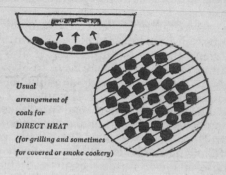

Usual
arrangement of
coals for
DIRECT HEAT
(for grilling and sometimes
for covered or smoke cookery)

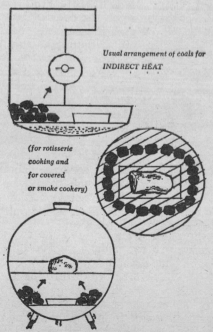

Usual arrangement of coals for
INDIRECT HEAT

(for rotisserie
cooking and
for covered
or smoke cookery)

Controlling the Heat

Bringing the fire to the right temperature—and keeping it there—is one of the most important steps in outdoor cooking. And it's at this point that experience really begins to tell.

The fire's temperature is affected by many elements, and they must all be taken into consideration. A brisk wind will cause the fire to burn faster; it also carries the heat away faster, so you may have to allow more cooking time. Temperature and humidity affect the fire. So do the dryness of the fuel and the size and shape of the fire itself. The barbecue "pro" takes these factors into account and controls the heat accordingly. Heat control does call for skill, but a little practice with the following methods will show you how you, too, can raise or lower the heat easily and efficiently. A watchword: Don't overdo it! If the fire's right, leave it alone.

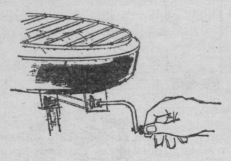

Change the cooking distance—All but the simplest of grills are equipped with grids or fireboxes that can be moved to adjust the space between the coals and the food. (Even an inch can make a marked difference in the amount of heat reaching the food.) The experienced chef who has learned to disturb his fire as little as possible usually uses this method of heat control. He raises or lowers the grid or firebox, or he pulls items toward or away from the hot center of the firebed.

Change the shape of the fire—A new shape means a quick change in heat. Separating the coals lowers the heat over the entire cooking area; raking them closer together or layering them raises the temperature immediately above them. This method is good if you want to cook one course over hot coals at one end of the grill and another course over medium or low coals at the other end of the grill. Always use long-handled tongs to handle hot coals.

Add or remove fuel—This method is especially useful when cooking for a long period of time or when coals are arranged in a specific manner, as in rotisserie cooking. Always add new fuel to the edge of the bed of coals; don't risk lowering the heat by putting cold fuel in the center.

Tap ash off the coals—Grey layers of ash form as briquets burn. Usually this ash flakes off by itself without affecting the overall temperature of the fire. However, if the ash building up on the briquets is gently knocked off without disturbing the shape of the fire, the heat will rise rapidly.

Adjust the dampers or draft doors—Open dampers to bring up the heat; partially close them to lower it. Opened wide, dampers get a fire off to a fast start; almost closed, they help to maintain the lower, steady heat needed for long cooking periods. These are an integral part of hibachis, covered units and most stationary fireplaces. Today, many relatively simple braziers have them, too.

Use windbreaks—Windbreaks shield the fire from wind and also reflect heat. Metal hoods and movable collars are built-in parts of many grills, but if yours is not so equipped, you can fashion your own windbreak. A strip of tin rigged to the side of the grill will do the job easily. A wide band of heavy-duty aluminum foil, held to the rim of the grill with metal clips, makes a good reflector, too—but don't expect it to withstand a very strong wind.

Controlling Drips and Flare-ups

Fats and juices that drip onto the hot coals in the firebox will often cause flare-ups. And these flare-ups, which cause meat to taste of burned fat, must be controlled.

Control starts before you begin cooking. Cut off most of the outside fat on steaks and chops before putting them on the grill. Leave a ½- to 1-inch space between briquets to help cut down on flare-ups. But when grilling kabobs, arrange the coals in parallel rows in the firebox. Stagger the skewers on the grid, right above the spaces between the briquet rows, so fats will not drip on the hot coals.

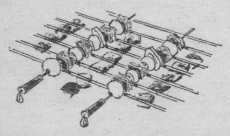

On a rotisserie, meats baste themselves as they revolve in front of the coals. Any dripping fats and juices must be collected in a drip pan set under the meat. The pan must be deep enough to keep the fats from running into the coals.

Certain types of grills have helpful built-in flare-up controls. With some, the grids can be tilted so that the fat drains into a cup; others are so constructed that the fat runs off at opposite sides of the grid, away from the bed of coals. With vertical grills, flare-ups are virtually impossible.

Many outdoor chefs find a water pistol useful for knocking out unwanted flames. Water bulbs, like those used for sprinkling clothes or potted plants, work well, too. Use water sparingly. Otherwise food may end up steamed instead of broiled and the heat of the coals may be lowered too much for good results.

All Done?

Don't let the still-burning coals go to waste; charcoal can be used again. Before you sit down to your outdoor feast, smother the fire. In a covered unit, just close the hood and dampers, top and bottom. If you have an uncovered grill, put the coals in a big pail and cover it tightly. For insurance, douse the coals with water. Later, spread them out to dry *thoroughly*. Or easier still, leave the coals in the firebox. Remove the grid and choke the fire by covering the coals with a metal cover, perhaps an ashcan lid.

Clean your grill after every cookout. The grid, if it was lightly greased, will probably wipe clean with newspaper or a damp cloth. Use a scouring brush only if you must. And then, before you put the unit away, give the grid a light veil of oil.

Barbecue Equipment

Every year more people are cooking more meals out of doors, and more kinds of equipment—from the simplest gadgets to the most sophisticated installations—are making it more fun and more foolproof. Hardware and department stores stock proliferating supplies of helpful gear for easy cooking and handsome serving. There are all kinds of grills at all prices, every sort of grill accessory and an endless variety of barbecue tools. And somewhere in this array the barbecue chef, novice or old hand, is bound to find the answer to his every need.

If you're new to outdoor cooking, be guided by basic needs and budget. If you're a fully equipped barbecuer, let your fancy take over.

Grills

Of course, the grill itself is the first and most important purchase you'll make for your outdoor cooking needs.

If you're in the market for your first grill, choose a relatively inexpensive mobile one, perhaps a compact grill or a simple brazier. Spend at least one or two summers experimenting with this unit before you lay the foundation for a brick and fieldstone stationary fireplace or move up to an expensive, dazzling cooking wagon with all the attachments. Move the small grill around in your yard. Find out if cooking in one location means filling the whole house with smoke. Find out which eating area is sheltered from blowing smoke. Most important, learn from experience whether you really like outdoor cooking as much as you think you will. Will you do as much of it as you hope to? Will your outdoor dining room be reserved for simple family meals or will you use it for entertaining, too?

This first grill need not be discarded or passed on to another fledgling barbecuer. Keep it to supplement the new grill—use it as a warmer for foil-wrapped breads or desserts, for keeping coals ready to be added to the firebed, for grilling appetizers or another course that might otherwise crowd the main grill. And if your "learning" grill is the folding type, it will come in handy for picnics and camping trips.

Following are some of the types of grills you'll want to consider. No matter what type you finally buy, follow the manufacturer's directions.

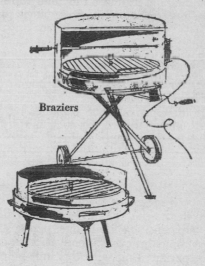

Braziers

Braziers are the most popular barbecue units on the market today, and you can choose from a wide variety. In its simplest form, a brazier is a shallow firebowl set on three or four legs. Many have adjustable grids and draft doors in the bottom of the firebowl—features which are a major advantage in controlling cooking heat. Some models have collars and half-hoods to shield the fire from wind, and some come with covers. More elaborate braziers boast electric rotisserie units, and wheels and stout handles for easy mobility.

Hibachis

These decorative firebowls from the Orient are often used on patios and porches. All have draft doors; many have adjustable grids. Hibachis come in several sizes, and the tiniest tabletop ones are especially nice for guests who like to grill their own appetizers. Traditionally, hibachis are made of cast iron, but today they are also available in aluminum.

Bucket Grills

Light and easily portable, bucket grills are about the size of large pails. They lend themselves particularly well to away-from-home cooking—the fuel, all ready to be lighted, can be safely transported right in the unit. Some have tops that can double as skillets.

Folding Grills

These simplest of all outdoor cooking units are small, grid-topped fireboxes supported by folding legs. Although folding grills are primarily used for turning out simple meals, experts have been known to team them up and produce feasts. Like all tabletop grills, they are light and easy to clean, transport and store.

Cooking Kettles

Cooking kettles often have been described as huge Dutch ovens on legs. They are made of heavy cast metal and have all-important dampers in both bowl and lid. Cooking kettles are relatively expensive, but they are adaptable to so many types of outdoor cooking that you'll find them well worth the price.

Cooking Wagons

The most elemental cooking wagon is a grill with an attached working surface. The really elegant ones have countless attachments and gadgets—built-in charcoal starters, warming ovens, full hoods, smoke chambers, motor-driven rotisseries and skewers; even cutting boards, storage drawers, towel and utensil racks and rubber tires. They are truly magnificent, but at last report they have not yet been programmed to cook by themselves.

Stationary Barbecue Fireplaces

A permanent fireplace of brick or brick and fieldstone can be an attractive addition to many backyards. Take a heartfelt word of advice: Plan the design and location of your fireplace carefully. Remember, it is a permanent structure, and it may be a permanent white elephant if it is so placed that it smokes you or your neighbors out of house and garden. As a matter of fact, stationary fireplaces are not nearly as common as they once were because so many people have found the movable units more practical.

Gas Grills

Gas grills are familiar appliances in many modern kitchens; now these new-fashioned grills are becoming very popular for year-round outdoor cooking as well. The gas can be piped in underground to a stationary unit, or you can have a mobile grill with a portable gas tank. Like all grills, they can be simple or elaborate. In some, the gas is fed in under a bed of ceramic briquets; in others, it is supplied to infra-red units in the lid. Fast starting and quick control of heat are among the main advantages of the gas grill.

Other Noteworthy Grills

New grills or new variations of standard grills appear every year. Some are frankly gimmicky; some are intended for a limited type of cooking; others are widely adaptable. You might be interested in investigating some of these: smoke ovens and various versions of the Chinese smoker, frypan-style grills, vertical grills and paper-fueled cookers.

Valuable Small Equipment

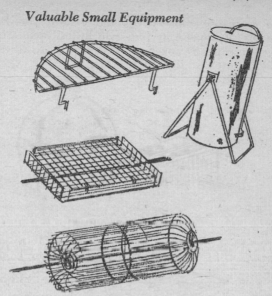

The number and variety of grill attachments and barbecue tools is constantly growing. Remember: An item that one barbecuer considers useless may be another's indispensable helper. Much depends on your grill (how it is equipped and how it can be supplemented), your pocketbook and your cooking needs.

Which of the following items would be just right for your barbecue plans? Which would be a perfect gift from the weekend houseguest? Attractive specialty holders for fish, frankfurters and hamburgers; a vegetable rack to fit around the grill, leaving the center of the grid free for the main course; a rib rack; an elevated half grid; a unique brace for poultry that fits around the bird and eliminates trussing; a basket rack for the rotisserie; a branding iron to mark steaks for rare, medium and well-done; whimsical asbestos mitts for the chef's hands; a storage unit for briquets; a protective covering for the grill.

It goes without saying that the majority of barbecuers can manage very successfully without any of the above-listed extras. The following aids, however, are more familiar items and are frequently used by outdoor chefs.

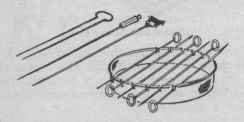

Skewers and Skewer Racks

Skewers range from long peeled green sticks to handsome rapierlike weapons with sterling silver handles. To be sure, the most practical skewers are made of steel. Some have little twists that provide a firm hold for the kabob ingredients; two-tined skewers also help to hold pieces of food securely. Chopsticks or pieces of bamboo make especially attractive skewers for rumaki or other Oriental-style appetizers. Before using these, sharpen one end for easy piercing and soak them thoroughly in water. Many elaborate barbecue units are equipped with motorized skewers at grilling level or as attachments to the rotisserie unit.

Although kabobs broil very nicely when placed directly on the grid, some cooks prefer to use simple non-mechanical skewer racks on the grid or even over the coals. Notches in these metal frames support the skewers. Since the food does not rest on the grid, there is less pressure on delicate pieces and the kabobs can be turned easily.

Tongs

The well-equipped outdoor cook should have two pairs of long-handled tongs: one for handling the coals and one for handling food. The long handles are "musts" for working over any kind of fire.

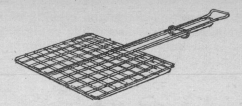

Hinged and Basket Grills

If your grill lacks an adjustable firebox or grid, you'll swear by these long-handled grills as a means of heat control, for changing the distance between the food and fire. And in case of flare-ups, simply snatch the grill away until the flare is under control.

Hinged grills can be adjusted to hold a thin slice of bread or expanded to accommodate a thick steak. They are invaluable for dealing with items such as frankfurters that need frequent turning and are bothersome to handle individually. Hinged grills are also useful for handling small or delicate foods that may slip through the regular grid or may break and fall into the fire when turned.

Deep enough to hold irregularly shaped foods such as chicken pieces, basket grills serve the same purpose as hinged grills. They are especially good for heating foods like French fried potatoes that need constant tossing and toasting.

Basting Brushes

Look for the special long-handled barbecue basters. It's nice to have brushes in several sizes: small ones for delicate kabobs and fish, large ones for big roasts. A good paintbrush with firmly attached bristles (not plastic) is a practical baster. A long-handled cotton or sponge dish mop makes a good dauber for large surfaces. The leafy green top of a celery stalk or a bunch of parsley firmly tied to a long stick also serve as dramatic basters. Discriminating barbecuers like to use bunches of fresh thyme, sage, marjoram or other herbs tied to a long stick for a basting tool with a built-in seasoning.

Grill and Meat Thermometers

A thermometer for the grid or spit rod will register the heat of the fire at meat level. This is the most accurate way for the cook to determine if the fire is ready or if he must raise or lower its heat.

A meat thermometer is even more useful in outdoor cooking than in indoor cooking since the charcoal fire is so variable. Your roast may look done on the outside, but only a meat thermometer will indicate the degree of doneness inside. There is even a special thermometer to use in a thick steak—a red light in its handle flashes when the steak is cooked to the degree preset on the dial. With this gadget, you won't lose a drop of juice by slitting and peeking to see if the meat's done.

Aluminum Foil

Experienced outdoor cooks consider aluminum foil to be second in importance as a tool only to a good sharp knife. There is almost no end to its uses. (See page 217 for ways to use foil at a campsite.) There are two points to remember about aluminum foil: heavy-duty foil is recommended as the most practical weight for outdoor cooking, and the shiny side of foil is the side that reflects heat—always keep it facing the food.

• Make a covered cooker out of a simple brazier by loosely tucking foil over the grid. (Leave some spaces for the air to get in to keep the fire going.) Or drape foil from a windbreak or half-hood to hold in heat and smoke.

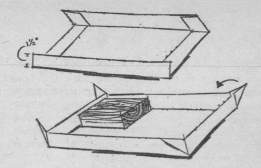

• Use a double thickness of heavy-duty foil to fashion a drip pan of just the right size—you'll want it to extend at least an inch beyond each end of a big roast. Grease and fold up foil about 1½ inches on all sides. Pinch the corners firmly against the sides of the pan—this keeps the collected drippings from trickling out.

• Line the bowl of the brazier with foil for extra reflected heat and for quick, neat handling of ashes.

• Secure a band of aluminum foil around the edge of the grill as a windbreak and for more reflected heat.

• Wrap cooked foods in foil to keep them warm.

• Mold foil into a keep-hot lid for a casserole, pot or pan.

• Foil is perhaps most famous as-a "utensil" for cooking foods on the grill or directly on the coals. A *well-sealed* foil packet acts like a steamer, and foods cook faster in it than if cooked unprotected over the same heat.

Place the food off-center on a double thickness of foil. (Don't be stingy. Tear off enough foil to cover the food completely.) Bring the long end of the foil up and over the food so all edges meet; seal the edges with two or three ½-inch folds. Don't pull the foil taut over the food; it's best to wrap foil packets loosely to allow for the expansion of steam. But be sure to pinch the folds tightly so the steam will be sealed in the package. Successful cooking in foil also calls for care in handling the package—don't puncture the foil during cooking and turning.

To open the foil packet, simply cut off the folded sides, or snip an X on the top of the packet and fold the ends back to make a cook-and-serve container.

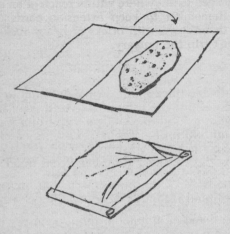

• Just for fun, make a spectacular serving cart by lining a wheelbarrow with foil. Let the edges, cut in points, scallops or fringes, fall over the sides. The wheelbarrow will look like a gigantic silver bowl. Fill it with cracked ice or ice cubes and wedge in glasses of iced tea, canned and bottled drinks, watermelon slices or cantaloupe halves. Wheel it around and let guests serve themselves. •

Electric Appliances

Many people find that charcoal-grilled meat tastes doubly delicious if all the accompanying courses are not permeated with the same smoky flavor. Use electric appliances to add this change-of-pace taste to an outdoor meal. You can cook in them right on the patio, in the garden or anywhere within reach of an electrical outlet. Remember to keep extension cords dry, and weight them down with bricks or heavy rocks so that they don't trip the unwary.

• Electric skillets are one of the most adaptable of cookers. They are superb for preparing pancakes, omelets, bacon, sausages and many other foods—they can even produce corn bread.

• A deep fat fryer is a helpful supplement to the charcoal grill. Corn fritters and French fried eggplant, zucchini, onion rings and parsley make excellent complements to barbecued meats and fish.

• An electric coffee maker—or two—is a blessing to the chef and his guests.

• Use your appliances as warmers, too. Many of the most successful backyard barbecues feature some foods prepared in advance and kept warm on the serving table in a big electric skillet or on a hot tray.

• As long as you're thinking electrically, why not bring out the electric knife? Use it for the fast, easy carving and slicing of roasts and steaks.

A Checklist of Tools for the Outdoor Chef

At least half the fun of cooking outdoors is lost if the chef is missing a needed tool and wastes time running to the kitchen or improvising. The most successful barbecuer assembles everything needed for cooking and serving in advance and then ignores the kitchen for the next few hours.

How many of the following items will you need to handle the fire and food for your outdoor dinner? Any others?

• Plenty of fuel

• A fire starter (and matches)

• A table or some type of work surface near the grill

• Water pistol or sprinkler for controlling flare-ups

• Pliers for adjusting holding forks

• Hinged or basket grills.

• Skewers

• Grill thermometer—for the grid or spit

• Meat thermometer

• Big serving spoons

• Cutting board for carving

• Carving knife and fork

• Paring knife

• Long-handled tongs (you'll need two, one for the coals and one for the food)

• Long-handled forks

• Basting brushes

• Long-handled pots, pans and skillets

• Work gloves for handling unlighted fuel

• Asbestos mitts or gloves for holding skewers, pots, tongs and other hot items

• Carry-all box of herbs and spices

• Pepper grinder and salt shaker

• Heavy-duty aluminum foil

• Paper towels

• A container of water and a sponge

• Damp towel for the chef's hands

• Covered garbage pail

Setting Out the Spread

There's no nicer finish to a fine summer's day than an outdoor cookout—for family or for friends. And like any other successful meal, the key to a bang-up barbecue is in its planning. Outline your menu in detail, right down to the salt and pepper. Then jot down a time schedule for food preparation so that everything will be ready for serving at the same time.

See that your outdoor dining room is adequately furnished. Use your patio table, and supplement it with card tables or TV trays, if necessary. Place chairs near any surface that can hold some of the "extras." Eating from a hot plate on the lap is no treat, and no one has yet invented a way to hold a glass, knife, fork, plate and napkin at the same time. Informality should not mean discomfort.

Set up a roomy working surface for outdoor cheffing. A cookout is no fun if the cook is constantly on the run to the kitchen for seasonings and tools. Collect all the items needed for cooking and serving—tongs, gloves, basting brush, cutting board—and set them out near the grill. A folding aluminum table makes a good work spot, but lacking one of these, you can keep everything handy in a big carton or picnic hamper. Keep your outdoor party out of doors.

Traditionally, casual buffet service is the best barbecue plan. Set up the table a reasonable distance from the grill and on it arrange the plates, main course, vegetables, salads, relishes, condiments, eating utensils, napkins and beverages. Keep hot foods hot in their foil wrappings or on warming trays. Keep bowls of salads and relishes cold by nesting them in larger bowls of cracked ice.

If you're having guests, leave a little something for them to do. You might invite them to grill their own

31

appetizers on a separate grill or on tabletop hibachis. But keep the company away from the main grill; the cook needs all the elbow room he can get.

Accord the chef the honor of serving the grill course, or courses. Arrange the buffet in the usual manner but stack the plates near the grill and let him serve the meat, right from the coals or cutting board. The guests then move on to the buffet to help themselves to the rest of the feast.

A buffet table is easy to set up. A picnic table would be perfect, but two or three card tables will do the job, too. Set pairs of adjacent legs in one small tin can to keep the tables from spreading apart and, if the tables are on the lawn, to keep them from sinking unevenly into the grass. Cover the table with a pretty cloth—fabric, paper or plastic.

It's perfectly all right to use your "indoor" linens, china and silver for any outdoor meal. But nearly everyone seems perfectly happy with gay paper napkins and paper or plastic plates with coordinated cups. Paper-plate holders are so handsome and sturdy that more and more people are using them, too. Barbecue-keyed knives, forks and spoons, with wooden or bone handles, are great to use if you have them.

And why not a few decorator touches? Deck napkin holders with real flowers. Use bright terry cloth hand towels as unusual but practical napkins for eat-with-the-hand items. Half-fill an outsized bucket or huge scooped-out watermelon with ice cubes and wedge in chilled canned or bottled drinks. Use the other half of the watermelon (also scooped out) as a flowerboat. Arrange fresh-cut flowers in low vases or glasses and put them in the watermelon. Fill in the empty spots and camouflage the glasses with greens.

Barbecue
Favorites

Sizzling from the Grill

Grilling is undoubtedly the quickest and easiest method of cooking over a charcoal or wood fire. But it looks so simple that many beginning barbecuers are deceived into thinking that the wonderful flavor of grilled foods comes from cooking over any flames and any kind of smoke. On the contrary, the tantalizing taste of charcoal-grilled food is the result of *controlled* charring of the exterior by smokeless, high heat.

"Controlled charring" is the key phrase. Look out for the flare-ups that burn meat—and then control them. Remember, it's fat dripping onto hot coals that causes the flare-ups. So steer clear of grilling meats like bacon which are very fatty. Trim the excess fat from all meats, especially pork and lamb. Stick to lean ground beef for burgers. Avoid cooking over coals that are raked closely together. A ½- to 1-inch space between briquets is ideal.

The actual techniques of grilling are both few and simple. To begin with, start with the right fire (see pages 2-15). Once the coals have reached the ash-grey stage, space them out in the firebox so that they cover an area slightly larger than that of the food on the grid. But make sure the temperature of the fire is correct. So keep an eye on the grill thermometer, or check the temperature with your hand from time to time.

Temperature Guide for Grilling		
Coals	Thermometer Registers	Hand Withdrawn
Low	about 300°	between 4 and 5 seconds
Medium	about 350°	between 3 and 4 seconds
Hot	about 400°	in less than 3 seconds

Of course, you must handle the grilled foods properly, too. Just about any meat that you can broil, panbroil or panfry in the kitchen can be grilled outdoors. Undoubtedly, steak is the most popular choice for barbecue fare. But easy as it is to grill, treat it with respect. Slash the outside fat at intervals to keep the edges from curling. (Do this with chops, too.) Use tongs to turn the steak. A fork puncture allows precious juices to escape. And salting draws out moisture, so season each side after it has been browned.

Chicken halves and pieces are also great for grilling. We grill them bone side down first as the bone helps to distribute heat throughout the meat.

But there's no reason in the world to limit yourself to these tried-and-true grill favorites. For a pleasant, and perhaps needed, change of pace, try your hand with another type of meat. Look over the chart below.

When cooking small or delicate foods, experienced outdoor chefs swear by long-handled hinged grills. They make turning a snap, and there's no danger of food falling into the fire. These grills are especially useful for handling fish.

Great for the Grill

Beef: steaks of all kinds; tenderloin; ground; cubed (for kabobs)

Pork and Ham: chops; tenderloin; steaks; Canadian-style bacon; canned ham; fully cooked ham slice; smoked pork shoulder butt; spareribs; back ribs (loin backs)

Lamb: chops; cubed (for kabobs); ground; shanks (tenderized)

Veal: steaks; chops; cutlets; cubed (for kabobs)

Miscellaneous Meats: frankfurters and other sausages; canned luncheon meats

Poultry: chicken halves, quarters, pieces; turkey pieces; Rock Cornish hen halves; duckling halves

Fish and Seafood: whole, fillets or steaks; whole lobster; lobster tails; shrimp; scallops; oysters

Beef

CHARCOAL-GRILLED STEAK

Choose 1-, 1½- or 2-inch-thick steak for best results. For each person, allow 1 pound of any steak with a bone, such as sirloin, porterhouse, club or T-bone; allow ½ pound of boneless cuts, such as tenderloin. For a small group, select individual steaks if your grill can accommodate all at once; if not order one large, thick steak so everyone can start eating together.

Trim excess fat from edge of steak; slash remaining fat at 2-inch intervals to prevent curling. Grill steak 4 inches from hot coals suggested time (see chart below). Handle steak with tongs (a fork releases juices). Season with salt and pepper after turning and after removing from grill. Test doneness by making a knife slit alongside bone. Serve steak piping hot topped with Blue Cheese Topping (below) or spread with Sesame Butter (below).

Grilling Time for Each Side		
1 inch thick	1½ inches thick	2 inches thick
Rare 4 to 5 minutes	7 to 8 minutes	12 to 13 minutes
Medium 7 to 8 minutes	10 to 12 minutes	15 to 17 minutes
Well Done 10 to 11 minutes	14 to 15 minutes	22 to 25 minutes

Blue Cheese Topping

Mix about 1 ounce blue cheese with about ¼ teaspoon Worcestershire sauce or bottled steak sauce.

Sesame Butter

Beat ¼ cup soft butter, 1 teaspoon Worcestershire sauce and ½ teaspoon garlic salt until fluffy. Stir in 1 tablespoon toasted sesame seed.

BEEF TENDERLOIN ROAST

Though expensive, this tender, juicy roast is solid meat and shrinks very little during its short cooking period.

Grill a 4-pound beef tenderloin 4 to 5 inches from medium coals. Cook 12 minutes on each side for rare, 15 to 17 minutes on each side for medium rare or 18 to 23 minutes on each side for medium, basting frequently with melted butter or margarine. Serve rare for best flavor and tenderness. *8 to 12 servings.*

STARTLING STEAK

3-pound beef arm steak, 1½ inches thick
Unseasoned instant meat tenderizer
1 can (4 ounces) dry mustard
1½ cups cornstarch
3 tablespoons salt
¾ cup water

Trim fat from meat. Sprinkle steak with tenderizer as directed on bottle. Mix mustard, cornstarch and salt thoroughly. Add water; stir until smooth (mixture will be stiff). Place steak in large shallow glass dish. Cover top and sides of steak completely with ⅔ of the mustard paste. Chill uncovered about 30 minutes, or until paste is firm. Turn steak carefully and cover second side with remaining paste; chill 30 minutes, or until paste is firm. Fill firebox with a double layer of coals, making coals as level as possible. When coals are very hot, use 2 large spatulas to place steak directly on coals, leaving enough hot coals on which to turn the steak. Cook 15 minutes on each side. Paste will be completely charred. Remove steak to board; remove outer crust. Cut meat across the grain into ¼-inch slices; serve immediately. Meat will be rare. *4 to 6 servings.*

STEAK WITH SAUCE LAFFITE

    1 can (12 ounces) beer
    ½ cup chili sauce
    ¼ cup salad oil
    2 tablespoons soy sauce
    1 tablespoon Dijon-style mustard
    ½ teaspoon red pepper sauce
    ⅛ teaspoon liquid smoke
    1 medium onion, coarsely chopped
    2 cloves garlic, crushed
    3-pound sirloin steak, 1½ to 2 inches thick
    1 teaspoon salt
    ½ teaspoon pepper

Mix all ingredients except steak, salt and pepper; simmer 30 minutes. Brush meat with hot sauce. Grill steak 4 inches from medium-hot coals 15 minutes on each side; baste frequently with sauce. Season with salt and pepper after turning and after removing from grill. Serve with remaining sauce. *8 servings.*

STEAK, BORDER STYLE

    2-pound round steak, ½ inch thick
    1 envelope (⅘ ounce) instant meat marinade
    ¼ cup catsup
    1 tablespoon Worcestershire sauce
    ⅛ teaspoon red pepper sauce
    1 can (15½ ounces) refried beans
    1 can (4 ounces) roasted and peeled green
    chili peppers

Score each side of steak ⅛ inch deep in diamond pattern. Prepare instant meat marinade as directed on envelope except—stir in catsup, Worcestershire sauce and pepper sauce. Marinate steak as directed on envelope. Heat beans in aluminum foil pan 15 to 20 minutes on side of grill. Grill steak 2 inches from hot coals 5 minutes on each side, brushing frequently with marinade mixture. Cut steak into serving pieces; top each serving with slice of chili pepper and large spoonful of beans. *6 servings.*

BARBECUED CHUCK ROAST

Select a 3- to 4-pound chuck roast, 2½ to 3 inches thick, of U.S. Choice grade. Prepare California Marinade (below). Place roast in shallow glass dish and pour marinade over roast. Cover dish with plastic wrap. Refrigerate 24 hours, turning meat frequently. Remove meat from marinade. Stir 2 tablespoons catsup into marinade; heat through on grill. Brush marinade on meat. Place roast on grill 4 inches from medium coals. Cook 1 to 1¼ hours or until tender, turning frequently and basting every 5 to 6 minutes with hot marinade. Serve roast rare in center, browned on the outside. *6 to 8 servings.*

California Marinade

  2 cloves garlic, crushed
¼ cup olive oil or salad oil
  1 teaspoon rosemary leaves, crushed
½ teaspoon dry mustard
  2 teaspoons soy sauce
¼ cup wine vinegar
¼ cup sherry or apple juice

Cook and stir garlic in oil; add rosemary, mustard and soy sauce. Remove from heat and stir in vinegar and sherry. *Makes about ¾ cup.*

GRILLED CUBE STEAKS

Place 6 cube steaks in shallow glass dish; pour California Marinade (above) over the meat. Cover dish with plastic wrap. Let stand 20 minutes. Remove meat from marinade. Place steaks in hinged grill. Cook 2 to 3 inches from hot coals 2 minutes on each side. Season and serve between slices of buttered toast. *6 servings.*

MINUTE STEAKS ON ONION ROLLS

Select 8 minute steaks, ¼ inch thick. Grill 2 inches from hot coals 4 to 5 minutes, turning once. Slice and butter lightly 8 onion rolls. Toast cut side down on grill 3 minutes. Spread with bottled blue cheese salad dressing. Season steaks with salt and pepper and serve on onion rolls. *8 servings.*

LONDON BROIL WITH ONIONS

1½ pounds flank steak
⅓ cup vinegar
⅓ cup salad oil
3 tablespoons brown sugar
3 tablespoons soy sauce
2 medium onions, sliced
1 clove garlic, crushed
½ teaspoon coarsely ground pepper

Place steak in shallow glass dish. Mix remaining ingredients; pour over steak. Cover dish with plastic wrap. Refrigerate at least 8 hours or overnight, turning steak occasionally. Remove steak and onions from marinade. Grill steak 2 inches from medium coals until medium rare, about 6 minutes on each side. At same time, cook and stir onions in aluminum foil pan or skillet on grill. To serve, cut meat diagonally across the grain into very thin slices; top with onions. *4 servings.*

Pork and Ham

GRILLED PORK CHOPS

For each serving, trim excess fat from 1- to 1½-inch-thick pork chop. Place on grill 4 inches from medium coals. Cook 60 to 70 minutes, turning every 15 minutes, or until meat is done—no pink in center. If desired, chops may be brushed with a glaze, such as Rainbow Glaze (page 106), after initial 30 minutes of grilling. Season with salt and pepper after removing from grill.

PEANUTTY PORK CHOPS

    1 cup croutons
    ½ cup finely chopped salted peanuts
    2 tablespoons instant minced onion
    2 tablespoons snipped parsley
    1 teaspoon crushed red chili pepper
    ⅓ cup butter or margarine, melted
    1 tablespoon water
    ¾ teaspoon salt
    8 loin or rib pork chops, 1¼ inches thick,
       with pockets
    1 teaspoon salt
    ¼ teaspoon pepper
    1 jar (10 ounces) apple jelly
    2 tablespoons lemon juice

Combine croutons, peanuts, onion, parsley and chili pepper in bowl. Stir together butter, water and ¾ teaspoon salt; pour over crouton mixture and toss gently. Trim excess fat from pork chops; sprinkle with 1 teaspoon salt and the pepper. Stuff crouton mixture in pockets; close opening with skewers. Heat jelly and lemon juice just to boiling, stirring constantly. Place chops on grill 4 inches from medium coals. Cook 1 hour, turning every 15 minutes, or until done—no pink in center. Baste with jelly sauce during last 30 minutes of cooking period. *8 servings.*

BARBECUED SPARERIBS

   4½ pounds spareribs
    3 cups water
   ½ cup soy sauce
  1½ tablespoons cornstarch
       Sweet and Sour Sauce or Texas Barbecue Sauce
       (below and right)

Place spareribs with water in large kettle; cover. Heat to boiling; boil 5 minutes. Remove spareribs from water; drain. Combine soy sauce and cornstarch. Place ribs in shallow glass dish; brush with soy-cornstarch mixture. Cover dish with plastic wrap; refrigerate 1 hour, turning meat occasionally. Grill bone side down 3 inches from medium coals 30 minutes. Turn and cook 30 to 40 minutes longer, turning and basting frequently with Sweet and Sour or Texas Barbecue Sauce. *4 to 6 servings.*

Sweet and Sour Sauce

    1 cup catsup
    1 cup water
   ¼ cup brown sugar (packed)
   ¼ cup vinegar
   ¼ cup Worcestershire sauce
    1 tablespoon celery seed
    1 teaspoon chili powder
    1 teaspoon salt
      Dash pepper
   ⅛ teaspoon red pepper sauce

Combine all ingredients in small saucepan. Heat to boiling. Baste spareribs during cooking period and use remaining sauce as a dip for barbecued spareribs. *Makes 2¾ cups.*

Texas Barbecue Sauce

1 cup tomato juice
½ cup water
¼ cup catsup
¼ cup vinegar
2 tablespoons Worcestershire sauce
2 tablespoons brown sugar
1 tablespoon paprika
1 teaspoon dry mustard
1 teaspoon salt
¼ teaspoon chili powder
⅛ teaspoon cayenne pepper

Combine all ingredients in small saucepan. Heat to boiling; simmer 15 minutes or until slightly thickened. *Makes 2¼ cups.*

SPUNKY SHOULDER SLICES

Prepare Spunky Spice Sauce (below). Cut ¾-inch-thick slices of smoked boneless pork shoulder butt. Place meat in shallow glass dish; pour sauce over meat. Cover dish with plastic wrap. Refrigerate at least 8 hours or overnight. Remove meat from sauce; reserve sauce. Place on grill 4 inches from medium coals. Cook, turning and basting frequently with sauce; 15 to 18 minutes or until done. *1½-pound butt makes 5 or 6 servings.*

Spunky Spice Sauce

1½ cups orange juice
½ cup vinegar
¼ cup brown sugar (packed)
2 tablespoons ground cloves
1 tablespoon dry mustard
1 tablespoon ginger
1 tablespoon molasses
2 tablespoons brandy, if desired

Measure ingredients into bowl; mix well with rotary beater.

CHARCOAL-GRILLED PORK TENDERLOIN

Have meatman cut pork tenderloin into 1-inch slices; allow 1 to 2 slices for each serving. Grill meat 4 inches from medium coals 8 to 10 minutes on each side or until done—no pink in center. While grilling, brush with mixture of ¼ teaspoon red pepper sauce and ¼ cup soft butter. Season slices with salt and pepper.

GLAZED PORK TENDERLOIN

This versatile meat can be a main dish on one occasion, an appetizer another. As an outdoor entrée, pair it with snow peas or a sweet and sour vegetable. When it's an appetizer, pass party rye bread or petite buns.

>   3 pork tenderloins, trimmed (10 to 12 ounces each)
>   ½ teaspoon salt
>   3 tablespoons tomato preserves

Place tenderloins on grill 6 inches from hot coals; close cover of barbecue. After meat begins to brown, sprinkle with salt. Cook covered 45 to 55 minutes or until done (no pink in the center), turning every 10 to 12 minutes. (Meat thermometer will register 185°.) During last 10 minutes of cooking period, brush each tenderloin with 1 tablespoon preserves. To serve, cut diagonally into thin slices. If desired, heat additional tomato preserves and serve as sauce with pork. *4 to 6 servings or 16 appetizer servings.*

PORK TERIYAKI

Have meatman cut fresh pork butt or shoulder into ¼- or ½-inch slices; allow 1 slice for each serving. Place meat in shallow glass dish. Prepare Teriyaki Sauce (page 111); pour over meat. Cover dish with plastic wrap. Refrigerate at least 8 hours or overnight, turning meat occasionally. Remove meat from marinade. Place on grill 6 to 8 inches from hot coals. Cook 20 to 30 minutes, turning every 3 or 4 minutes, or until pork is done—no pink in center.

CINNAMON-GLAZED HAM

Mix ⅔ cup honey and 2 teaspoons cinnamon; set aside. Place 2- to 4-pound canned ham on grill 4 inches from medium coals. Cook 45 minutes until thoroughly heated and nicely glazed, turning and basting frequently with cinnamon honey. Serve immediately. *2-pound ham makes 6 to 8 servings.*

HAM HAWAIIAN

> 1 fully cooked center ham slice, 1½ inches thick (about 3 pounds)
> 1 jar (8 ounces) coconut syrup*
> 1 can (11 ounces) mandarin orange segments, drained (reserve syrup)
> ¼ teaspoon allspice
> 1 tablespoon cornstarch
> 1 tablespoon vinegar
> ½ cup raisins
> ¼ cup flaked coconut

Score fat around edge of ham. Combine ⅓ cup coconut syrup with 2 teaspoons mandarin orange syrup and the allspice. Place ham on grill 4 inches from medium coals. Grill 15 minutes on each side, basting frequently with coconut syrup mixture. In saucepan, add enough cold water to remaining mandarin orange syrup to make 1 cup liquid. Stir in cornstarch and remaining coconut syrup. Cook, stirring constantly, until mixture thickens and boils. Boil and stir 1 minute. Stir in vinegar, orange segments, raisins and coconut. (This sauce may be made ahead and reheated, covered, in an 8-inch aluminum foil pan 15 minutes on side of grill.) Serve hot sauce over ham. *6 servings.*

* *Coconut syrup is available in gourmet shops and specialty food departments.*

SUGAR-CRUSTED HAM

> 2 fully cooked center ham slices, each 1 inch thick
>   (about 3½ pounds)
> 1 cup brown sugar (packed)
> ⅓ cup horseradish
> ¼ cup lemon juice

Score each side of ham ¼ inch deep in diamond pattern. Combine remaining ingredients; heat to boiling. Grill ham 3 inches from medium coals 15 minutes on each side, basting frequently with sugar mixture. *6 to 8 servings.*

Veal and Lamb

GRILLED VEAL CHOPS AND STEAKS

Don't confuse veal chops with cutlets. Veal loin chops are porterhouse or T-bones cut from veal instead of beef and are considered a great delicacy.

> 8 veal loin or kidney chops or 4 veal sirloin steaks,
>   1 inch thick
> ¾ cup salad oil
> ½ cup soy sauce
> ¼ cup wine vinegar
> 2 tablespoons Worcestershire sauce
> 2 tablespoons lemon juice
> 1 tablespoon dry mustard
> 2 teaspoons coarsely ground black pepper
> 1½ teaspoons salt
> 1 teaspoon parsley flakes
> 2 cloves garlic, crushed

Place veal in shallow glass dish. Mix remaining ingredients; pour over veal. Cover dish with plastic wrap. Refrigerate several hours. Remove meat from marinade; store remaining marinade in refrigerator for future use. Place veal on grill 4 inches from medium coals. Cook 10 to 12 minutes on each side. *4 servings.*

POLYNESIAN VEAL CUTLETS

    1 can (8¾ ounces) crushed pineapple, drained
      (reserve syrup)
    1 can (5 ounces) water chestnuts, coarsely chopped
    6 veal cutlets (about 2 pounds), pounded
    6 slices bacon
1½ cups catsup
    ½ cup soy sauce
    3 cloves garlic, crushed
    1 tablespoon bottled steak sauce

Combine pineapple and water chestnuts. Spread about 3 tablespoons pineapple mixture on half of each cutlet; fold in half. Wind 1 slice bacon around each cutlet; tie securely with string. Combine remaining ingredients and reserved pineapple syrup. Grill cutlets 4 inches from medium coals 20 to 30 minutes on each side, basting frequently with catsup mixture. 6 *servings.*

GRILLED LAMB CHOPS

Choose loin, rib or shoulder lamb chops, allowing 1 or 2 chops for each person. Trim excess fat from chops. Place chops on grill 4 inches from medium coals. Grill as directed in Timetable (below). Test for doneness by making a knife slit alongside bone; meat should be juicy and slightly pink. If desired, chops may be basted with a sauce, such as Orange Sauce (page 106), during last half of cooking period.

Grilling Time for Each Side	
¾-inch chops	10 to 12 minutes
1-inch chops	14 to 16 minutes
1½-inch chops	16 to 18 minutes
2-inch chops	20 to 22 minutes

LAMB CHOPS BHARATI

    8 lamb chops, 1 inch thick
½ cup soft butter
¼ cup snipped parsley
½ teaspoon curry powder

Trim excess fat from chops. Mix remaining ingredients. Grill chops 4 inches from medium coals 14 minutes on each side, basting frequently with butter mixture. Just before serving, top each sizzling chop with remaining butter mixture. *4 servings.*

LEG O' LAMB BARBECUE

    4- to 5-pound leg of lamb, boned but not tied
2 small cloves garlic, peeled and slivered
½ cup red wine vinegar
⅓ cup salad oil
⅓ cup brown sugar (packed)
2 tablespoons tarragon leaves
1 teaspoon salt
2 green onions (with tops), cut into 2-inch slices
1 can (8 ounces) tomato sauce

Trim excess fat from lamb; if necessary, cut to lay flat. Stud with garlic slivers. Place lamb in large plastic bag or shallow glass dish. Mix remaining ingredients except tomato sauce; pour over lamb. Fasten bag securely or cover dish with plastic wrap. Refrigerate at least 8 hours or overnight, turning meat several times. Remove lamb from marinade. Combine tomato sauce with marinade. Place lamb flat on grill 5 inches from medium coals. Grill 50 to 60 minutes, turning every 10 minutes. Baste with marinade during last 20 minutes of cooking period. *6 to 8 servings.*

KING ARTHUR LAMB SHANKS

      4 meaty lamb shanks (about 12 ounces each)
   1½ cups buttermilk
      2 tablespoons instant minced onion
      1 teaspoon salt
    ¾ teaspoon ginger
    ¾ teaspoon ground coriander
    ½ teaspoon celery seed
    ½ teaspoon pepper

Place lamb shanks in shallow glass dish. Mix remaining ingredients and pour over shanks. Cover dish with plastic wrap. Refrigerate at least 8 hours or overnight, turning meat occasionally. Place shanks on 35x18-inch piece of double thickness heavy-duty aluminum foil. Turn foil up around meat; pour in remaining marinade. Wrap shanks securely in foil. Place on grill 5 inches from medium coals. Cook 1 hour, turning once. Remove shanks from packet; place directly on grill; cook 3 or 4 minutes longer or until browned. *4 servings.*

Hamburgers

BEEFBURGER SPECIALS

   1½ pounds ground beef
    ¾ cup soft bread crumbs
    ⅓ cup milk
    ¼ cup catsup
      1 medium onion, finely chopped
      1 tablespoon prepared mustard
      2 teaspoons Worcestershire sauce
      2 teaspoons horseradish
   1½ teaspoons salt

Combine all ingredients; mix lightly. Shape into 6 large patties. Place in hinged grill. Grill 4 inches from hot coals about 7 minutes on each side or until browned outside and medium inside. If desired, serve in toasted hamburger buns. *6 servings.*

CAPRI BURGERS

    1 beef bouillon cube
    ½ cup boiling water
    1 pound ground beef
    ⅓ cup dry bread crumbs
    1 teaspoon grated lemon peel
    1 teaspoon lemon juice
    ½ teaspoon salt
    ½ teaspoon pepper
    ½ teaspoon ground sage
    ½ teaspoon ginger
    4 or 5 hamburger buns, toasted

Dissolve bouillon cube in boiling water; mix thoroughly
with beef, crumbs, lemon peel and juice, and seasonings. Shape into 4 or 5 patties; chill thoroughly. Grill
4 inches from hot coals until done, about 7 minutes on
each side. Serve in toasted hamburger buns. *4 or 5
servings.*

BARBECUED CHEESEBURGERS IN FOIL

    2 pounds ground beef
    1 teaspoon salt
    ⅛ teaspoon pepper
    1 envelope (1½ ounces) dry onion soup mix
    ½ cup water
    6 slices process American cheese
    6 hamburger buns, toasted

Mix meat and seasonings; shape into 12 patties. Combine soup mix and water; stir until dissolved. For each
of 6 packets, use 12x10-inch piece of heavy-duty aluminum foil. Place a meat patty on each piece of foil;
spread with 2 teaspoons onion sauce. Top with a cheese
slice and second patty. Press edges of hamburgers
together. Spread with another 2 teaspoons onion sauce.
Wrap securely in foil. Cook directly on hot coals 8 to
10 minutes on each side. Serve in toasted buns. *6
servings.*

GRILLED HAMBURGER "STEAKS"

    2 pounds ground beef or ground round steak
    1 egg
    1 medium onion, chopped
    ½ cup cracker crumbs
    ¼ cup catsup
    2 tablespoons brown sugar
    1 teaspoon prepared mustard
    Bar-B-Q Sauce (below)

Mix beef, egg, onion and crumbs. Blend catsup, sugar and mustard; stir into meat mixture. Divide mixture in half; shape each to resemble a steak, about 8x4½x1 inch. Brush top side of each with Bar-B-Q Sauce; place "steaks" sauce side down on grill 4 inches from medium coals. Cook 7 to 8 minutes. Brush "steaks" with Bar-B-Q Sauce and carefully turn, using a large spatula or two smaller spatulas. Cook 7 to 8 minutes longer. *Makes 6 servings.*

Bar-B-Q Sauce

  ¼ cup catsup
  3 tablespoons brown sugar
  1 teaspoon dry mustard
  ¼ teaspoon nutmeg

Mix all ingredients.

ORIENTAL HAMBURGER STEAKS

Shape 1½ pounds ground beef into 6 large patties. Place meat in shallow glass dish. Pour Soy-Garlic Marinade (page 111) over meat. Cover dish with plastic wrap. Refrigerate 2 to 3 hours, turning patties occasionally. Remove meat from marinade; place in hinged grill. Grill 4 to 5 inches from hot coals 8 minutes on each side for medium, 10 to 12 minutes on each side for well done. Serve in sesame hamburger buns, if desired. *6 servings.*

ZESTY HAMBURGERS ON RYE

> 1 pound ground beef
> 1 pound ground veal
> ¼ cup catsup
> 1 tablespoon instant minced onion
> 2 teaspoons salt
> 1 teaspoon pepper
> 1 teaspoon celery seed
> ¼ teaspoon garlic powder
> 2 medium red onions, thinly sliced
> ½ cup red wine vinegar
> ¼ cup salad oil
> ½ teaspoon dill weed
> Sliced rye bread *or* 8 rye buns

In large bowl mix thoroughly beef, veal, catsup, minced onion, salt, pepper, celery seed and garlic powder. Shape mixture into 16 thin patties; chill. Place onion slices in shallow glass dish. Combine vinegar, oil and dill weed; pour over onions. Cover dish with plastic wrap; refrigerate at least 30 minutes. Wrap rye bread securely in heavy-duty aluminum foil. Twenty minutes before starting to cook hamburgers, place bread on grill; turn occasionally to heat on all four sides. Drain onions, reserving marinade. Grill hamburgers 4 inches from medium coals 5 minutes on each side or until done, brushing frequently with reserved marinade. To serve, place a hamburger patty on slice of warm bread; top with onion slices, a second patty and second slice of bread. Serve immediately. *8 servings.*

DOUBLE-DECKER HAMBURGERS

Set out the thin hamburger patties with a variety of fillings and let guests make their own.

>   2 pounds ground beef
>   2 eggs
>   ½ cup bread crumbs
>   2 teaspoons salt
>   Dash pepper
>   Fillings (below)

Mix beef, eggs, bread crumbs and seasonings lightly; shape into 20 thin patties. On half the patties spread one or more fillings; top with remaining patties and seal edges. Place on grill 4 to 6 inches from hot coals, or wrap individually in squares of heavy-duty aluminum foil and place directly on hot coals. Cook 15 minutes or until done, turning once. If desired, serve in toasted hamburger buns. *10 servings.*

FILLINGS TO MIX AND MATCH—Dill pickle slices, pickle relish, prepared mustard, catsup, horseradish, chopped onions, onion slices, Cheddar cheese slices, shredded process American cheese.

ONION FILLING—Mix 1 envelope (1½ ounces) dry onion soup mix with ¼ cup water.

PEPPY CHEESE FILLING—Combine 2 ounces crumbled blue cheese or 2 ounces shredded process American cheese, 2 tablespoons mayonnaise or salad dressing, 1 teaspoon salt, 1 teaspoon Worcestershire sauce, ½ teaspoon prepared mustard and ¼ teaspoon pepper.

Frankfurters

FILLED FRANKFURTER VARIATIONS

Special somethings slipped inside bacon-wrapped franks. For a party arrange a trayful of fillings and fix franks to order.

For each serving, panfry 1 strip bacon 2 minutes on each side. Split frankfurter lengthwise, not cutting completely through. Place your choice of the following fillings in cut. Wrap frank with bacon; secure with wooden picks. Place frankfurter on grill 4 inches from medium coals. Cook 12 to 15 minutes, turning frequently, until franks are heated through.

TAHITIAN FRANKS—Place pineapple spear in cut.

MELONED FRANKS—Place cantaloupe spear in cut.

ORIENTAL FRANKS—Place 3 mandarin orange segments in cut.

FRANKS 'N ONIONS—Place green onion in cut.

FRANKS 'N MUSHROOMS—Place 3 pickled mushrooms in cut.

FRANKS 'N PICKLES—Place thin dill pickle in cut.

POPULAR FRANKFURTER BASTES

Make diagonal cuts in frankfurters, not cutting completely through. Place franks on grill 4 inches from medium coals. Cook 12 to 15 minutes, turning frequently, until franks are heated through. While cooking, brush liberally with your choice of the following bases.

SUGAR-SWEET BASTE—Mixture of 1 part horseradish and 2 parts brown sugar.

WAIKIKI BASTE—Bottled pineapple preserves.

CONEY ISLANDS

    1 can (1 pound 4 ounces) chili con carne
    1 can (6 ounces) tomato paste
    1 teaspoon prepared mustard
    ½ teaspoon salt
    1 pound frankfurters
    8 to 10 frankfurter buns, split and buttered

In saucepan or aluminum foil pan, mix chili, tomato paste, mustard and salt. Make diagonal cuts ¼ inch deep in each frankfurter. Place franks and pan of chili mixture on grill 4 inches from medium coals. Cook 7 to 10 minutes, turning franks and stirring chili frequently. During last 3 to 4 minutes, toast buns buttered side down on grill. To serve, place a frank in each bun and cover with chili mixture. *8 to 10 servings.*

FRANKS 'N HERBED BUNS

    ½ cup soft butter or margarine
    ¼ cup sliced green onions
    ½ teaspoon crushed thyme leaves
    1 pound frankfurters
    8 to 10 frankfurter buns, split

Mix butter, green onion and thyme. Grill franks 4 inches from hot coals 15 minutes, turning frequently. Spread butter mixture on cut surface of buns; grill cut side down 4 minutes. *8 to 10 servings.*

BAR-B-Q FRANKS AND KRAUT

For each serving, split 2 frankfurters lengthwise, not cutting completely through. Spread cut surface of one frankfurter with mustard; spread the other with catsup. Arrange 3 to 4 tablespoons drained sauerkraut on one frankfurter; top with second frank, cut side down. Fasten ends with wooden picks. Wrap securely in 18x12-inch piece of double thickness heavy-duty aluminum foil. Cook directly on hot coals 3 to 4 minutes on each side.

CHEESEBOATS

10 slices bacon
1 pound frankfurters
Liquid smoke
⅔ cup shredded Cheddar cheese
3 tablespoons chili sauce

Panfry bacon 2 minutes on each side. Split frankfurters lengthwise, not cutting completely through. Brush cut surface lightly with liquid smoke. Mix cheese and chili sauce; fill each frank with 2 teaspoons of the mixture. Wrap each with a slice of bacon; secure with wooden picks. Grill 4 inches from medium coals 12 to 15 minutes, or until bacon is crisp, turning occasionally. If desired, serve in toasted buttered frankfurter buns. *8 to 10 servings.*

PLUM GOOD FRANKS

½ cup plum preserves
1 tablespoon lemon juice
¼ teaspoon ginger
1 pound frankfurters
8 to 10 frankfurter buns, split and buttered

Combine preserves, lemon juice and ginger in saucepan; simmer 5 minutes, stirring constantly. Make diagonal cuts ¼ inch deep in each frankfurter. Grill frankfurters 4 inches from medium coals 7 to 10 minutes, turning franks and basting frequently with preserve mixture. During last 3 to 4 minutes, toast buns buttered side down on grill. *8 to 10 servings.*

Specialty Meats

HEIDELBERG DINNER

1 small head (1½ pounds) red cabbage,
  coarsely shredded (about 6 cups)
4 unpared tart apples, thinly sliced
½ cup apple cider
¼ cup salad oil
2 tablespoons red wine vinegar
1 teaspoon pickling spice
1 teaspoon brown sugar
1 teaspoon salt
¼ teaspoon crushed thyme leaves
1 package (1 pound) Polish sausages
1 package (1 pound) bratwurst sausages

Combine all ingredients except sausages on 24-inch square of double thickness heavy-duty aluminum foil. Wrap securely. Place on grill 4 inches from medium coals. Cook 1 hour, turning once. During last 10 minutes of cooking period, place sausages on grill; turn frequently. *6 to 8 servings.*

Temperature Guide for Grilling		
Coals	Thermometer Registers	Hand Withdrawn
Low	about 300°	between 4 and 5 seconds
Medium	about 350°	between 3 and 4 seconds
Hot	about 400°	in less than 3 seconds

LIVER WITH SNIPPETS OF GREEN ONION

    ¼ cup catsup
    1 tablespoon water
    1 tablespoon dark molasses
    2 teaspoons vinegar
    1 teaspoon salt
    ¼ teaspoon pepper
    2 pounds sliced calf or beef liver
    ½ cup sliced green onions (with tops)

Combine all ingredients except liver and onions. Place liver on grill 4 inches from medium coals. Cook 5 to 6 minutes on each side, basting with sauce. To serve, sprinkle with green onions. *6 to 8 servings.*

GLAZED LUNCHEON MEAT GRILL

    2 cans (12 ounces each) pork luncheon meat
    1 jar (10 ounces) red currant jelly
    ½ cup boiling water
    1 chicken bouillon cube
    1 tablespoon lemon juice
    ½ teaspoon salt
    ½ teaspoon mace
    ½ teaspoon ginger

Remove luncheon meat from cans; cut each loaf lengthwise into 5 slices. Score each side ⅛ inch deep in diamond pattern. Combine remaining ingredients in saucepan; simmer 10 minutes, stirring occasionally. Place meat on grill 3 inches from hot coals. Grill 20 minutes, turning once and basting frequently with jelly mixture. *4 or 5 servings.*

Chicken

MEXICAN CHICKEN

1 can (8 ounces) tomato sauce
1 tablespoon parsley flakes
1 tablespoon sugar
1 teaspoon salt
½ teaspoon chili powder
⅛ teaspoon pepper
⅛ teaspoon red pepper sauce
2 broiler-fryer chickens (2 pounds each), split in half

Combine tomato sauce and next 6 seasonings. Place chicken halves bone side down on grill 5 inches from medium coals; cook 20 to 30 minutes. Turn chicken and cook 30 to 40 minutes longer, turning and brushing frequently with tomato mixture. *4 servings.*

CHARCOAL-GRILLED CHICKEN HALVES

1 cup sherry or apple juice
½ cup salad oil
1 large onion, grated
1 tablespoon prepared mustard
1 tablespoon mixed herbs
1 teaspoon garlic salt
½ teaspoon coarsely ground pepper
¼ teaspoon salt
1 tablespoon Worcestershire sauce
1 teaspoon soy sauce

3 broiler-fryer chickens (2 pounds each), split in half

Measure sherry, oil, onion and next 7 seasonings into large jar; shake well to blend. Place chicken in shallow glass dish; pour marinade over chicken. Cover dish with plastic wrap. Refrigerate several hours, turning meat occasionally. Remove chicken from marinade; reserve marinade. Place chicken halves bone side down on grill 5 inches from medium coals; cook 20 to 30 minutes. Turn chicken and cook 30 to 40 minutes longer, basting frequently with marinade. *6 servings.*

ISLAND-IN-THE-SUN CHICKEN

> 2 broiler-fryer chickens (2½ pounds each),
>   quartered
> 2 teaspoons salt
> ¼ teaspoon pepper
> ¼ cup butter or margarine, melted
> 1 cup bottled barbecue sauce
> ½ cup honey
> ¼ cup lemon juice
> 2 tablespoons soy sauce
> 1 clove garlic, crushed
> ½ teaspoon ginger

Season chicken with salt and pepper; brush with melted butter. Combine remaining ingredients. Place chicken bone side down on grill 5 inches from medium coals; cook 20 to 30 minutes. Turn chicken and cook 30 to 40 minutes longer, turning and brushing frequently with sauce mixture. *4 servings.*

BARBECUED CHICKEN

> 2 broiler-fryer chickens (2 to 2½ pounds each),
>   cut up
> 1½ cups tomato juice
> ⅓ cup lemon juice
> ¼ cup butter or margarine
> 1 tablespoon Worcestershire sauce
> ½ cup minced onion
> 1 tablespoon paprika
> 1 teaspoon sugar
> 1 teaspoon salt
> ½ teaspoon pepper

Place chicken pieces bone side down on grill 5 inches from medium coals; cook 20 to 30 minutes. In saucepan mix remaining ingredients and heat just to boiling; keep sauce hot for basting. Turn chicken and cook 30 to 40 minutes longer, turning and basting frequently with sauce. *4 to 6 servings.*

CHICKEN TERIYAKI

Select a 2- to 2½-pound broiler-fryer chicken; cut into serving pieces. Place meat in shallow glass dish; pour Teriyaki Sauce (page 111) over meat. Cover dish with plastic wrap. Refrigerate at least 8 hours or overnight. Remove meat from marinade. Place chicken pieces bone side down on grill 5 inches from medium coals; cook 20 to 30 minutes. Turn chicken and cook 30 to 40 minutes longer, turning and brushing frequently with sauce. Chicken will be quite dark. *2 or 3 servings.*

GOLDEN CHICKEN AND CHUTNEY APPLES

 1 tablespoon curry powder
 1 teaspoon salt
 8 meaty chicken pieces (legs, thighs and breasts),
  about 2 pounds
 ⅓ cup honey
 ⅓ cup prepared mustard
 Chutney Apples (below)

Combine curry powder and salt in paper or plastic bag. Shake 2 pieces of chicken at a time in the bag until they are thoroughly coated. Combine honey and mustard. Grill chicken bone side down 5 inches from medium coals 20 to 30 minutes. Turn chicken and cook 30 to 40 minutes longer, turning and brushing frequently with honey mixture. Serve with Chutney Apples. *4 servings.*

Chutney Apples

Core 4 apples and remove 1 inch of peel at stem end. Fill each center with 1 tablespoon chopped chutney. Wrap each apple in a 10-inch square of heavy-duty aluminum foil. Grill 5 inches from medium coals 30 minutes or until apples are soft, turning once.

CHICKEN ITALIAN

Meal in foil, Italian style. For added eating pleasure, serve with crusty rolls to be dipped into the sauce.

    2 meaty chicken pieces (thighs, legs or breasts)
    1½ teaspoons salad oil
    ¼ teaspoon salt
    1 medium potato, pared
      Salt
    1 medium zucchini
    3 large pitted ripe olives
    2 tablespoons tomato sauce
    ½ teaspoon crushed oregano leaves
    1 tablespoon butter or margarine

Brush chicken pieces with oil; sprinkle with ¼ teaspoon salt. Cut potato lengthwise into ⅛-inch slices. Place potato slices on 18x12-inch piece of double thickness heavy-duty aluminum foil; sprinkle with salt. Cut unpared zucchini into ¼-inch rounds. Place squash on potatoes; sprinkle with salt. Top with chicken pieces, olives, tomato sauce and oregano. Dot with butter. Wrap securely in foil. Place on grill 5 inches from medium coals. Cook 25 to 30 minutes on each side, or until chicken and vegetables are tender. If desired, open packet and sprinkle with Parmesan cheese before serving.

Fish and Seafood

BARBECUED FISH FILLETS

Clean and fillet a 3-pound fish (such as bass, pike, mackerel or trout). Wash and pat dry with paper towels; brush with salad oil. Place in hinged grill or on well-greased grill 3 to 4 inches from medium coals. Grill 5 to 7 minutes on each side, or until fish flakes easily with a fork. Baste frequently with mixture of ½ cup melted butter and ¼ cup lemon juice. Just before serving, sprinkle with salt and pepper. *4 to 6 servings.*

NOTE—Thawed frozen fish fillets are equally delicious grilled this way.

HALIBUT FILLETS, COUNTRY STYLE

For each serving:

    ½ pound fresh or frozen halibut fillets
    ¼ teaspoon salt
       Pepper and paprika
    ¼ cup shredded carrot
    ¼ cup coarsely chopped celery
    2 tablespoons chopped green onion (with top)
    ½ teaspoon salt
    1 tablespoon butter or margarine
    1 teaspoon lemon juice

If fillets are frozen, thaw in refrigerator. Sprinkle fillets with ¼ teaspoon salt, the pepper and paprika. Place vegetables on 12-inch square of double thickness heavy-duty aluminum foil. Sprinkle with ½ teaspoon salt; top with fillets. Dot with butter and sprinkle with lemon juice. Wrap securely in foil. Place on grill 4 inches from medium coals. Cook 10 minutes on each side.

WHITEFISH WITH STUFFING

    1 whole whitefish (2½ to 3 pounds), cleaned and
       head removed
    3 cups cooked rice
    ½ cup salad dressing
    1 can (5 ounces) water chestnuts, sliced
    ⅓ cup chopped green onion
    1 jar (2 ounces) chopped pimiento, drained
    ¾ teaspoon monosodium glutamate
    ¾ teaspoon salt
    ¼ teaspoon pepper
    Melted butter or margarine

Wash fish and pat dry with paper towels. Mix remaining ingredients except melted butter. Stuff fish with rice mixture. Close opening with skewers; lace. Place fish in lightly greased hinged grill 5 inches from medium coals. Cook 50 minutes, turning once. Baste frequently with melted butter. Garnish with lemon wedges, if desired. *6 servings.*

Note—Extra stuffing may be heated 50 minutes in covered aluminum foil pan at side of grill.

MONTEREY BROILED SWORDFISH

    4 swordfish steaks (6 to 8 ounces each),
       1 inch thick
    1 teaspoon salt
    ¼ teaspoon pepper
    ¼ cup butter or margarine, melted
    1 tablespoon lemon juice
    1 teaspoon crushed chervil leaves
    Avocado Sauce (right)
    Lemon wedges

Sprinkle fish with salt and pepper. Combine butter, lemon juice and chervil. Place steaks on lightly greased grill 4 inches from medium coals. Grill 10 minutes on each side, brushing frequently with butter mixture.

Serve steaks with Avocado Sauce and lemon wedges. *4 servings.*

Avocado Sauce

1 small ripe avocado, peeled and pitted
⅓ cup dairy sour cream
1 teaspoon lemon juice
¼ teaspoon salt
Few drops red pepper sauce

Combine all ingredients in blender or beat with rotary beater until smooth.

FISH STEAKS

Your choice of two delicious butters to enhance the flavor of broiled fish. The Mustard Butter is particularly good with salmon.

Mustard Butter or Lemon-Parsley Butter (below)
8 pounds fresh or frozen fish steaks (salmon, tuna, halibut or swordfish), ¾ to 1 inch thick

Prepare your choice of the butters. Place steaks on lightly greased grill (or use hinged grill for easier turning) 4 inches from medium coals. Cook, basting frequently with butter sauce, 6 to 8 minutes on each side, or until fish flakes easily with a fork. Do not overcook. If desired, garnish with lemon wedges. Serve with remaining butter sauce. *6 servings.*

Mustard Butter

Melt ½ cup butter or margarine; combine with 1½ teaspoons salt, 2 teaspoons lemon juice, 1 teaspoon prepared mustard and dash pepper.

Lemon-Parsley Butter

Melt ½ cup butter or margarine; combine with ¼ cup lemon juice, 1½ tablespoons snipped parsley, 1½ teaspoons salt and dash pepper.

FILLET OF SOLE EN PAPILLOTE

1 pound fresh or frozen fillets of sole
1 teaspoon salt
½ cup thinly sliced washed and trimmed fresh
    mushrooms
2 tablespoons butter or margarine
1 cup dry sherry
2 teaspoons instant minced onion
1 tablespoon cornstarch
⅓ cup cold water
2 tablespoons lemon juice
7 ounces cleaned raw shrimp, fresh or frozen*
4 teaspoons snipped parsley

If fillets are frozen, thaw in refrigerator. Divide fillets
into 4 equal portions; sprinkle each with ¼ teaspoon
salt. Cook and stir mushrooms in butter until tender
but not brown. Add sherry and onion. Blend cornstarch with water; stir into mixture in skillet. Cook,
stirring constantly, until mixture thickens and boils.
Boil and stir 1 minute. Stir in lemon juice. For each
of 4 packets, use 14x9-inch piece of double thickness
heavy-duty aluminum foil. Place ¼ of the sole on each
piece of foil; top with ¼ of the shrimp. Turn foil up
around fish; pour ¼ of sauce over shrimp. Sprinkle
with 1 teaspoon parsley. Wrap food securely in foil.
Place on grill 4 inches from medium coals; cook 20 to
25 minutes, or until fish flakes easily with a fork. *4
servings.*

* *Rinse frozen shrimp under running cold water to remove ice glaze.*

BARBECUED STUFFED WHOLE FISH

8- to 10-pound whole fish (such as tuna, salmon,
    cod, pike, snapper or lake trout), cleaned
Salt and pepper
Garden Vegetable Stuffing (below)
Salad oil
½ cup butter or margarine, melted
¼ cup lemon juice

Wash fish quickly in cold water and pat dry with paper
towels. Rub the cavity of the fish with salt and pepper.
Stuff with Garden Vegetable Stuffing. Close opening
with skewers; lace. Brush fish with salad oil. Mix butter
and lemon juice; set aside. Place fish in wire basket on
grill 4 inches from medium coals. Cook 45 minutes, or
until fish flakes easily with a fork, turning three times
and basting with butter mixture. *12 servings.*

Garden Vegetable Stuffing

1 cup finely chopped onion
¼ cup butter or margarine
2 cups dry bread cubes
1 cup shredded carrot
1 cup cut-up washed and trimmed fresh mushrooms
½ cup snipped parsley
1½ tablespoons lemon juice
1 egg
1 clove garlic, crushed
2 teaspoons salt
¼ teaspoon marjoram
¼ teaspoon pepper

Cook and stir onion in butter until onion is tender.
Lightly mix remaining ingredients with onion and
butter. If you have extra stuffing, place in aluminum
foil pan; cover and heat on grill 20 minutes before
serving.

NOTE—If you do not have a wire basket, one may be
improvised with chicken wire. When fish is done, open
this rack with wire snippers and pliers.

SHRIMP INTERNATIONALE

It's exciting. It's unusual. It looks like a salad. It tastes like a main dish. It's sure to establish your reputation as a creative cook.

    7 to 8 ounces cleaned raw shrimp, fresh or frozen*
    ½ cup bottled creamy Italian salad dressing
    1 tablespoon soy sauce
    1 teaspoon parsley flakes
    1 medium onion, diced (about 1 cup)
    ¼ cup chopped green pepper
    ¼ pound fresh mushrooms, washed, trimmed and
        sliced, *or* 1 can (2 ounces) mushroom pieces,
        drained
    2 tablespoons salad oil
    2 cups cooked rice
    1 can (8¾ ounces) crushed pineapple, drained
    1 tablespoon soy sauce
        Cabbage leaves
    ⅓ cup slivered almonds
        Cherry tomatoes
        Lime wedges

Place shrimp on 12-inch square of double thickness heavy-duty aluminum foil. Combine dressing, 1 tablespoon soy sauce and the parsley flakes; spoon over shrimp. Wrap securely in foil.

In skillet or aluminum foil pan, cook and stir onion, green pepper and mushrooms in oil on grill 2 inches from medium coals 30 minutes, or until onion is tender. Remove pan from grill. Stir in rice, pineapple and 1 tablespoon soy sauce; cover tightly with lid or aluminum foil. Raise grill to 4 inches. Place pan of rice mixture and packet of shrimp on grill. Cook over medium coals 15 minutes, or until shrimp is tender. Line a salad bowl with green cabbage leaves. Stir almonds into rice mixture; pour into bowl. Top with shrimp and sauce. Garnish with cherry tomatoes and lime wedges. *6 servings.*

* *Rinse frozen shrimp under running cold water to remove ice glaze.*

SHRIMP CARMEL

  ½ cup butter
  2 teaspoons garlic salt
  ⅛ teaspoon red pepper sauce
  3 pounds cleaned raw shrimp, fresh or frozen*
  2 cans (5 ounces each) water chestnuts,
    drained and sliced
  1 large green pepper, cut into rings
  1 tablespoon minced onion
  ½ teaspoon salt
  ½ teaspoon tarragon

Form a pan, 11x11x½ inch, from double thickness heavy-duty aluminum foil. Combine butter, garlic salt and pepper sauce in pan; place on grill 4 to 6 inches from medium coals until butter melts. Remove pan from grill; add remaining ingredients. Cover pan with piece of heavy-duty aluminum foil, sealing edges well. Return to grill; cook 20 to 30 minutes, or until shrimp is done. *6 servings.*

* *Rinse frozen shrimp under running cold water to remove ice glaze.*

LOBSTER TAILS ON THE GRILL

  6 fresh or frozen medium lobster tails
  ½ cup butter or margarine, melted
  ⅓ cup lemon juice
  2 teaspoons Worcestershire sauce
  ½ teaspoon onion salt
  ½ cup butter or margarine, melted
  Lemon wedges

Thaw frozen lobster tails. Cut away thin undershell with kitchen scissors. Bend each tail backward toward shell; crack. (This prevents tails from curling while they grill.) Mix ½ cup butter, melted, the lemon juice, Worcestershire sauce and onion salt. Place lobster tails shell side down on grill 4 inches from hot coals. Cook 10 minutes, basting frequently with butter mixture. Turn shell side up; cook 5 minutes or until meat is opaque, basting frequently. Serve with melted butter and the lemon wedges. *6 servings.*

Kabobs

The combination of meat and vegetables on skewers produces an exceptionally colorful, flavorful and easily served barbecue dinner with a gourmet air. Easy-to-do kabobs are also easy on the budget, getting maximum mileage from minimum meat.

Lean lamb is the classic choice of meat for skewer cooking, but chunks of tender beef, lobster or canned meats are also delicious cooked in this way. However, the long grilling of small pieces of meat can leave them dry and wooden, so meats that cook through quickly or that can be served on the rare side are best for kabobs. This means that vegetables that are good on the crisp side—mushroom caps, green peppers, zucchini—make excellent kabob companions. Small whole onions, potatoes, chunks of carrot and acorn squash may need brief parboiling before skewering.

It's a good idea to grill foods with widely different cooking times on separate skewers. (See our recipe for Skewered Lamb, Tomatoes and Corn on page 71.) If your skewer supply is limited, try adding faster-cooking foods to the skewers after the other ingredients are partly cooked.

When threading a skewer, be careful to pierce each chunk of food through its center of gravity; this will prevent the pieces from flopping when the skewer is turned. Cut unpeeled tomatoes and other soft vegetables into good-size chunks. Thin pieces of green pepper or onion will stay put if wedged firmly between cubes of meat. But don't overcrowd the skewer—the kabob elements will be more evenly cooked if a little space is left between them. Double skewers and skewers with twists help to put a firm hold on the food and reduce slippage. (For more about skewers and skewer racks, see page 24.)

As a rule, kabob meat is best if marinated before it is cooked, and meat alone or meat and vegetables together will need some basting during grilling.

To reduce flare-ups when grilling kabobs, arrange coals in parallel rows in the firebox. On the grill, stagger the skewers so that they rest directly over the coal-less rows.

Following are six sure-fire recipes. Try them, then go ahead and make your own combinations. Or present a kabob buffet, and let each guest create his own skewered dinner.

SKEWERED LAMB, TOMATOES AND CORN

    ½ cup salad oil
    ⅓ cup lemon juice
    1 clove garlic, crushed
    2 teaspoons salt
    1 teaspoon dill weed
    ¼ teaspoon coarsely ground pepper
1½ pounds boneless lamb, cut into 1¼-inch cubes
    4 small whole tomatoes
    2 large ears corn, cut into 2-inch pieces
    2 slices French bread, cut in half and buttered on both sides

Combine oil, lemon juice, garlic, salt, dill weed and pepper. Place meat in shallow glass dish; pour lemon mixture over meat. Cover dish with plastic wrap. Refrigerate 4 hours or overnight, turning meat occasionally. Remove meat from marinade; reserve marinade. Place lamb cubes, vegetables and bread on skewers, using separate skewers for each kind of food. (To keep the tomatoes from slipping when they are turned, insert two skewers parallel and about ½ inch apart through center of tomatoes.) Place lamb kabobs on grill 4 inches from hot coals; cook 20 minutes, turning once. After 5 minutes add vegetable kabobs; cook 15 minutes, turning and basting frequently with reserved marinade. Grill bread until golden brown, 5 to 7 minutes on each side. *4 servings.*

LAMB SHISH KABOBS

For these superb kabobs we recommend a two-step grilling process so that both lamb and vegetables are done to perfection. Serve with pilaf.

    2 pounds boneless lamb shoulder, cut into 1½-inch
      cubes
    1 small onion, thinly sliced
    2 teaspoons salt
    ¼ teaspoon coarsely ground pepper
    ½ to 1 teaspoon crushed oregano leaves
    2 medium green peppers, cut into squares
    1 pound large fresh mushroom caps, washed and
      trimmed

Place lamb in bowl. Tuck in onion slices; sprinkle with seasonings. Cover with plastic wrap. Refrigerate 1 to 2 hours. Thread lamb on 4 to 6 skewers. Grill 4 inches from hot coals 15 to 20 minutes. Complete kabobs by threading green pepper and mushrooms on skewers with partially cooked lamb. Cook, turning often, about 15 minutes, or until meat and vegetables are done. *4 to 6 servings.*

AUTUMN SUPPER EN BROCHETTE

    1 can (6 ounces) frozen orange juice concentrate
    ½ cup honey
    ¼ cup cut-up crystallized ginger
    ¾ teaspoon crushed marjoram leaves
    2 pounds boneless veal, cut into 1-inch cubes
    1 medium acorn squash (unpared), cut into
      2-inch pieces
    4 medium unpared apples, quartered

Combine orange juice concentrate, honey, ginger and marjoram. Place veal cubes in shallow glass dish. Pour orange juice mixture over veal. Cover dish with plastic wrap. Refrigerate several hours or overnight, turning meat occasionally. Cook squash in small amount of water 10 minutes. Remove veal from marinade; reserve marinade. Alternate veal, squash and apples on 6 skewers. Place on grill 3 inches from medium coals. Cook, turning and basting frequently with reserved marinade, 30 minutes, or until meat is browned and squash and apples are tender. *4 servings.*

BEEF ON A SKEWER

   1½ pounds sirloin steak, cut into 1-inch cubes
      2 cups tomato juice
      ½ cup vinegar
      ¼ cup prepared mustard
      2 teaspoons sugar
      2 teaspoons salt
      ½ teaspoon pepper
      ½ pound fresh mushroom caps, washed and trimmed
      1 large green pepper, cut into 1-inch pieces
      1 pint cherry tomatoes
      ½ fresh pineapple, cut into pieces

Place steak cubes in shallow glass dish. Combine tomato juice, vinegar and seasonings; pour over meat. Cover dish with plastic wrap. Refrigerate 2 hours. Remove meat from marinade; reserve marinade. Alternate meat, vegetables and pineapple on skewers. Place on grill 4 inches from hot coals. Cook, turning and basting frequently with reserved marinade, 12 to 15 minutes, or until meat is browned and vegetables are tender. *4 servings.*

FRANK-A-BOBS

Cut each frankfurter into 5 pieces; alternate with pineapple chunks on skewers. Brush with salad oil. Grill 4 inches from medium coals 7 to 10 minutes, turning frequently, until browned. During last 3 to 4 minutes, toast buttered frankfurter buns cut side down on grill. Serve kabobs in buns with mustard or barbecue sauce.

SCALLOP KABOBS

    1 pound fresh or frozen scallops
    1 can (4 ounces) button mushrooms, drained
    2 tablespoons salad oil
    2 tablespoons soy sauce
    2 tablespoons lemon juice
    2 tablespoons snipped parsley
    ½ teaspoon salt
    Dash pepper
    12 bacon slices
    1 can (13½ ounces) pineapple chunks, drained

Thaw scallops, if frozen; wash and remove any shell particles. Place scallops and mushrooms in shallow glass dish. Combine oil, soy sauce, lemon juice, parsley and seasonings; pour over scallops. Cover dish with plastic wrap. Let stand 30 minutes, turning scallops and mushrooms once. Partially fry bacon; cut each slice in half. Remove scallops and mushrooms from marinade. Alternate scallops, mushrooms, bacon and pineapple on skewers. Grill 4 inches from medium coals 6 to 8 minutes on each side. *4 servings.*

Done to a Turn
on the Rotisserie

When the main course of an alfresco meal is to be a good-sized roast or a whole chicken or turkey—or, for that matter, any meat that gives off large amounts of fat, like pork or duckling—head straight for the rotisserie. Since spit-cooked meat bastes itself constantly as it turns, it can be counted on to be especially juicy.

Electrically driven spits to be used with charcoal fires come in a wide range of styles and prices. There are relatively inexpensive ones for use over a simple brazier and elaborate units complete with their own movable fireboxes, drip pans and reflectors. And there's the whole range in between. A number of helpful, though certainly not necessary, attachments for the spit rod are also readily available. They include a basket in which disjointed pieces of chicken can be held, a double grid for chops and other small meats, a unit for turning kabob skewers and a rotary rack for a large roast or turkey.

The ideal fire for cooking any sizable piece of meat on a revolving spit should be a little lower than for broiling on the grill. For good results, start with medium-hot coals. If the heat is right, a spit thermometer will read about 300° (your hand can remain at spit level between 4 and 5 seconds). But the fire must be arranged so that it will give off an even heat for the entire cooking time—which may run to several hours. For this steady, moderate heat, hardwood briquets are by far the most practical type of fuel. The temperature of the fire is controlled by removing or adding fuel and, with some equipment, by adjusting the distance between the spit and the fire. Experienced outdoor cooks often keep a standby supply of briquets going on a nearby brazier or shallow metal pan and then, when needed, add a few ready-and-waiting hot ones to the bed of coals.

For rotisserie cooking the coals are never placed directly under the meat; they are usually arranged at the back of the firebox so the fat from the meat can fall freely into a drip pan. The drip pan is naturally placed directly under the spit. Use heavy-duty aluminum foil to make an unbeatable drip pan; you can fashion one of just the right size to catch all of the meat's fat juice and bastings (see page 26).

Concentrate on mounting the meat correctly. (Always make sure the spit will turn away from you at the top of the turn. This allows the fat to drip off on the up-turn farthest from the fire.) The usual method of mounting meat for spit cooking is to spear it on the main rod and hold it firmly in place with adjustable holding forks. But the meat must be balanced so the spit can turn without strain. It is essential, then, to insert the rod through the center of gravity so that the meat will turn *with* the rod and thus prevent the flopping which tears meat and stalls the motor. Check the balance by holding the mounted meat with the ends of the spit rod across your palms. If the spit and meat do not rotate easily, simply remove the holding forks and rod, and remount.

Before mounting, a bird must be well trussed with heavy strings or skewers so the wings and legs will not fall away from the body. There are many ways to do this; the important point is to keep the bird together as a compact package. (See step-by-step pictures at right.) Insert the spit rod through the trussed bird from neck end to tail. You'll find that it's best to roast spinning birds without a stuffing. Simply sprinkle the cavity with salt and some herbs, or stuff with just an apple or onion for flavor.

A rolled roast or other large piece of boneless meat should be tied firmly at intervals with heavy string. A leg of lamb or other bone-in roast need not be trussed; but because of their bones, such meats are tricky to balance. To spit any bone-in roast more

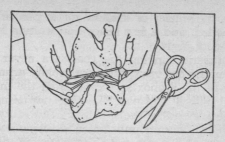

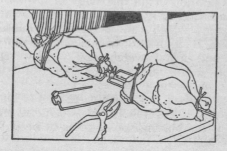

Just Right for the Rotisserie

Beef: rib roasts (rolled or standing); Delmonico roast;
  rolled rump roast (high quality)

Pork and Ham: rolled fresh pork roast (shoulder, loin,
  ham); smoked boneless ham; spareribs; back ribs (loin
  backs); Canadian-style bacon

Veal: boned and rolled roast (shoulder, loin, sirloin, leg)

Lamb: boned and rolled roast (shoulder, loin, sirloin,
  leg); rack

Poultry: chicken, turkey, duckling; Rock Cornish game
  hens

Miscellaneous Meats: bologna (whole or cut) and other
  sausages

---

easily, try running the rod through the meat in an off-center position or on the diagonal.

Fortunately, some spits come with their own weight compensators, which can be adjusted quickly and easily. The compensator unit clamps right on the turnspit, and metal weights of varying sizes are screwed to it to equalize the balance of the meat. Weight compensators are especially helpful when dealing with meats that lose a great deal of fat during cooking and so need rebalancing—a messy and difficult task if the blazing-hot iron has to be pulled out and reset.

Once the meat has been properly mounted, insert a meat thermometer, always making sure it does not touch bone, fat or the spit rod. For turkeys or chickens, insert the thermometer in the thickest part of the breast meat or at the center of the inside thigh muscle; for roasts, insert it at an angle or into the end, parallel to the spit rod. Check, too, to see that the thermometer will clear both the drip pan and the reflector when it rotates with the meat. A meat thermometer is the safest guide to the doneness of any roast, especially one cooked over a charcoal fire.

For easier carving, allow the roast to "set" awhile. To do this properly, remove the meat from the rotisserie when the thermometer registers 5 to 10° below the desired doneness. Even though it has been removed from the source of heat, the meat will continue to cook while "setting."

Beef

RUMP ROAST CALIFORNIAN

> 5-pound rolled beef rump roast (U.S. Choice grade)
> 1 cup orange juice
> 1 cup tomato juice
> ¼ cup salad oil
> 1 clove garlic, crushed
> 2 teaspoons salt
> ½ teaspoon allspice
> ¼ teaspoon chili powder
> 3 tablespoons flour
> ⅓ cup water

Place the roast in a plastic bag or in a deep bowl. Combine all ingredients except flour and water; pour over roast. Fasten bag securely or cover bowl with plastic wrap; refrigerate 4 hours or overnight, turning occasionally. Remove roast from marinade; reserve 2 cups marinade. Insert spit rod lengthwise through center of roast. Secure meat on spit with holding forks. Check balance by rotating spit in palms of hands. Insert meat thermometer in center of meat, making sure it doesn't touch fat or spit. Arrange medium-hot coals at back of firebox; place foil drip pan under spit area. Cook roast on rotisserie 2½ to 3 hours, or until meat is of desired doneness. (Meat thermometer should register 150 to 170°.) Add coals, if necessary, to maintain even heat. Blend flour and water; stir into reserved 2 cups marinade. Heat to boiling, stirring constantly. Boil 1 minute. Slice roast thinly; serve with gravy. *10 to 12 servings.*

BEEF ROAST ON THE TURNSPIT

Select a 5-pound rolled rib roast of beef. Insert spit rod lengthwise through center of roast. Secure meat on spit with holding forks. Check balance by rotating spit in palms of hands. Insert meat thermometer in center of meat, making sure it doesn't touch fat or spit. Arrange medium-hot coals at back of firebox; place foil drip pan under spit area. Cook roast on rotisserie as directed in Timetable (below), using thermometer reading as the final guide to correct doneness. (Roast will be easier to carve if allowed to "set" about 15 minutes in a warm place. Since meat continues to cook during this time, it should be removed from rotisserie and the spit rod taken out when the thermometer registers about 5 to 10° below the desired doneness.) Serve with Easy Horseradish Sauce (below). *10 to 12 servings.*

Timetable for Roast	
Internal Temperature	**Minutes per Pound**
Rare (140°)	20 to 25
Medium (160°)	30 to 35
Well done (170°)	40

Easy Horseradish Sauce

Whip ½ cup whipping cream until stiff; fold in 3 tablespoons well-drained horseradish and ½ teaspoon salt. *Makes 1 cup.*

TANGY SHORT RIBS

> 4 pounds short ribs, cut into 2-inch pieces
> ½ cup lemon juice
> ½ cup salad oil
> 1 clove garlic, crushed
> 1 teaspoon salt
> 1 teaspoon ground cumin
> ½ teaspoon monosodium glutamate
> ¼ teaspoon pepper
> ⅓ cup bottled steak sauce

Place ribs in shallow glass dish. Combine remaining ingredients except steak sauce; pour over meat. Cover dish with plastic wrap. Refrigerate at least 24 hours, turning meat occasionally. Remove meat from marinade. Place ribs in spit basket; fasten securely. Arrange medium-hot coals at back of firebox; place full drip pan under spit area. Cook ribs on rotisserie 2 hours or until well done. Add coals, if necessary, to maintain even heat. Baste with steak sauce during last 30 minutes of cooking period. *4 servings.*

Pork and Ham

SPIT-BARBECUED RIBS

> 3 to 4 pounds loin back ribs
> 1 cup soy sauce
> ½ cup sherry or pineapple juice
> 2 tablespoons honey
> 1 clove garlic, crushed
> ½ cup honey

Place ribs in plastic bag or shallow glass dish. Combine remaining ingredients except ½ cup honey; pour over meat. Fasten bag securely or cover dish with plastic wrap. Refrigerate at least 8 hours or overnight, turning ribs occasionally. Remove ribs from marinade;

reserve marinade. Lace ribs on spit rod; secure with holding forks. Check balance by rotating spit in palms of hands. Arrange medium-hot coals at back of firebox; place drip pan under spit area. Cook ribs on rotisserie 1½ to 2 hours or until done, basting frequently with reserved marinade. Add coals, if necessary, to maintain even heat. Brush ribs with the ½ cup honey during last 30 minutes of cooking period. *4 servings.*

FRUIT-FULL SPARERIBS

    2 cups cut-up cooked prunes
    1 can (13½ ounces) pineapple tidbits, drained
      (reserve syrup)
    1 can (1 pound 1 ounce) apricot halves, drained
    2 tablespoons brown sugar
    3 tablespoons flour
    ½ teaspoon cinnamon
    2 racks (1¾ pounds each) spareribs, untrimmed
1½ teaspoons salt
    ½ teaspoon pepper
    ½ cup honey

Combine fruits, sugar, flour and cinnamon. Sprinkle ribs with salt and pepper. Spoon fruit onto bony side of one rack of ribs; top with other rack of ribs, bony side down. (Ribs may fit more compactly if wide end of top rack of ribs is placed over narrow end of bottom rack of ribs.) Secure in spit basket. Arrange medium-hot coals at back of firebox; place foil drip pan under spit area. Cook ribs on rotisserie 1 hour 45 minutes, or until the ribs are done. Add coals, if necessary, to maintain even heat. During last 30 minutes of cooking period, brush ribs with mixture of honey and 2 tablespoons reserved pineapple syrup. *4 servings.*

ROAST PORK WITH ORANGE SAUCE

    1 can (12 ounces) frozen orange juice concentrate
    2 cups water
    ½ cup brown sugar (packed)
    2 teaspoons salt
    1 teaspoon crushed marjoram leaves
    1 teaspoon crushed rosemary leaves
    ½ teaspoon coarsely ground pepper
    6-pound pork sirloin roast, hip bone removed and
      backbone loosened
    ¼ cup water
    1 tablespoon cornstarch

Combine orange juice concentrate, 2 cups water, the sugar, salt, herbs, pepper. Place roast in large plastic bag or shallow glass dish; pour orange juice mixture over meat. Fasten bag securely or cover dish with plastic wrap. Refrigerate at least 8 hours or overnight, turning meat occasionally. Remove meat from marinade; reserve marinade. Tie meat with string. Insert spit rod lengthwise through center of roast. Secure meat on spit with holding forks. Check balance by rotating spit in palms of hands. Insert meat thermometer in center of meat, making sure it doesn't touch fat or spit. Arrange medium-hot coals at back of firebox; place foil drip pan under spit area. Cook roast on rotisserie 2½ to 3 hours, or until meat is done—no pink in center. (Meat thermometer should register 185°.) Add coals, if necessary, to maintain even heat. During last 1½ hours of cooking period, baste with 2 cups of the reserved marinade. For sauce, blend ¼ cup water and the cornstarch; stir into remaining reserved marinade. Cook, stirring constantly, until mixture thickens and boils. Boil and stir 1 minute. Serve over roast. *8 to 10 servings.*

BARBECUED HAM ON THE SPIT

    6-pound fully cooked boneless ham
    1 can (8¾ ounces) crushed pineapple *or* 1 cup
        pineapple juice
    1 cup brown sugar (packed)
    1 tablespoon prepared mustard
    2 tablespoons lemon juice

Score fat on ham in diamond pattern. Insert spit rod through ham. Secure meat on spit with holding forks. Check balance by rotating spit in palms of hands. Insert meat thermometer in center of ham, making sure it doesn't touch the spit rod. Arrange medium-hot coals at back of firebox; place foil drip pan under spit area. Combine remaining ingredients. Cook ham on rotisserie 2 hours and 45 minutes. (Meat thermometer should register 130°.) Baste ham with pineapple mixture during last 30 minutes of cooking period. Add coals, if necessary, to maintain even heat. *12 to 15 servings.*

Veal and Lamb

LIMED VEAL ROAST

    4½ - to 5-pound veal leg, boned and rolled with
        fat covering
    ½ cup butter or margarine, melted
    1 tablespoon grated lime peel
    ¼ cup lime juice
    1 teaspoon marjoram
    ½ teaspoon thyme
    Lime wedges

Insert spit rod lengthwise through center of roast. Secure meat on spit with holding forks. Check balance by rotating spit in palms of hands. Insert meat thermometer in center of roast, making sure it doesn't touch spit rod. Arrange medium-hot coals at back of firebox; place foil drip pan under spit area. Combine remaining ingredients except lime wedges. Cook roast on rotisserie 3 to 3½ hours or until done, basting with lime juice mixture occasionally. (Meat thermometer should register 170°.) Add coals, if necessary, to maintain even heat. Garnish roast with lime wedges. *8 to 10 servings.*

ROLLED STUFFED LAMB SHOULDER

> 3- to 3½-pound lamb shoulder, boned and well trimmed
> Salt
> 1 cup fine bread crumbs
> ⅓ cup soft butter or margarine
> 1 clove garlic, crushed
> 1 teaspoon rosemary leaves, crushed
> 1 teaspoon salt
> ½ teaspoon pepper
> 1 egg
> Salt and pepper

Spread meat flat; sprinkle with salt. Mix bread crumbs, butter, garlic, rosemary, 1 teaspoon salt, ½ teaspoon pepper and the egg. Spread bread mixture evenly over meat. Roll meat tightly; tie with string. Insert spit rod lengthwise through center of meat. Rub roast with salt and pepper. Secure meat on spit with holding forks. Check balance by rotating spit in palms of hands. Insert meat thermometer in center of roast, making sure it doesn't touch fat or spit. Arrange medium-hot coals at back of firebox; place foil drip pan under spit area. Cook roast on rotisserie 2 to 2½ hours or until done. (Meat thermometer should register 175 to 180°.) Add coals, if necessary, to maintain even heat. Slice to serve. *8 servings.*

APRICOT-GLAZED LAMB SHOULDER

> 4-pound lamb shoulder, boned, rolled and tied
> 1 teaspoon salt
> ¼ teaspoon pepper
> 2 jars (4¾ ounces each) strained apricots
>   (baby food)
> ¼ cup mint-flavored apple jelly

Insert spit rod lengthwise through center of roast. Rub roast with salt and pepper. Secure meat on spit with holding forks. Check balance by rotating spit in palms of hands. Insert meat thermometer in center of roast, making sure it doesn't touch fat or spit. Arrange medium-hot coals at back of firebox; place foil drip pan under spit area. Cook roast on rotisserie 2½ hours or until done. (Meat thermometer should register 175 to 180°.) Add coals, if necessary, to maintain even heat. Mix apricots and jelly. After roast has cooked 1 hour, baste with apricot mixture every 20 minutes during remaining cooking period. Slice the roast and serve with the remaining apricot sauce. *8 servings.*

LAMB ROAST COSMOPOLITAN

> 5-pound leg of lamb, boned and flattened
> 3 tablespoons flour
> 2 tablespoons olive oil
> 1 tablespoon salt
> ½ teaspoon *each* ginger, sage, marjoram, thyme and
>   pepper
> 2 cloves garlic, crushed

Trim excess fat from meat if necessary. Mix remaining ingredients to a smooth paste. Spread half of paste over inside surface of meat; roll meat tightly and tie with cord. Insert spit rod lengthwise through center of roast. Secure meat on spit with holding forks. Check balance by rotating spit in palms of hands. Spread remaining paste over outer surface of meat. Insert meat thermometer in center of meat, making sure it doesn't touch fat or spit. Arrange medium-hot coals at back of firebox; place foil drip pan under spit area. Cook roast on rotisserie 3 hours, or until meat is done. (Meat thermometer should register 175 to 180°.) Add coals, if necessary, to maintain even heat. *10 servings.*

Poultry

CHICKENS ON THE ROTISSERIE

    2 broiler-fryer chickens (about 3 pounds each)
    4 teaspoons salt
    Pepper
    ⅓ cup butter or margarine, melted

Wash chickens and pat dry with paper towels. Rub cavity of each with 2 teaspoons salt and dash pepper. Fasten neck skin to back with skewer. Flatten wings over breast; tie with string to hold wings securely. Tie drumsticks securely to tail. Insert spit rod through center of each bird from breast end toward tail. Secure each with holding forks. Check balance by rotating spit in palms of hands. Arrange medium-hot coals at back of firebox; place foil drip pan under spit area. Cook chickens on rotisserie 2½ hours, or until leg bone moves easily, brushing frequently with butter during last 30 minutes of cooking period. (Meat thermometer should register 185°.) Add coals, if necessary, to maintain even heat. *4 to 6 servings.*

CHICKEN WITH PÂTÉ DRESSING—Follow recipe above except—before mounting chickens on spit, rub cavity of each with ½ teaspoon salt. Fill cavities of chickens with mixture of 3 cups cooked rice, 8 ounces fresh liverwurst, cubed, ¼ cup butter or margarine, melted, 2 tablespoons parsley flakes, ½ teaspoon salt and ½ teaspoon thyme. Close openings with skewers. Sprinkle chickens with paprika before roasting. If you have extra stuffing, heat on grill in covered aluminum foil pan 20 minutes.

TURNABOUT TURKEY

    8- to 10-pound turkey
    2 to 2½ tablespoons salt
    Pepper
    ½ cup butter or margarine, melted

Wash turkey and pat dry with paper towels. Rub cavities with salt; sprinkle with pepper. Fasten neck skin to back with skewer. Flatten wings over breast; tie with string to hold wings securely. Tie drumsticks securely to tail. Insert spit rod through center of bird from breast end toward tail. Secure breast and tail areas with holding forks. Check balance by rotating spit in palms of hands. Arrange medium-hot coals at back of firebox; place foil drip pan under spit area. Insert meat thermometer in heavy part of breast. Brush turkey with melted butter. Cook turkey on rotisserie 3½ to 4 hours, or until leg bone moves easily. (Meat thermometer should register 185°.) Add coals, if necessary, to maintain even heat. *10 to 14 servings.*

TURKEY ROAST, 'FRISCO STYLE

    1 frozen boneless turkey roast, about 4 pounds
    ⅔ cup salad oil
    ½ cup lemon juice
    2 cloves garlic, crushed
    1 teaspoon crushed mint leaves
    1 teaspoon coarsely ground pepper
    1 lemon, thinly sliced

Place frozen roast in plastic bag or shallow glass dish. Combine remaining ingredients; pour over roast. Fasten bag securely or cover dish with plastic wrap. Refrigerate at least 8 hours or overnight, turning roast occasionally. Remove roast from marinade; reserve marinade. Insert spit rod lengthwise through center of roast. Secure meat on spit with holding forks. Check balance by rotating spit in palms of hands. Insert meat thermometer in center of meat, making sure it doesn't touch spit rod. Arrange medium-hot coals at back of firebox; place foil drip pan under spit area. Cook roast on rotisserie until done, following cooking directions printed on package. Add coals, if necessary, to maintain even heat. Baste frequently with reserved marinade. *8 servings.*

CORNISH GAME HENS

> 4 Rock Cornish game hens (about 1 pound 2 ounces each)
> 2 teaspoons salt
> ½ cup butter or margarine, melted
> Paprika
> 1 can (8¾ ounces) pitted Bing cherries, drained (reserve ¼ cup syrup)
> 1 teaspoon cornstarch
> ⅛ teaspoon salt
> ¼ cup orange marmalade
> 3 tablespoons brandy or reserved mandarin orange syrup
> 1 can (11 ounces) mandarin orange segments, drained

Wash hens and pat dry with paper towels. Rub cavity of each with ½ teaspoon salt. Flatten wings over breast; tie with string to hold wings securely. Tie drumsticks securely to tail. Insert spit rod through center of each bird from breast end toward tail, securing each with holding forks. Check balance by rotating spit in palms of hands. Brush hens with melted butter; sprinkle with paprika. Arrange medium-hot coals at back of firebox; place foil drip pan under spit area. Cook hens on rotisserie 1 to 1½ hours, brushing frequently with butter. Blend reserved cherry syrup, the cornstarch and salt in small saucepan; add orange marmalade. Cook, stirring constantly, until mixture thickens and boils. Boil and stir 1 minute. Add brandy, cherries and orange segments; heat through. To serve, spoon fruit sauce over hens. *4 servings.*

GAME HENS ON THE SPIT

Wash and dry Rock Cornish game hens (about 1 pound 2 ounces each). Rub cavity of each with ½ teaspoon salt. Place ¼ small apple and ¼ small onion in cavity of each. Close openings with skewers; lace. Flatten wings over breast; tie with string to hold wings securely. Tie drumsticks securely to tail. Insert spit rod through center of each bird from breast end toward tail, securing each with holding forks and arranging up to 4 game hens on spit. Check balance by rotating spit in palms of hands. Arrange medium-hot coals at back of firebox; place foil drip pan under spit area. Cook hens on rotisserie 1 to 1½ hours, brushing frequently with doubled recipe Tabasco Butter (page 44). *1 game hen per serving.*

SAVORY DUCKLING

  5-pound ready-to-cook duckling
  2 teaspoons salt
  1 small onion
  3 sprigs parsley
  ½ cup dry vermouth or apple juice
  ½ cup dark corn syrup
  1 tablespoon lemon juice
  1 teaspoon ground coriander

Wash duckling and pat dry with paper towels. Rub cavity with salt; place onion and parsley in cavity. Combine remaining ingredients in saucepan; simmer 15 to 20 minutes or until reduced about half. Fasten neck skin of duckling to back with skewer. Flatten wings over breast; tie string around breast to hold wings securely. Tie drumsticks securely to tail. Insert spit rod through center of bird from breast end toward tail. Secure duckling on spit with holding forks. Check balance by rotating spit in palms of hands. Arrange medium-hot coals at back of firebox; place large foil drip pan under spit area. Just before placing duckling on rotisserie, use a baster to force ¼ cup of the sauce into cavity of duckling. If needed, use additional skewers to keep cavity closed securely. Cook duckling on rotisserie 2 hours or until tender; prick skin with a fork frequently to allow excess fat to drain away. Add coals, if necessary, to maintain even heat. During last 20 minutes of cooking period, brush duckling every 5 minutes with sauce. *2 or 3 servings.*

Specialty Meats

WHIRLING FRANKS

   1 pound frankfurters
 10 whole sweet or dill pickles
  ½ cup bottled barbecue sauce
  2 tablespoons prepared mustard
  1 teaspoon horseradish
    Warm frankfurter buns

Make crosscut in center of each frankfurter and pickle. Alternating frankfurters and pickles, insert spit rod through cuts. Combine remaining ingredients except buns. Arrange hot coals at back of firebox; place foil drip pan under spit area. Cook frankfurters and pickles on rotisserie 20 minutes, brushing frequently with barbecue sauce mixture. Serve in buns. *8 to 10 servings.*

ORANGE-GLAZED BOLOGNA CUTS

Remove casing from 1-pound ring bologna; cut on the diagonal into 1-inch slices. Insert spit rod through center of slices, leaving ¼-inch space between each slice. If necessary, secure meat on spit with holding forks. Check balance by rotating spit in palms of hands. Arrange medium-hot coals at back of firebox; place foil drip pan under spit area. Combine ¼ cup orange marmalade and 1 teaspoon soy sauce. Cook bologna on rotisserie 30 minutes, brushing frequently with orange sauce. *4 or 5 servings.*

BARBECUED BOLOGNA

Prepare Chef's Special Sauce (below). Remove casing from a 2-pound large bologna, unsliced. Score bologna ½ inch deep in diamond pattern. Insert a whole clove in center of each diamond. Insert spit rod through center of bologna. Secure meat on spit with holding forks. Check balance by rotating spit in palms of hands. Arrange medium-hot coals at back of firebox; place foil drip pan under spit area. Cook on rotisserie 30 to 40 minutes, brushing frequently with sauce. *6 to 8 servings.*

Chef's Special Sauce

Mix ¼ cup prepared mustard, ¼ cup pineapple juice, 2 tablespoons brown sugar, ½ teaspoon horseradish and dash salt in saucepan. Heat, stirring occasionally. If desired, double recipe for extra sauce to serve with bologna.

Foods with a Smoky Flavor

There is a big difference between smoke cookery and the curing of meats and fish in smoke. Smoke curing is a method of preserving but not necessarily of cooking. For example, ham treated in a smokehouse still needs cooking after its slow aging in cool smoke is finished. What we are concerned with here, then, are the various methods by which the outdoor chef produces a smoky flavor in his food *while* he is cooking it.

An easy and popular way to obtain the flavor of smoke is by artificial means—by adding a few drops of liquid smoke seasoning to a basting sauce or by sprinkling meat or fish with smoke-flavored salt and then cooking it over a fire that does not, itself produce a smoky taste.

However, classic smoke cookery calls for a smoldering fuel that *will* produce an appetizing smoke flavor. And the word "appetizing" should be emphasized. Smoke from burning fat adds only the taste of burned fat; smoke from resinous woods like pine produces a sharp acrid flavor that can be extremely unpleasant. Although oak, maple, nut and fruit woods are widely used and produce excellent results, hickory is the favored choice of wood for smoke cookery. And many people add hickory chips, available in handy packages, to briquets to get that characteristic flavor.

Whether the food and fire are close together in a covered barbecue unit or the food is hung in a chimney away from the fire to be cooked *only* in its hot smoke, as in a Chinese smoker (see page 101), the standard procedure is first to get the fire burning with even, smokeless heat. Then the coals are arranged to suit the food and your grill. (Always follow any recommendations for covered cooking that accompany the grill.) Small, quick-cooking meats may be grilled directly over the coals. A roast that cooks for several hours, however, should be done over indirect heat.

There are various ways to achieve indirect heat, depending on your grill. (See page 12.)

Regardless of the location of the coals, once they are in position, toss a handful or so of *damp* wood chips, *damp* hardwood sawdust or other suitable smothering materials over them. And continue to add the chips or sawdust at regular intervals throughout the cooking period to maintain the dense smoke. For proper smoking, give wood chips a 30-minute soaking before adding them to the hot coals. If they should catch fire, simply remove them with tongs and soak again.

In most covered units, dampers are used to control the heat and maintain an even cooking temperature. Opening the dampers will raise the temperature; nearly closing them lowers it. And, of course, when cooking a roast, it will probably be necessary to add more fuel from time to time.

Marvelous flavors can also be produced by partly smothering your fire with fresh herbs. The herbs may be added at regular intervals while cooking a big piece of meat. But when dealing with small meats, fish steaks or even a rather large fish, wait until near the end of the cooking period. About ten minutes or so before the food is done, put generous handfuls of the fresh herbs directly on the coals. Lower the lid and close all dampers, top and bottom. This method of driving the smoke of herbs quickly into food is widely used in California, where one species of the bay tree grows wild and so the fresh leaves are readily available. (Somewhat the same results can be achieved with dry bay leaves that have been soaked in water.) Fresh rosemary twigs are also good used in this fashion, as are fresh thyme, marjoram and mint.

Although the smoky taste in your food will certainly be less emphatic, you can add these smothering materials to the coals in an open brazier. Or let wide bands of aluminum foil, tucked around the grid or weighted down with stones, serve as a makeshift hood.

Try your hand at smoke cookery with any of the following recipes—for appetizers, vegetables, meat, fish and poultry. We know you'll like them.

Appetizers

TENDERLOIN ORIENTALE

    1 can (13½ ounces) pineapple chunks, drained
       (reserve syrup)
    ¼ cup pineapple syrup
    ¼ cup dry sherry
    2 tablespoons soy sauce
    2 tablespoons chili sauce
    ½ teaspoon salt
    2 cloves garlic, crushed
    1 green onion, cut into thick slices
    2 slices ginger root, smashed
    2 pork tenderloins (10 to 12 ounces each)
    1 cup honey

Combine all ingredients except tenderloins and honey. Place tenderloins in plastic bag or shallow glass dish. Pour pineapple mixture over meat. Fasten bag securely or cover dish with plastic wrap. Refrigerate 2 hours, turning tenderloins once. Soak wood chips in water about 30 minutes. Remove meat from marinade. Pour marinade into foil pan. Insert meat thermometer in tenderloin. Arrange hot coals around edge of firebox; place water-filled foil drip pan under roast area. Drain half of chips; add to hot coals. Place meat and pan of marinade on grill about 6 inches from coals; cover grill. Cook 1¼ hours, turning meat every 15 minutes until desired degree of doneness. (Meat thermometer should register 185°.) At 30-minute intervals, add drained wood chips and, if necessary, hot coals to maintain smoke and even heat. During last 30 minutes of grilling, brush meat with honey 4 times. To serve, cut tenderloins diagonally into ¼-inch slices. Place a pineapple chunk on each slice and spear with a wooden pick. *24 appetizers.*

SMOKED TROUT APPETIZERS

1 large trout (3 to 4 pounds)
Salt
2 tablespoons soy sauce
2 slices bacon
1 lemon, thinly sliced

Soak wood chips in water about 30 minutes. Remove head and clean trout, if necessary. Sprinkle cavity of fish with salt and soy sauce. Lay a slice of bacon on each side of cavity; place lemon slices in center. Close opening with skewers; lace. Place fish on greased piece of wire mesh. Arrange hot coals around edge of firebox; place foil drip pan under cooking area. Drain half of chips; add to hot coals. Place fish on grill about 4 inches from coals; cover grill. Cook 1 to 1½ hours, or until fish is tender and flakes easily with a fork. At 30-minute intervals, add drained wood chips and, if necessary, hot coals to maintain smoke and even heat. Remove bones from trout and cut into squares. Serve on buttered crackers. *24 appetizers.*

SMOKED CEREAL MIX

1½ cups corn puffs cereal
1½ cups O-shaped puffed oat cereal
2 cups pretzel sticks
½ pound mixed nuts
¼ cup butter or margarine, melted
½ teaspoon Worcestershire sauce
¼ teaspoon garlic salt
¼ teaspoon celery salt

Soak wood chips in water about 30 minutes. Combine cereals, pretzel sticks and nuts. Form a pan, 18x12 inches, from double thickness heavy-duty aluminum foil; place cereal mixture in pan. Stir together remaining ingredients; pour over cereal mixture. Stir and salt lightly. Arrange hot coals around edge of firebox. Drain chips; add to hot coals. Place pan on grill about 4 inches from coals; cover grill. Cook 15 to 20 minutes. *Makes 6 cups.*

SMOKY SNACKS

Soak wood chips in water about 30 minutes. Form a pan, 18x12 inches, from double thickness heavy-duty aluminum foil. Measure 3 cups corn-cheese snacks and 3 cups horn-shaped corn snacks into pan; stir together. Arrange hot coals around edge of firebox. Drain chips; add to hot coals. Place pan on grill about 4 inches from coals; cover grill. Cook 15 minutes. *Makes 6 cups.*

Meat, Fish and Poultry

SMOKE-FLAVORED BURGERS

　1 can (8 ounces) tomato sauce
　¼ cup Worcestershire sauce
　2 tablespoons butter or margarine
　1 teaspoon sugar
　1 teaspoon salt
　½ teaspoon pepper
　½ teaspoon instant coffee
　¼ cup chopped onion
　1 pound ground beef
　　Smoked Buns (below)

Soak wood chips in water about 30 minutes. Combine first 7 ingredients in saucepan; heat to boiling. Stir together ¼ cup sauce mixture and the onion. Shape ground beef into 8 thin patties. Spread about 2 tablespoons of onion mixture on half the patties. Top with remaining thin patties and seal edges. Arrange hot coals in bottom of the firebox. Drain chips; add to hot coals. Place patties on grill about 4 inches from coals; cover grill. Cook 7 to 10 minutes on each side. Brush patties with sauce; serve in Smoked Buns. *4 servings.*

Smoked Buns

Butter 4 hamburger buns lightly. Place buns on grill when patties are turned.

HICKORY SMOKED CHICKEN

  6-pound roasting hen
  1 teaspoon poultry seasoning
  1 teaspoon crushed rosemary leaves
  1 orange, sliced
  1 cup chopped celery
  3 onions, quartered
  1 teaspoon crushed rosemary leaves
  ½ cup butter or margarine, melted

Soak wood chips in water about 30 minutes. Wash chicken and pat dry with paper towels. Rub cavity with poultry seasoning and 1 teaspoon crushed rosemary leaves. Stuff cavity with orange slices, celery and onions. Close opening with skewers; lace. Tie legs securely to tail. Fasten neck skin to back with skewer. Lift wings up and over back; tie with string to hold securely. Insert meat thermometer in hen, making sure it does not touch fat or bone. Arrange hot coals around edge of firebox; place foil drip pan under roast area. Drain half of chips; add to hot coals. Place hen breast side up on grill about 4 inches from coals; cover grill. Stir 1 teaspoon rosemary into melted butter. Cook hen 3 to 3½ hours or until tender, basting frequently with rosemary butter. (Meat thermometer should register 185°.) At 30-minute intervals, add drained wood chips and, if necessary, hot coals to maintain smoke and even heat. *8 to 10 servings.*

PAUL BUNYAN FRANK

  3½ - to 4-pound piece large bologna
  1 cup catsup
  ½ cup vinegar
  ½ cup molasses
  ⅓ cup prepared mustard
  2 tablespoons Worcestershire sauce
  ¼ to ½ teaspoon red pepper sauce

Soak wood chips in water about 30 minutes. Arrange hot coals around edge of firebox; place foil drip pan under roast area. Remove casing from bologna. Mix catsup and remaining ingredients. Drain half of chips; add to hot coals. Place bologna on grill about 4 inches from coals; cover grill. Cook 1¼ hours, basting bologna frequently with catsup mixture. At 30-minute intervals, add drained wood chips and, if necessary, hot coals to maintain smoke and even heat. Cut bologna into small pieces and serve with remaining sauce as appetizers. Or cut into slices and, if desired, serve with remaining sauce in individual French rolls. *12 to 15 servings.*

MINTED LEG OF LAMB

In this unique recipe fresh mint leaves thrown on the hot coals impart a subtle flavor to the lamb.

> ½ cup brown sugar (packed)
> ½ cup salad oil
> 1 teaspoon grated lemon peel
> ¼ cup lemon juice
> 3 tablespoons vinegar
> ¼ cup chopped fresh mint leaves
> 1 teaspoon tarragon leaves
> 1 teaspoon salt
> 1 teaspoon dry mustard
> 4- to 5-pound leg of lamb, boned, rolled and tied
>   Fresh mint leaves

Mix sugar, oil, peel and juice, vinegar and next 4 seasonings. Heat to boiling; reduce heat and simmer 5 minutes. Cool. Place lamb in plastic bag or shallow glass dish. Pour cooled marinade over meat. Fasten bag securely or cover dish with plastic wrap. Refrigerate 24 hours or longer, turning meat occasionally. Remove meat from marinade. Insert meat thermometer in roast. Arrange hot coals around edge of firebox; place water-filled foil drip pan under roast area. Add fresh mint leaves to hot coals. Place on grill about 4 inches from coals; cover grill. Cook 3 hours, or until meat is desired degree of doneness. (Meat thermometer should register 175°.) At 30-minute intervals, add fresh mint leaves and, if necessary, hot coals to maintain smoke and even heat. *8 servings.*

PUGET SOUND SMOKED SALMON

    2 limes, thinly sliced
    1 lemon, thinly sliced
    3 pounds fresh or frozen salmon steaks, 1 inch thick
½ cup butter or margarine, melted
    1 teaspoon curry powder
½ teaspoon salt
¼ teaspoon pepper

Soak wood chips in water about 30 minutes. Form a pan, 18x18 inches, from double thickness heavy-duty aluminum foil. Arrange lime and lemon slices in pan; place salmon steaks on slices. Combine butter and curry powder; pour over salmon. Sprinkle with salt and pepper. Arrange hot coals around edge of firebox. Drain chips; add to hot coals. Place foil pan on grill about 4 inches from coals; cover grill. Cook 40 to 50 minutes, or until fish flakes easily. *6 servings.*

Vegetables

FULL O' SMOKE EARS

Soak wood chips in water about 30 minutes. Remove husks and silk from tender young sweet corn. Arrange hot coals around edge of firebox. Drain chips; add to hot coals. Place corn on grill about 4 inches from coals; cover grill. Cook 15 to 20 minutes, or until corn is tender.

HICKORY BAKED POTATOES

Soak wood chips in water about 30 minutes. For each serving, brush 1 large baking potato with oil. Arrange hot coals around edge of firebox. Drain half of chips; add to hot coals. Place potatoes on grill about 4 inches from coals; cover grill. Cook 2 hours. At 30-minute intervals, add drained wood chips and, if necessary, hot coals to maintain smoke and even heat.

Especially for the Chinese Smoker

CHINESE SMOKED CHICKEN

   2- to 2½-pound broiler-fryer chicken
   ¼ cup soy sauce
   ¼ cup honey
   ½ teaspoon pepper
   ¼ teaspoon garlic salt

Arrange hot coals in center of firebox in Chinese smoker; add hardwood. Close lid on firebox. Insert meat thermometer in chicken, making sure it does not touch bone. Suspend chicken by wires in chimney. Combine remaining ingredients. Cook 2½ to 3 hours, or until chicken is tender, basting chicken frequently with soy mixture. (Meat thermometer should register 185°.) At 30-minute intervals, add hardwood and hot coals to maintain smoke and even heat. *4 servings.*

CHINESE SMOKED RIBS

   1 rack spareribs, about 3¼ pounds
   ⅓ cup salad oil
   ¼ cup soy sauce
   ¼ cup dry sherry or pineapple juice
   1 tablespoon brown sugar
   1 small onion, chopped
   1 clove garlic, crushed

Place ribs in plastic bag or shallow glass dish. Combine remaining ingredients; pour over ribs. Fasten bag securely or cover dish with plastic wrap. Refrigerate at least 8 hours or overnight, turning ribs occasionally. Remove ribs from marinade. Arrange hot coals in center of firebox in Chinese smoker; add hardwood. Close lid on firebox. Suspend ribs by wires in chimney. Cook 3 hours, or until meat is tender. At 30-minute intervals, add hardwood and hot coals to maintain smoke and even heat. *3 or 4 servings.*

CHINESE SMOKED POTATOES

For each serving, scrub 1 baking potato; rub with butter. Arrange hot coals in center of firebox in Chinese smoker; add hardwood. Close lid on firebox. Suspend potato by wires in chimney. Cook 2 hours, or until potato is tender. At 30-minute intervals, add hardwood and hot coals to maintain smoke and even heat.

One of the best pieces of equipment for smoke-cooking large pieces of meat is the Chinese smoker. Like all equipment for outdoor cooking, the smoker can range from a relatively simple makeshift unit to an elaborate brick structure with dampers, a grill section and the oven-chimney. Movable metal ones are also available and are very popular. Regardless of the trimmings, a Chinese smoker is basically L-shaped. The smoke from the hot fire rises up a flue or chimney set at one side of the firebox. The food, suspended in the heated chimney portion, cooks in the hot smoke rather than directly over the fire.

Sauces and Marinades

A just-right barbecue sauce or marinade can make all the difference between an ordinary meal and an unforgettable one. A basting sauce, brushed on the meat as it cooks, adds its own special flavor and keeps the meat juicy and succulent. Hold up on basting with a tomato-y sauce or one high in sugar until the last half hour—such sauces burn easily.

A marinade flavors meat, and sometimes tenderizes it, before cooking. Marinate in a tightly covered *non-metal* dish, and use tongs—never a fork—to turn the meat. Or use a large plastic bag; simply turn the bag to redistribute the marinade. We usually recommend marinating for several hours in the refrigerator, but an hour or two may be enough time, and a whole day or night is not too long.

When choosing from among these bastes, marinades and serve-with sauces, be sure to select one that will complement, not overpower, the meat.

Basting Sauces

PANTRY-SHELF BARBECUE SAUCE

For beef. Remember this sauce for your next cookout.

    2 tablespoons Worcestershire sauce
    2 tablespoons vinegar
    1 tablespoon butter or margarine, melted
    ⅛ teaspoon red pepper sauce

Combine all ingredients; brush on both sides of hamburgers or steaks; let stand 15 minutes. While grilling, brush meat with sauce. *Makes ⅓ cup.*

STEAK SAUCE, EASTERN STYLE

  ¼ cup vinegar
  2 tablespoons brown sugar
  1 tablespoon prepared mustard
1½ teaspoons salt
  1 teaspoon crushed tarragon leaves
  ¼ teaspoon pepper
  1 lemon, cut into thick slices
  1 medium onion, sliced
  ½ cup red wine or apple juice
  ¼ cup butter
  2 tablespoons Worcestershire sauce

In small saucepan simmer all ingredients except wine, butter and Worcestershire sauce 20 minutes. Stir in remaining ingredients; heat to boiling. Baste steak. *Makes 1 cup.*

NEW ORLEANS TOMATO SAUCE

With the rich, mellow flavor of molasses—here's a sauce for beef, spareribs or lamb.

  1 can (15 ounces) tomato sauce
  1 envelope (7/10 ounce) onion salad dressing mix
  ¼ cup vinegar
  ¼ cup light molasses
  2 tablespoons salad oil
  1 teaspoon dry mustard

Combine all ingredients in small saucepan. Cook and stir 3 minutes. Baste spareribs, beef or lamb during last half of cooking period. *Makes about 2 cups.*

RANCHO-RED SAUCE

A sauce to enhance grilled beef, ham, pork or lamb.

Melt contents of 1 jar (10 ounces) red currant jelly in small saucepan over low heat, stirring constantly. Blend in 2 tablespoons Worcestershire sauce. Baste meat during last 20 minutes of cooking period. Serve remaining sauce hot. *Makes 1 cup.*

SPARKLE 'N SPICE BARBECUE SAUCE

A new variation on the tomato barbecue sauce theme. A generous recipe for a big hamburger or chicken grilling party.

½ cup chopped onion
1 clove garlic, crushed
2 tablespoons salad oil
1 can (10½ ounces) tomato puree
1 cup chili sauce
1 cup vinegar
1 bottle (7 ounces) ginger ale
¼ cup sugar
2 teaspoons salt
2 teaspoons seasoned pepper
2 teaspoons allspice
1 teaspoon mace
⅛ teaspoon red pepper sauce

Cook and stir onion and garlic in oil until onion is tender. Add remaining ingredients; simmer 15 minutes. Baste hamburgers or chicken during last half of cooking period. *Makes 4 cups.*

SMOKY SAUCE

For beef. To add an unusual flavor.

1 teaspoon brown sugar
¾ teaspoon salt
½ teaspoon prepared mustard
¼ teaspoon pepper
¼ cup water
2 tablespoons vinegar
2 tablespoons butter or margarine
1 thin slice lemon
1 slice onion
¼ cup catsup
1 tablespoon Worcestershire sauce
¾ teaspoon liquid smoke

Mix first 9 ingredients in small saucepan. Heat to boiling and simmer 20 minutes uncovered; strain. Add remaining ingredients. Heat to boiling. Baste beef during last half of cooking period. *Makes ¾ cup.*

RAINBOW GLAZE

Green mint jelly and pink grenadine syrup are the "rainbow" ingredients that flavor pork or lamb.

   1 jar (8 ounces) mint-flavored apple jelly
   ½ cup grenadine syrup
   ½ cup vinegar
   1 teaspoon ginger

Combine all ingredients in small saucepan; simmer about 5 minutes. Baste pork or lamb during last 30 minutes of cooking period. Just before serving, brush again with sauce. *Makes 1½ cups.*

ORANGE SAUCE

For lamb or ham. This sauce really perks up the flavor of meat.

   1 jar (10 ounces) red currant jelly
   1 teaspoon grated orange peel
   ¼ cup orange juice
   1 tablespoon prepared mustard
   1 teaspoon salt
   ¼ teaspoon pepper

Combine all ingredients in saucepan. Simmer 5 minutes, stirring constantly. Baste lamb or ham during last 30 minutes of cooking period. *Makes about 1 cup.*

SAUCE O' GOLD

The sweetness of honey and the fragrance of rosemary mingle with mustard in a basting sauce. Perfect for ham, pork or lamb.

   ½ cup prepared mustard
   ½ cup honey
   1 teaspoon salt
   ½ teaspoon crushed rosemary leaves
   ¼ teaspoon pepper

Combine all ingredients. Baste lamb chops, pork chops or ham during last half of cooking period. Top with remaining sauce just before serving. *Makes 1 cup.*

SUGAR-SWEET BASTING SAUCE

Here's how to give ham and pork a spicy glaze.

> ¼ cup brown sugar (packed)
> 2 tablespoons salad oil
> 2 tablespoons honey
> 2 tablespoons lemon juice
> 1 teaspoon allspice
> 1 teaspoon cinnamon

Combine all ingredients in small saucepan. Heat to boiling, stirring constantly. Baste ham or pork chops during last half of cooking period. *Makes about ½ cup.*

LEMON SAUCE

For chicken or fish. A slightly different, snappy sauce.

> ½ cup butter or margarine
> ½ clove garlic, crushed
> 2 teaspoons flour
> ⅓ cup water
> 3 tablespoons lemon juice
> 1½ teaspoons sugar
> 1 teaspoon salt
> ⅛ teaspoon pepper
> ⅛ teaspoon poultry seasoning
> ⅛ teaspoon red pepper sauce

Melt butter in small saucepan. Add garlic; cook and stir a few minutes. Stir in flour; cook over low heat, stirring until mixture is bubbly. Remove from heat. Add remaining ingredients; cook over medium heat, stirring constantly, until mixture thickens and boils. Cool and refrigerate. Baste chicken or fish during cooking period. *Makes 1 cup.*

SAUCE PARISIAN

For chicken. Basting sauce par excellence.

  ½ cup salad oil
  ½ cup vermouth or other dry white wine
   1 teaspoon garlic salt
   1 teaspoon onion salt

In small saucepan heat all ingredients to boiling. Baste chicken during last half of cooking period. *Makes 1 cup.*

Marinades

SWEET 'N PUNGENT MARINADE

For beef or pork. Doubly good because it's first a glaze, then a serve-with sauce.

   1 can (8¾ ounces) crushed pineapple
   1 medium onion, cut into slices and separated
  ½ cup vinegar
  ½ cup molasses
  ¼ cup soy sauce
   1 clove garlic, crushed
  ½ teaspoon ginger
  ¼ teaspoon red pepper sauce
   1 can (8 ounces) tomato sauce

Combine all ingredients except tomato sauce. Marinate pork chops, pork tenderloin or beef; reserve marinade. Grill meat. Pour marinade into saucepan during last 30 minutes of cooking period. Cook on side of grill, stirring occasionally, until mixture is reduced to 1 cup. Stir in tomato sauce; heat just to boiling. Serve with meat. *Makes 3½ cups.*

HERB MARINADE

For beef. Its flavor fulfills the promise made by its tantalizing aroma.

> ½ cup chopped onion
> ½ cup lemon juice
> ¼ cup salad oil
> ½ teaspoon salt
> ½ teaspoon celery salt
> ½ teaspoon ground thyme
> ½ teaspoon crushed oregano leaves
> ½ teaspoon rosemary leaves, crushed
> 1 clove garlic, crushed

Combine all ingredients. Marinate beef; reserve marinade. Baste meat with remaining marinade during cooking period. *Makes 1 cup.*

RIVIERA MARINADE

For steak. To challenge the steak connoisseurs.

> 1 cup dry red wine
> 1 cup salad oil
> 2 tablespoons vinegar
> ¼ cup chopped green onions
> 1 tablespoon grated lemon peel
> 1 clove garlic, crushed
> 1 tablespoon salt
> 1 teaspoon pepper
> ½ teaspoon dry mustard
> ¼ teaspoon thyme
> ¼ teaspoon basil

Combine all ingredients. Marinate steak; reserve marinade. Baste steak with remaining marinade during cooking period. *Makes 2½ cups.*

SPICED APPLE MARINADE

For pork chops. The often-wasted syrup from spiced apple rings is first a marinade, then a sauce.

> 1 jar (14 ounces) spiced apple rings, drained
> (reserve syrup)
> ¼ cup white vinegar
> ½ teaspoon salt
> 1 medium green pepper, finely chopped
> 1 tablespoon water
> 2 teaspoons cornstarch

Mix apple syrup, vinegar, salt and green pepper; marinate pork chops 8 hours or overnight. Remove meat from marinade; reserve marinade. Grill meat. Stir water into cornstarch. Mix with reserved marinade. Cook, stirring constantly, until mixture thickens and boils. Boil and stir 1 minute. Add apple rings; heat through. Serve with grilled pork chops. *Makes 1½ cups.*

CATSUP-CURRY MARINADE

For spareribs, chicken or lamb. Tangy . . . tasty.

> 1 chicken bouillon cube
> ½ cup boiling water
> 1 cup catsup
> 1 tablespoon lemon juice
> 1½ teaspoons curry powder
> 1 teaspoon pepper

Dissolve bouillon cube in boiling water; stir in remaining ingredients. Marinate spareribs, lamb or chicken; reserve marinade. Baste with remaining marinade during last half of cooking period. *Makes 2 cups.*

ORIENTAL MARINADE

For chicken, spareribs or ham. The kumquat syrup adds an authentic Cantonese touch.

> 1 can (12½ ounces) kumquats
> 1 tablespoon grated orange peel
> ⅓ cup orange juice
> ¼ cup honey
> ¼ cup soy sauce
> ½ teaspoon ginger

Drain kumquats, reserving 2 tablespoons syrup. Combine reserved kumquat syrup with orange peel, orange juice, honey, soy sauce and ginger. Marinate chicken, spareribs or ham. Baste with remaining marinade during last half of cooking period. Garnish meat with kumquats. *Makes ¾ cup.*

SOY-GARLIC MARINADE

For pork, beef, chicken. A sauce with character.

> ¼ cup salad oil
> ¼ cup soy sauce
> 2 tablespoons catsup
> 1 tablespoon vinegar
> ¼ teaspoon pepper
> 2 cloves garlic, crushed

Mix all ingredients. Marinate meat. *Makes ¾ cup.*

TERIYAKI SAUCE

A famous favorite for pork, beef or chicken.

Mix ½ cup soy sauce, ¼ cup honey, ½ teaspoon monosodium glutamate and 1 clove garlic, crushed, or ½ teaspoon ginger. Marinate meat. *Makes ¾ cup.*

TOMATO-SOY MARINADE

For lamb. With a whisper of garlic.

> ½ cup tomato juice
> ¼ cup lemon juice
> 2 tablespoons soy sauce
> 1 tablespoon salt
> ½ teaspoon garlic salt

Combine all ingredients and marinate lamb. *Makes 1 cup.*

PRINCESS MARINADE

For fish fillets. So named because it's pretty and pink in color and delicate in flavor.

> ¾ cup rosé wine or apple juice
> ¼ cup lemon juice
> 2 tablespoons instant minced onion
> ½ teaspoon monosodium glutamate
> ¼ teaspoon aromatic bitters

Combine all ingredients and marinate fish fillets 1 to 2 hours. *Makes 1 cup.*

Serve-With Sauces

CHERRY-ORANGE SAUCE

> 1 can (1 pound 5 ounces) cherry pie filling
> 1 teaspoon grated orange peel
> ¼ cup orange juice
> ¼ teaspoon nutmeg

Combine all ingredients in saucepan; heat through, stirring constantly. Serve hot sauce with ham or pork. *Makes 2⅓ cups.*

ORANGE-MINT SAUCE

Combine ½ cup orange marmalade and ¼ cup prepared mustard in small saucepan. Heat slowly, stirring constantly, until marmalade melts. Stir in ¼ cup chopped mint leaves. Serve warm or cold with lamb or pork. *Makes about 1 cup.*

TROPICAL SAUCE

2 tablespoons butter or margarine
1 tablespoon soy sauce
1 teaspoon finely cut-up crystallized ginger
1 can (6 ounces) frozen pineapple-orange juice concentrate
1 can (8¾ ounces) crushed pineapple
⅓ cup flaked coconut
½ cup finely chopped macadamia nuts

Melt butter in small saucepan. Add remaining ingredients except nuts; heat to boiling. Reheat at serving time; stir in nuts. Serve with chicken. *Makes 2 cups.*

CREAMY CUCUMBER SAUCE

½ cup finely chopped pared cucumber
¼ cup dairy sour cream
¼ teaspoon salad seasoning
¼ teaspoon salt

Combine all ingredients; chill. Serve with shrimp, lobster or grilled fish. *Makes ⅔ cup.*

Barbecue Go-withs

A main course from the grill does not a dinner make. What to serve with it? Certainly not a plain lettuce wedge. Not an uninspired vegetable. Make the whole meal a success, from appetizer to dessert. A word to the wise: Outdoor cooking can be tricky; don't try to prepare an *entire* meal over the coals.

Here, then, are outstanding selections for every course—some to be prepared in the kitchen, some to go along on the grill. They're all sure to please.

Appetizers

GAZPACHO

>   2 cans (5½ ounces each) tomato juice
>   1 beef bouillon cube
>   1 tomato, unpeeled and chopped (about ¾ cup)
> ¼ cup chopped unpared cucumber
>   2 tablespoons chopped green pepper
>   2 tablespoons chopped onion
>   2 tablespoons wine vinegar
>   1 tablespoon salad oil
> ½ teaspoon salt
> ½ teaspoon Worcestershire sauce
>   3 drops red pepper sauce

Heat tomato juice to boiling; dissolve bouillon cube in juice. Stir in remaining ingredients; chill several hours. For accompaniments, fill small bowls with chopped unpeeled tomato, chopped unpared cucumber, chopped green pepper, chopped onion and herbed croutons. To serve, pour chilled soup into cups and sprinkle with accompaniments. *6 servings.*

"RARE 'N" TO GO STEAK APPETIZERS

½ pound ground sirloin
1 egg
1 green onion, finely chopped
½ teaspoon salt
2 drops red pepper sauce
    Soft butter or margarine
5 slices bread

Mix meat, egg, onion, salt and pepper sauce thoroughly. Butter one side of each bread slice. Cover unbuttered side of bread with meat mixture. Carefully spread butter on meat mixture. Place bread side down on grill 2 inches from medium coals. Grill 1½ minutes, or until bread is toasted. Turn and grill 1½ minutes longer. Cut each into 9 bitesize pieces with kitchen shears. *45 appetizers.*

SURPRISE MEATBALLS

½ pound ground sirloin
2 tablespoons grated Parmesan cheese
2 tablespoons catsup
½ teaspoon salt
36 small cocktail onions

Combine sirloin, cheese, catsup and salt; mix thoroughly. Drain onions well on paper towels; pat dry. Shape meat mixture around each onion, making balls about twice as large as the onions. Place 3 or 4 meatballs on each bamboo skewer. Chill. Place skewers on well-greased grill 2 inches from hot coals; cook 10 to 15 minutes, turning once. *9 to 12 appetizers.*

CHEESE PASTRY SQUARES

Prepare pastry for Two-crust Pie as directed on package of pie crust mix except—add ½ cup shredded Cheddar cheese to crumbled mix. Divide dough in half. On lightly floured cloth-covered board, roll each half into a rectangle, 15x10 inches; cut each rectangle in half. Place pastry strips directly on grill about 4 inches from medium coals; cover grill. If covered grill is not available, use a foil tent. Cook 35 to 40 minutes, or until pastry is golden brown. To serve, cut each strip into 6 appetizers. If hickory-smoked flavor is desired, add damp hickory chips to hot coals. *24 appetizers.*

EASY PIZZA APPETIZERS

>   4 large slices salami
>   2 long slices mozzarella cheese
>   1 can (2 ounces) mushroom stems and pieces,
>   drained
>   ½ cup canned pizza sauce
>   8 slices day-old bread
>   Soft butter or margarine

Coarsely chop salami and cheese; mix with mushrooms. Spread 1 tablespoon pizza sauce on each slice of bread. Spread 4 slices of the bread with salami mixture, making sure filling is spread to edge of bread. Top with remaining slices of bread, sauce side down. Generously butter both sides of sandwiches. Place in hinged sandwich grill. Grill 4 inches from medium coals about 5 minutes on each side or until browned on both sides. Cut each sandwich into 9 pieces with sharp knife or kitchen shears. *36 appetizers.*

FRUITED SALAMI KABOBS

>   ½ pound unsliced salami, cut into ½-inch cubes
>   (48 cubes)
>   ½ small cantaloupe, pared and cut into ¾-inch cubes
>   (48 cubes)
>   48 pickled mushroom caps (about 6 ounces)
>   ¼ cup butter or margarine, melted

Alternate salami, cantaloupe and mushrooms on bamboo skewers. Place on grill 2 inches from medium coals. Cook 5 to 6 minutes, turning once and basting frequently with butter. *24 appetizers.*

SWEETBREAD HORS D'OEUVRES

> 1 pound sweetbreads
> 1 teaspoon salt
> 1 teaspoon vinegar
> ½ teaspoon red pepper sauce
> 12 slices bacon, cut in half

Rinse sweetbreads in cold water. Combine 1 quart water with salt and vinegar; heat to boiling. Add sweetbreads; reduce heat and simmer 35 minutes. Drain; rinse sweetbreads with cold water. Dry on paper towels. Remove tough membranes. Cut into bite-size pieces; sprinkle with pepper sauce. Fry bacon 2 minutes on each side. Wrap each sweetbread with a bacon slice; secure with wooden pick. Grill on hibachi or in hinged grill 2 inches from hot coals 12 minutes, turning once, until bacon is crisp. *24 appetizers.*

RUMAKI ON THE HIBACHI

> 6 chicken livers
> 4 water chestnuts
> Soy-Garlic Marinade (page 111)
> 6 slices bacon
> Brown sugar

Cut chicken livers in half; cut each water chestnut into 3 slices. Pour Soy-Garlic Marinade over chicken livers and water chestnuts in bowl; marinate about 4 hours. Drain; cut bacon slices in half. Wrap a piece of chicken liver and water chestnut in each bacon slice. Secure with wooden pick; roll in brown sugar. Grill on hibachi over hot coals. Cook 15 to 20 minutes, turning often, until bacon is crisp. *12 appetizers.*

SHRIMP EN BROCHETTE

Delicious served with a hot mustard sauce and cocktail sauce.

> 1 pound fresh or frozen shrimp, cooked
> 6 to 8 bacon slices, cut in half
> ¼ cup butter or margarine
> ¼ cup lemon juice

If necessary, peel and devein shrimp. Wrap each shrimp in bacon slice; secure with wooden pick. If very small shrimp are used, wrap 2 or 3 together. Heat butter and lemon juice in small saucepan until butter melts. Grill bacon-wrapped shrimp on hibachi or in hinged grill 3 inches from hot coals 15 minutes, turning and basting frequently with butter mixture, until the bacon is crisp. *12 to 16 appetizers.*

LOUISIANA BOILED SHRIMP

> 2 quarts water
> 3 cups diced celery
> 1 cup chopped onion
> 2 lemons, quartered
> 2 cloves garlic, crushed
> 6 bay leaves
> 3 tablespoons salt
> 1 tablespoon whole allspice
> 2 teaspoons cayenne pepper
> 3 pounds fresh or frozen raw shrimp (in shells)

Heat water to boiling in large kettle. Add all ingredients except shrimp. Simmer 15 minutes. Add shrimp; heat to boiling and simmer 5 minutes, or until shell turns pink and shrimp is tender. Remove from heat. Let shrimp stand 20 minutes in shrimp boil; drain. Peel off shell; remove black vein. Serve on cracked ice with favorite cocktail sauce. *6 to 8 appetizer servings; 3 or 4 main-dish servings.*

CHICKEN BITES

    2 cans (4¾ ounces each) chicken spread
    2 tablespoons mayonnaise or salad dressing
    1 tablespoon parsley flakes
    2 teaspoons instant minced onion
    ¼ teaspoon crushed thyme leaves
    8 slices pumpernickel bread

Mix all ingredients except bread thoroughly. Spread mixture on slices of pumpernickel. Place bread side down on grill 2 inches from hot coals. Grill 3 minutes; turn and grill 3 minutes longer. With kitchen shears, cut each slice into 6 pieces; serve hot. *48 appetizers.*

Beverages

SPARKLING TOMATO JUICE

At serving time, pour 2 bottles (7 ounces each) carbonated lemon-lime beverage and 1 can (8 ounces) tomato sauce into pitcher. Serve over ice cubes. *6 servings.*

GRAPE CRUSH

    1 bottle (1 pint 8 ounces) grape juice, chilled
    1 cup orange juice, chilled
    ¼ cup lemon juice, chilled
    ½ cup sugar
    1 quart ginger ale, chilled
    Cracked ice

Combine all ingredients except ginger ale and ice; stir until sugar is dissolved. Just before serving, pour ginger ale down side of punch bowl or large pitcher; stir gently. Serve over cracked ice in tall glasses. *8 to 10 servings.*

MELONADE

    4 pounds watermelon
    ¼ cup sugar
    3 tablespoons lemon juice
    1 quart carbonated lemon-lime beverage
      Lime ice
      Fresh mint leaves
      Maraschino cherries

Remove rind and seeds from watermelon. Puree melon with blender or rotary beater. Stir in sugar and lemon juice; chill thoroughly. To serve, pour about ⅓ cup puree mixture into tall glass; fill with carbonated beverage. Top with scoop of lime ice; garnish with mint leaves and cherries. (Or combine puree mixture and carbonated beverage in punch bowl or scooped-out watermelon half.) *12 servings.*

CITRUS CIDER

    2 cups orange juice, chilled
    1 cup lemon juice, chilled
    4 cups apple cider, chilled
    ½ cup sugar
      Fresh mint leaves

Combine juices and cider with sugar; stir until sugar is dissolved. Pour over ice cubes. Garnish each glass with mint leaves. *7 or 8 servings.*

SPARKLING PUNCH

    1 can (6 ounces) frozen grape juice concentrate
    1 can (6 ounces) frozen orange juice concentrate
    1 can (6 ounces) frozen lemonade concentrate
    4 cups water
    1 quart ginger ale, chilled

Combine all ingredients except ginger ale; chill several hours. At serving time, slowly pour in ginger ale. Serve over cracked ice. *10 to 12 servings.*

PINK FRUIT PUNCH

Chill 1 can (46 ounces) pineapple-grapefruit drink, 1 quart cranberry cocktail and 1 quart ginger ale. Combine just before serving. Serve over ice in tall glasses. *14 servings.*

PERSIAN TEA PUNCH

    3 cups water
    3 orange pekoe tea bags
    1 teaspoon whole allspice
    ½ cup sugar
    ½ cup orange juice
    3 tablespoons lemon juice
    Fresh mint leaves

Heat water to boiling; remove from heat. Add tea bags and allspice. Cover and let stand 5 minutes. Remove tea bags; stir in sugar. Chill. Just before serving, remove allspice and stir in fruit juices. Serve over ice. Garnish with mint. *4 or 5 servings.*

LEMONADE

Stir together 3 cups water, 1 cup lemon juice (about 4 lemons) and ½ cup sugar. Pour over ice. *Makes 1 quart.*

MINTED LEMONADE—Prepare Lemonade (above) except—place bruised fresh mint leaves in glasses before pouring in lemonade. Garnish with mint.

PINK LEMONADE—Prepare Lemonade (above) except—add 2 teaspoons grenadine syrup and a little red food coloring.

LIMEADE—Prepare Lemonade (above) except—substitute lime juice (about 10 limes) for lemon juice and increase sugar to ¾ cup.

CRANBERRY-APPLE COOLER

> 6 cups water
> 1 cup sugar
> 1 quart cranberry cocktail
> 2 cups apple juice
> 1 cup orange juice
> 1 cup strong black tea
> 1 can (5½ ounces) frozen lemon juice concentrate

Heat water and sugar to boiling, stirring constantly until sugar is dissolved. Stir in remaining ingredients. Chill. Serve in tall glasses. *15 servings.*

FROSTY MOCHA

In small mixer bowl beat 2½ cups chilled strong coffee, 1 pint softened vanilla ice cream, ¼ cup chocolate syrup and ½ teaspoon aromatic bitters until smooth. Pour into small ice-frosted glasses. *8 servings.*

COFFEE À LA MODE

Fill mugs about ¾ full with steaming-hot strong coffee. Add a small scoop of vanilla or coffee ice cream. Serve at once. *(1 pint of ice cream is enough for about 6 servings.)*

Breads

BLUE CHEESE BREAD

½ cup soft butter
¼ cup crumbled blue cheese
1 loaf (1 pound) French bread
2 tablespoons grated Parmesan cheese

Blend butter and blue cheese thoroughly. Cut loaf
into 1-inch slices. Spread butter mixture on slices.
Reassemble loaf; spread remaining butter mixture over
top of loaf and sprinkle with Parmesan cheese. Wrap
in 28x18-inch piece of heavy-duty aluminum foil; seal
securely. Heat on grill 4 inches from medium coals 15
to 20 minutes, turning once. *Makes 24 slices.*

PARMESAN SLICES

¼ cup soft butter
½ cup grated Parmesan cheese
6 slices French or Vienna bread, 1 inch thick
1 tablespoon poppy seed

Blend butter and cheese. Spread both sides of bread
slices with butter mixture; sprinkle with poppy seed.
Place on grill 4 inches from medium coals. Toast 5 to
6 minutes on each side or until golden brown. *Makes
6 slices.*

SPICY ENGLISH MUFFINS

½ cup soft butter or margarine
1 teaspoon chili powder
½ teaspoon onion salt
4 large English muffins, split

Combine butter and seasonings; spread on cut surface
of muffins. Place muffins buttered side up on grill 4
inches from hot coals. Grill 3 minutes on each side
or until golden brown. *Makes 8 slices.*

HOT BREAD IN FOIL

Slice 1-pound loaf French bread (1-inch slices) or Vienna bread (½-inch slices) or split 8 large individual club rolls. Spread generously with one of the Butter Spreads (below). Reassemble loaf or rolls and wrap in heavy-duty aluminum foil (a 28x18-inch piece of foil is just right for loaf); seal securely. Heat on grill 4 inches from medium coals 10 to 12 minutes for rolls, 15 to 20 minutes for loaf, turning once. *Makes 24 to 28 slices or 8 rolls.*

Butter Spreads

Cream ½ cup (¼ pound) soft butter or margarine with one of the following:

GARLIC—1 medium clove garlic, crushed.

TARRAGON—1 teaspoon crushed tarragon leaves and ¼ teaspoon paprika.

ONION—2 tablespoons minced onion or snipped chives.

HERB-CHEESE—2 teaspoons snipped parsley, ½ teaspoon crushed oregano leaves, 2 tablespoons grated Parmesan cheese and ⅛ teaspoon garlic salt.

HERB-LEMON—2 teaspoons lemon juice and 1 tablespoon freshly minced herbs or 1 teaspoon dried herbs and dash salt.

SEEDED—1 to 2 teaspoons celery, poppy, dill or sesame seed.

MUFFINS EN BROCHETTE

Bake muffins as directed on 1 package (13.5 ounces) wild blueberry muffin mix. When muffins are cool, wrap in aluminum foil until ready to serve. Arrange muffins on a skewer; toast over medium coals until slightly browned and heated through. *Makes about 12 muffins.*

HOT BREAD INDIENNE

⅓ cup crunchy peanut butter
¼ cup mayonnaise or salad dressing
¾ teaspoon curry powder
1 loaf (1 pound) raisin bread, sliced

Mix peanut butter, mayonnaise and curry powder; spread mixture on one side of each slice of bread. Reassemble loaf with spread sides together. Wrap loaf securely in 18x15-inch piece of heavy-duty aluminum foil. Place on grill 5 inches from medium coals. Heat about 6 minutes on each of the four sides for a total of 25 minutes. *Makes 16 slices.*

CHEESE LOAF

1 package active dry yeast
¼ cup warm water (105 to 115°)
¼ cup lukewarm milk, scalded then cooled
1½ teaspoons sugar
1 teaspoon salt
½ cup butter or margarine
3 eggs
2¾ cups all-purpose flour°
1 cup diced natural Cheddar cheese
  (about 8 ounces)

Dissolve yeast in warm water. Combine dissolved yeast, milk, sugar, salt, butter, eggs and half the flour in large mixer bowl. Beat 10 minutes medium speed on mixer. Blend in remaining flour with spoon until smooth. Cover with cloth and let rise in warm place (85°) until double, 1 to 2 hours.

Punch down; cover and refrigerate overnight. Punch down; form flat ball. Knead in cheese until well distributed. Form round ball; place in greased 8-inch pie pan. Let rise until double, 1 to 2 hours.

Heat oven to 375°. Bake 30 minutes. *Makes 1 round loaf.*

° *If using self-rising flour, omit salt.*

ITALIAN BREADSTICKS

> 1 package active dry yeast
> ⅔ cup warm water (105 to 115°)
> 2½ cups buttermilk baking mix
> ¼ cup butter or margarine, melted
>   Caraway, poppy, celery or sesame seed or
>   garlic salt

Dissolve yeast in warm water. Mix in baking mix; beat vigorously. Turn dough onto surface well dusted with baking mix. Knead until smooth, about 20 times. Divide dough into 16 equal parts. Roll each piece between hands into pencil-like strip, 8 inches long. Spread part of butter in oblong pan, 13x9x2 inches. Place strips of dough in pan. Brush tops with remaining butter; sprinkle with seed or garlic salt. Cover and let rise in warm place (85°) until light, about 1 hour.

Heat oven to 425°. Bake breadsticks 15 minutes or until light golden brown. Turn off oven; allow breadsticks to remain in oven 15 minutes to crisp. *Makes 16 breadsticks.*

CHEESE TWISTS

> Biscuit dough
> ¼ cup soft butter or margarine
> ⅓ cup shredded process American cheese
>   Salt and paprika

Heat oven to 450°. Cover baking sheet with aluminum foil; grease foil lightly. Prepare Biscuit dough as directed on package of buttermilk baking mix except— use half the amounts of ingredients. Roll dough into a rectangle, 12x10 inches. Spread with butter and sprinkle with cheese. Fold lengthwise in half; pinch edges to seal. Cut into ¾-inch strips; twist each strip. Place on prepared baking sheet. Sprinkle with salt and paprika. Bake 6 to 8 minutes. Serve hot. *Makes 16 twists.*

CARAWAY-CHEESE TWISTS—Follow recipe above except—sprinkle caraway seed over cheese.

FRENCH BREAD

　　1 package active dry yeast
1¼ cups warm water (105 to 115°)
　　3 tablespoons shortening
1½ teaspoons salt
　　4 cups all-purpose flour°
　　Egg White Glaze (below)

In mixing bowl dissolve yeast in warm water. Stir in shortening, salt and half the flour until dough is easy to handle. Add remaining flour; mix with hand. Turn onto lightly floured board; knead until smooth and elastic, about 5 minutes. Round up in greased bowl; cover with towel. Let rise in warm place (85°) until double, 1½ to 2 hours. Test for rising: Stick 2 fingers in dough; if holes remain but top stays smooth, dough is ready. Punch down; roll into an oblong, 15x10 inches. Roll up tightly; seal edge. Roll to taper ends. Place on lightly greased baking sheet. Make slashes 2 inches apart. Let rise uncovered about 1 hour.

Heat oven to 375°. Fill loaf pan, 9x5x3 inches, with water; place on top shelf in oven 30 minutes before baking. Brush loaf with cold water. Bake 20 minutes. Brush loaf with Egg White Glaze. Return to oven and bake 25 to 30 minutes until golden. *Makes 1 loaf.*

° *Do not use self-rising flour in this recipe.*

Egg White Glaze

Mix 1 egg white and 2 tablespoons water in small bowl.

FRENCH ROLLS—Prepare dough for French Bread (above) except—after punching down dough, divide into 16 equal parts. Shape into rolls; place 2½ inches apart on ungreased baking sheet sprinkled with cornmeal. Let rise uncovered 30 minutes.

Heat oven to 425°. Fill loaf pan, 9x5x3 inches, with water; place on top shelf of oven 30 minutes before baking. Brush rolls with cold water. Bake 25 to 30 minutes or until brown. Remove from oven; brush with cold water. Cool in draft from open window or fan. Do not store in covered container. *Makes 16 rolls.*

HICKORY-CHEESE LOAF

>   1 loaf (1 pound) French bread
> ½ cup soft butter or margarine
>   1 cup shredded natural sharp Cheddar cheese
>   (4 ounces)
>   1 tablespoon snipped parsley
> ½ teaspoon hickory smoked salt
>   2 teaspoons Worcestershire sauce

Cut bread diagonally into 1-inch slices. Mix remaining ingredients; spread on slices. Reassemble loaf and wrap securely in 28x18-inch piece of heavy-duty aluminum foil. Place on grill 4 inches from medium coals. Heat 15 to 20 minutes, turning once. *6 to 8 servings.*

Vegetables

GREEN BEANS WITH MUSHROOMS AND ONIONS

>   2 packages (10 ounces each) frozen French-style
>   green beans
>   1 can (4 ounces) mushroom stems and pieces,
>   drained
> ¼ cup butter or margarine
>   Salt and pepper
>   1 package (4 ounces) frozen French fried onions *or*
>   1 can (3¼ ounces) French fried onions

Place frozen blocks of beans side by side on 18-inch square of double thickness heavy-duty aluminum foil. Top with mushrooms, butter and seasonings. Wrap securely in foil. Cook on medium coals 10 to 20 minutes or on grill 3 inches from hot coals 30 to 40 minutes or until tender, turning 2 or 3 times. Wrap frozen French fried onions in foil; 5 minutes before beans are done, place on grill. To serve, place onion rings on beans. (Canned onion rings will warm on the hot beans.) *6 servings.*

GREEN BEANS RIO

1 package (9 ounces) frozen cut green beans,
partially thawed
4 slices bacon, crisply fried and crumbled
½ cup chopped celery
1 green onion (with top), chopped
1 tablespoon sugar
1 tablespoon vinegar
1 tablespoon water
¾ teaspoon salt
⅛ teaspoon pepper

Break beans apart. Place beans, bacon, celery and
onion on 18x12-inch piece of double thickness heavy-
duty aluminum foil. Wrap food in foil, leaving one
side open. Combine remaining ingredients and pour
into foil packet; seal securely. Place on grill 4 inches
from medium coals. Cook, turning once, 25 to 30 minutes, or until beans are tender. *3 or 4 servings.*

SPEEDY BAKED BEANS

6 slices bacon, diced
1 cup minced onion
3 cans (1 pound 3 ounces each) baked beans
(with pork)
1½ teaspoons prepared mustard
⅓ cup chili sauce

Heat oven to 350°. Cook and stir bacon and onion
until bacon is crisp. Stir in remaining ingredients;
pour into 2-quart casserole. Bake uncovered 45 minutes, or until beans are heated through. *8 servings.*

NIPPY BEETS

1 can (1 pound) sliced beets, drained
(reserve 1 tablespoon liquid)
1 tablespoon instant minced onion
1 teaspoon salt
1 tablespoon butter or margarine
2 teaspoons horseradish

Place beets on 18x12-inch piece of double thickness heavy-duty aluminum foil. Sprinkle with onion, reserved liquid and the salt; dot with butter and horseradish. Wrap securely in foil. Cook 4 inches from medium coals 15 minutes, turning once. *3 or 4 servings.*

GRILLED SWEET CARROT STICKS

Sweet carrots complement ham or pork; the herbed variation is good with lamb. A recipe to remember when camping.

8 to 10 large carrots, pared
2 tablespoons butter or margarine
½ teaspoon salt
Dash pepper
¼ cup brown sugar (packed)

Cut carrots into sticks. Place on double thickness heavy-duty aluminum foil. Add butter, salt and pepper. Wrap securely in foil. Roast on medium coals 30 to 40 minutes or on grill 3 inches from hot coals 1 hour or until soft. Just before serving, sprinkle brown sugar over hot carrots. (Heat of the carrots will melt the sugar.) *6 servings.*

HERB-SEASONED GRILLED CARROTS—Follow recipe above except—sprinkle carrots lightly with dill weed or crushed thyme leaves before wrapping; omit brown sugar.

OUTDOOR CREAMY CABBAGE

For each serving, place 1 cup chopped cabbage on 10-inch square of heavy-duty aluminum foil. Season with salt and pepper and dot with ½ tablespoon butter or margarine. Wrap in foil, leaving one side open. Pour in 1 tablespoon light cream. Seal packet securely. Cook 4 inches from hot coals 30 minutes, turning once, or until cabbage is tender.

ROAST CORN

Juicy, buttery roasted sweet corn is almost a meal in itself. No one ever seems to get enough or tire of it during its brief season. Get young tender corn straight from the field if you possibly can.

Corn Roasted on Grill over Coals

Remove large outer husks; turn back inner husks and remove silk. Spread corn with soft butter. Pull husks back over ears, tying with fine wire. Roast on grill 3 inches from hot coals 20 to 30 minutes, turning frequently. Serve with salt, pepper and butter.

Corn Roasted in Foil on Coals

WITH HUSKS—Remove large outer husks; turn back inner husks and remove silk. Spread corn with soft butter. Pull husks back over ears. Wrap each ear securely in heavy-duty aluminum foil, twisting ends to make handles for turning. Roast corn directly on medium coals 10 to 15 minutes, turning once.

WITHOUT HUSKS—Remove husks and silk. Place each ear on piece of heavy-duty aluminum foil. Add 1 tablespoon butter and 1 ice cube (or about 2 tablespoons water). Wrap securely in foil, twisting ends to make handles for turning. Roast corn directly on medium coals 10 to 15 minutes, turning once.

EGGPLANT "COMBO"

    1 eggplant (about 1¼ pounds)
    1 green pepper, coarsely chopped
    1 medium onion, coarsely chopped (about 1 cup)
    1 tablespoon butter or margarine
    ¼ teaspoon crushed oregano leaves
    2 medium tomatoes, cut up
    ½ teaspoon salt
    ⅛ teaspoon pepper

Wash and prick surface of eggplant. Place green pepper, onion, butter and oregano on 18x12-inch piece of double thickness heavy-duty aluminum foil. Wrap securely. Place eggplant and foil packet directly on hot coals. Cook 10 to 15 minutes, turning eggplant once. (Eggplant will feel soft and skin will blacken.) Remove eggplant to chopping board; cut in half and scoop out pulp. Coarsely chop pulp. Combine with green pepper and onion mixture. Toss with tomatoes, salt and pepper. Serve immediately. *4 to 6 servings.*

MUSHROOMS LYONNAISE

Take down the "For Steak Only" sign and try these buttery mushrooms with other cuts of beef or with lamb.

    2 tablespoons instant minced onion
    ¼ cup water
    1 pound fresh mushrooms, washed, trimmed
      and sliced
    2 tablespoons snipped parsley
    ½ teaspoon salt
    ¼ teaspoon pepper
    ¼ cup butter or margarine

Mix onion and water. Place mushrooms on 18-inch square of double thickness heavy-duty aluminum foil; sprinkle with onion mixture, parsley, salt and pepper. Dot with butter. Wrap securely in foil. Place on grill 5 inches from medium coals; cook 10 minutes on each side. *6 servings.*

MUSHROOMS IN BUTTER

Wash and trim ½ pound fresh mushrooms; slice, if desired. Spread mushrooms on heavy-duty aluminum foil; dot with 1½ tablespoons butter. Wrap securely in foil. Place on grill 3 inches from hot coals. Cook sliced mushrooms 15 minutes; whole mushrooms 20 minutes; turn often. Serve with steak. *2 generous or 4 average servings.*

ROAST ONIONS

Here are two good and easy ways to cook whole onions outdoors. And they have a taste so different from those done in the kitchen that they seem almost like another vegetable. Plan on one onion for each serving.

Roasted Bermuda Onions

Choose large onions of uniform size. Place washed onions on low coals or on grill 3 to 4 inches from medium coals. Cook, turning occasionally, 30 to 45 minutes or until tender. To serve, squeeze the sweet, yellow "heart" out of the blackened crust.

Onions Roasted in Foil

For each serving, wash and cut stem end from one medium onion. Cut each onion into quarters, not cutting completely through. Place each onion on 9-inch square of heavy-duty aluminum foil. Pour ½ teaspoon Worcestershire sauce over onion or brush top with liquid smoke. Wrap securely in foil. Cook on medium coals 30 minutes or on grill 3 inches from hot coals 45 to 60 minutes, turning at 10-minute intervals. Onions are done when soft to touch with tongs or asbestos-gloved thumb. To serve, remove outer skin of onion.

PEAS ALMONDINE IN FOIL

>   2 packages (10 ounces each) frozen peas
> ⅓ cup slivered almonds
>   2 tablespoons butter
>   Salt and pepper

Place frozen blocks of peas side by side on 18-inch square of double thickness heavy-duty aluminum foil. Top with almonds and butter. Sprinkle with salt and pepper. Wrap securely in foil. Cook on medium coals 18 to 20 minutes or on grill 3 inches from hot coals 30 to 35 minutes or until tender, turning once. *6 servings.*

FOIL-GRILLED PEPPERS

Remove stems, seeds and membranes from 6 medium green peppers. Place each pepper on double thickness heavy-duty aluminum foil. Fill peppers with Chili Stuffing (below) or 1 can (24 ounces) Spanish rice. Wrap securely in foil. Cook on medium coals 15 to 20 minutes or on grill 3 to 4 inches from hot coals 30 to 40 minutes, turning once. *6 servings.*

Chili Stuffing

Combine 1 can (15 ounces) chili beans, drained, ¾ cup catsup and ½ cup whole kernel corn.

POTATOES ROASTED IN FOIL

Choose medium sweet potatoes, yams or white baking potatoes. Scrub potatoes and rub skins with salad oil or butter. Wrap each potato securely in heavy-duty aluminum foil. Roast potatoes on medium coals 45 to 60 minutes or on grill 3 inches from hot coals about 1 hour, turning frequently. Potatoes are done when soft to touch with asbestos-gloved thumb. To serve: make crosswise slits through foil and potato, fold back foil and squeeze gently until potato pops up through opening. Pass butter, salt and pepper.

POTATOES ROASTED ON THE COALS

Choose medium to large white baking potatoes, sweet potatoes or yams. Place scrubbed potatoes directly on medium coals. Roast, turning occasionally, 45 to 60 minutes or until tender. To serve, crack off the charred casing and serve the "heart" with lots of butter.

ZESTY GRILLED POTATOES

    4 medium unpared potatoes
    ½ cup bottled Italian dressing
    1 teaspoon salt
    ¼ teaspoon pepper

Scrub potatoes; cook in skins just until tender, about 30 minutes. While hot, cut unpeeled potatoes diagonally into ½-inch slices. Place in shallow glass dish; pour dressing over hot slices. Let stand 1 hour, turning slices once. Remove potatoes from dressing; place on grill 3 inches from hot coals. Grill 8 to 10 minutes on each side until golden brown; season with salt and pepper after turning. *4 to 6 servings.*

LEMON-TART POTATOES

    4 large potatoes, pared and cubed
    ¼ cup butter or margarine, melted
    ¼ cup lemon juice
    2 teaspoons salt
    1 teaspoon grated lemon peel
    ¼ teaspoon nutmeg
    ¼ teaspoon coarsely ground pepper
    1 green onion (with top), chopped

Cook potato cubes in boiling salted water just until tender. Combine remaining ingredients; toss gently with potatoes. Spoon onto 20x14-inch piece of double thickness heavy-duty aluminum foil. Wrap securely in foil. Let stand at room temperature 1 hour. Place on grill 4 inches from medium coals. Cook 30 minutes, turning once. *4 to 6 servings.*

ROAST POTATOES AND ONIONS

For each serving, pare 1 baking potato. Slice 1 inch thick; brush with melted butter and season with salt. Cut 1-inch slices of onion. Reassemble each potato with onion slices between slices of potato on double thickness heavy-duty aluminum foil. Brush top with melted butter; sprinkle with salt and pepper. Wrap securely in foil. Roast directly on medium coals about 45 minutes, turning frequently. Serve in foil.

GRILLED FROZEN POTATO PRODUCTS

Any of the many frozen potato products, such as French fries, shredded potato patties, rissoles and potato puffs, are delicious cooked out of doors. Wrap in heavy-duty aluminum foil with 1 tablespoon butter, salt and pepper to taste. Cook 4 to 5 inches from hot coals 20 to 25 minutes, turning once, until foil package is soft to touch with asbestos-gloved thumb.

CAJUN FRIED YAMS

Cook 2 pounds yams or sweet potatoes in boiling salted water 20 to 25 minutes or just until tender; cool. Peel; slice ¼ inch thick. Heat 2 tablespoons butter or bacon drippings in 10-inch skillet on grill. Place single layer of potato slices in skillet. Cook 5 to 8 minutes on each side or until golden brown. Remove from skillet; sprinkle immediately with granulated sugar. Cover to keep warm. Repeat procedure with remaining potatoes. *4 to 6 servings*.

STUFFED ACORN SQUASH

Select 3 medium acorn squash. Cut in half; remove seeds. Place each half on double thickness heavy-duty aluminum foil. In each half place ¾ cup chopped apple, 2 tablespoons chopped walnuts and 2 teaspoons brown sugar. Top each shell with 1 tablespoon butter. Wrap securely in foil. Cook on medium coals 40 to 50 minutes or on grill 3 inches from hot coals about 1 hour, turning once. Squash is done when soft to touch with asbestos-gloved thumb. *6 servings.*

ROASTED ACORN SQUASH HALVES—Follow recipe above except—omit apple and walnuts.

SQUASH WITH HONEY-CHILI SAUCE

Allow one acorn squash for two servings. Place whole squash directly on low coals. Roast 1 hour, turning occasionally. Outside of squash will char but inside will be moist and tender. When done, split and remove seeds. Serve hot with Honey-Chili Sauce (below).

Honey-Chili Sauce

½ cup butter or margarine, melted
½ cup honey
3 tablespoons sweet chow chow
1 tablespoon chili powder
1 clove garlic, crushed
1 teaspoon salt
⅛ teaspoon pepper
⅛ teaspoon nutmeg

Mix all ingredients; serve warm or cold. *Makes about 1 cup, enough for 8 servings.*

OUTDOOR PILAF

The perfect accompaniment for lamb or beef . . . adapted from the Middle East.

> ⅓ cup butter
> 1 cup uncooked regular long-grain rice
> 1 clove garlic, crushed
> 2½ to 3 cups beef bouillon
> ¼ cup raisins
> 2 tablespoons toasted slivered almonds

Heat butter in heavy 9-inch skillet on grill. Add rice and garlic. Cook and stir until rice is orange colored. Remove from heat; add bouillon. Cover (if skillet has no lid, fit piece of heavy-duty aluminum foil securely around edge); cook 30 minutes. Add additional bouillon if rice seems dry. Cook 15 to 20 minutes longer, or until liquid is absorbed and rice is tender. Remove from heat; uncover and sprinkle with raisins and almonds. Serve immediately. *4 servings.*

CHEESE-GRILLED TOMATOES

> 4 large or 8 medium firm tomatoes
> 1½ teaspoons salt
> ¼ cup dry bread crumbs
> ½ cup crumbled blue cheese or shredded natural
> Cheddar cheese
> 2 tablespoons butter or margarine

Cut tomatoes in half crosswise. Sprinkle each cut side with salt, bread crumbs and cheese. Dot with butter. Place on grill 4 inches from medium coals; cover loosely with aluminum foil "tent." Cook until skins pull away from edges of tomatoes, about 10 minutes. *6 to 8 servings.*

HERBED ZUCCHINI

> 4 zucchini, cut into ½-inch slices
> 2 medium tomatoes, cut into wedges
> 2 teaspoons instant minced onion
> 1½ teaspoons salt
> ¾ teaspoon crushed oregano leaves
> 1 tablespoon butter or margarine

Place squash on 20x14-inch piece of double thickness heavy-duty aluminum foil. Add tomatoes; sprinkle with onion, salt and oregano. Dot with butter. Wrap securely in foil. Place on grill 4 inches from medium coals. Cook 30 minutes, turning once. Serve with slotted spoon. *6 to 8 servings.*

ROMAN ZUCCHINI

> 1½ pounds zucchini
> 1 tablespoon Italian salad dressing mix
> ¼ cup salad oil
> Parmesan cheese

Cut squash lengthwise into ½-inch slices. Place slices in crisscross layers on 18x14-inch piece of double thickness heavy-duty aluminum foil, sprinkling each layer with salad dressing mix. Pour salad oil over top. Wrap securely in foil. Cook 4 inches from medium coals 20 to 30 minutes, turning once. Just before serving, sprinkle with Parmesan cheese. *4 or 5 servings.*

FOIL-GRILLED ZUCCHINI

Cut zucchini crosswise into ¼-inch slices. Place individual portions on double thickness heavy-duty aluminum foil. Sprinkle each serving with salt, freshly ground black pepper, grated Parmesan cheese and 1 tablespoon water; dot with 2 teaspoons butter. Wrap securely in foil. Cook on medium coals about 15 minutes or on grill 3 inches from hot coals 20 minutes, turning once.

Salads

TOSSED SALAD WITH CAULIFLOWERETS

1 medium head lettuce, torn into small pieces
  (about 6 cups)
¼ pound fresh mushrooms, washed, trimmed and
  sliced (about 2 cups)
1 small cauliflower, separated into tiny flowerets
1 small Bermuda onion, sliced and separated into rings
1 medium green pepper, diced (about ⅔ cup)
½ cup sliced pimiento-stuffed olives
½ cup crumbled blue cheese
  Classic French Dressing (below)

Toss gently all ingredients except Classic French
Dressing. Cover and chill at least 1 hour. Toss with
dressing; serve immediately. *8 to 10 servings.*

Classic French Dressing

¼ cup olive oil or salad oil
2 tablespoons wine or tarragon vinegar
¾ teaspoon salt
1 small clove garlic, crushed
  Generous dash freshly ground pepper
¼ teaspoon monosodium glutamate

Toss salad greens with oil until leaves glisten. Add
vinegar combined with remaining ingredients. Toss.

BEST TOSSED SALAD

1 large head lettuce (about 6 cups)
1 bunch leaf lettuce (about 2 cups)
½ small bag spinach (about 2 cups)
½ small bunch endive (about 1 cup)
  Classic French Dressing (above)

Use choice part of greens; discard stems and cores.
Tear greens into bite-size pieces (do not cut). Have
them dry and cold. Just before serving, toss greens
with Classic French Dressing. *6 to 8 servings.*

MEDITERRANEAN SALAD

2 medium tomatoes *or* 1 small (1 pound) eggplant
½ cup dairy sour cream
1 tablespoon lemon juice
1 tablespoon snipped parsley
½ teaspoon salt
½ teaspoon dill weed
¼ teaspoon coarsely ground pepper
1 small clove garlic, crushed
1 cup croutons
2 tablespoons butter, melted
4 cups torn salad greens
Pitted ripe olives

If using tomatoes, peel (if desired) and cut up; chill thoroughly. If using eggplant, pare and cube; cook covered in ½ inch boiling salted water 5 minutes or until just tender; drain well. Chill thoroughly. Mix sour cream, lemon juice and next 5 seasonings; chill thoroughly. Toss croutons with melted butter. Just before serving, gently toss tomatoes or eggplant with salad greens, sour cream mixture and croutons. Garnish with olives. *5 or 6 servings.*

BRUSSELS SPROUTS SALAD

2 packages (10 ounces each) frozen Brussels sprouts
¼ cup vinegar
¼ cup salad oil
1½ teaspoons chervil leaves
1 teaspoon salt
¼ teaspoon pepper
1 tomato, chilled and cut into wedges
Snipped parsley

Cook Brussels sprouts as directed on package; drain well. Combine remaining ingredients except tomato and parsley. Pour mixture over hot Brussels sprouts; toss gently until well coated. Chill thoroughly, at least 3 hours. Add tomato wedges; toss lightly. Sprinkle with parsley. Serve on spinach leaves, if desired. *6 servings.*

FIESTA SALAD

1 medium onion, thinly sliced
1 medium green pepper, coarsely chopped
(about 1 cup)
3 small tomatoes, coarsely chopped (about 2 cups)
4 slices bacon
¼ cup vinegar
1 teaspoon chili powder
½ teaspoon salt
2 to 3 drops red pepper sauce

Separate onion slices into rings; place in bowl with green pepper and tomatoes. Fry bacon until crisp; drain on paper towel. Pour off bacon drippings, reserving 2 tablespoons in skillet. Stir vinegar, chili powder, salt and pepper sauce into drippings; heat to boiling. Pour over vegetables; toss lightly. Crumble bacon and sprinkle over top; serve at once. If desired, serve over shredded lettuce. *6 servings.*

SALAD SENSATIONAL

4 cups bite-size pieces salad greens
1 cup shredded Swiss cheese
¼ cup sliced pimiento-stuffed olives
2 hard-cooked eggs, chopped
½ cup mayonnaise or salad dressing
2 tablespoons light cream
1 teaspoon dry mustard
½ teaspoon salt
¼ teaspoon pepper
2 tomatoes, cut into eighths

Combine greens, cheese, olives and eggs in large salad bowl. Blend mayonnaise, cream, mustard, salt and pepper; pour over salad greens. Toss lightly and garnish with tomatoes. Serve immediately. *6 to 8 servings.*

ZUCCHINI TOSSED SALAD

1 head lettuce (about 6 cups)
1 head romaine (about 5 cups)
2 medium zucchini, thinly sliced
1 cup sliced radishes
3 green onions, sliced (about 2 tablespoons)
1 ounce blue cheese, crumbled (about 2 tablespoons)
Classic French Dressing (page 140)

Tear greens into bite-size pieces, discarding stems and cores. Toss gently all ingredients except dressing, then toss with dressing. *6 to 8 servings.*

MOCK SLAW

1 can (1 pound) sauerkraut, drained
1 cup diagonally sliced celery
⅔ cup short green pepper strips
½ cup chopped onion
¼ cup sugar
⅓ cup dairy sour cream *or* ¼ cup light cream
½ teaspoon celery seed

Chop sauerkraut into short pieces. Mix in remaining ingredients. Cover and chill at least 24 hours, stirring occasionally. *8 servings.*

FRUIT 'N CHEESE SLAW

4 cups shredded cabbage (about ½ head)
2 cups sliced unpared apples, cut into strips
   (about 1½ apples)
3 ounces blue cheese, crumbled
½ cup dairy sour cream
¼ cup mayonnaise or salad dressing
½ teaspoon seasoned salt

Toss cabbage, apples and cheese together lightly. Blend remaining ingredients; pour over cabbage mixture and toss. *6 to 8 servings.*

COLESLAW

4 cups shredded cabbage (about ½ head)
¼ cup chopped onion
½ cup dairy sour cream
¼ cup mayonnaise or salad dressing
½ teaspoon seasoned salt
½ teaspoon dry mustard
Dash pepper

Toss cabbage and onion together lightly. Blend remaining ingredients; pour over cabbage and toss. Sprinkle with paprika, if desired. *6 to 8 servings.*

HERBED SLAW—Follow recipe above except—substitute 1 teaspoon celery seed and ½ teaspoon chervil leaves for the mustard and pepper.

MARINATED BEAN AND EGG SALAD

2 cans (1 pound each) whole green beans, drained
½ cup chopped onion
⅓ cup salad oil
¼ cup vinegar
½ teaspoon salt
¼ teaspoon pepper
4 hard-cooked eggs, chopped
¼ cup mayonnaise or salad dressing
1 teaspoon prepared mustard
2 teaspoons vinegar
¼ teaspoon salt
4 slices bacon, crisply fried and crumbled
Lettuce
Paprika

Combine beans, onion, oil, ¼ cup vinegar, ½ teaspoon salt and the pepper; toss lightly. Cover and chill. In another bowl, stir together eggs, mayonnaise, mustard, 2 teaspoons vinegar and ¼ teaspoon salt. Just before serving, drain bean mixture; add bacon and toss lightly. Arrange lettuce on 6 salad plates. Top each with spoonful of beans and scoop of egg mixture. Sprinkle with paprika. *6 servings.*

BEAN BONANZA

⅓ cup sugar
½ cup vinegar
½ cup salad oil
1 teaspoon salt
¼ teaspoon pepper
1 can (1 pound) cut green beans, drained
1 can (1 pound) kidney beans, drained
1 green pepper, finely chopped (about ⅔ cup)
1 small onion, finely chopped (about ⅓ cup)
Lettuce cups

Combine sugar, vinegar, oil, salt and pepper; mix with remaining ingredients. Cover and refrigerate several hours or overnight; drain and serve in lettuce cups. *4 to 6 servings.*

CREAMY BEAN SALAD—Follow recipe above except— omit sugar, vinegar and salad oil. Stir 1 cup chopped dill pickle and ⅓ cup mayonnaise or salad dressing into the bean mixture with the salt.

DEVILED DIP WITH VEGETABLE RELISHES

1 cup dairy sour cream
1 can (4½ ounces) deviled ham
1½ tablespoons instant minced onion
1 teaspoon prepared mustard
½ teaspoon celery salt
Dash pepper
Radishes
Carrot sticks
Cauliflowerets
Celery sticks
Green onions

Combine first 6 ingredients; chill at least 1 hour. Arrange radishes, carrots, cauliflowerets and celery in four wedge-shaped sections on large round chop plate or platter; use the green onions as dividers between the sections. Center the platter with a bowl of the chilled dip. *Makes 1½ cups dip.*

TOMATOES VINAIGRETTE

>   4 very thick tomato slices
> ⅔ cup bottled oil and vinegar salad dressing
>   Instant minced onion
>   Parsley flakes
>   4 large lettuce leaves

Arrange tomatoes in pie pan or square baking dish. Pour dressing over tomatoes; sprinkle with onion and parsley. Cover with plastic wrap. Refrigerate 3 hours, basting occasionally. To serve, arrange lettuce on salad plates; top with a tomato slice and dressing. *4 servings.*

FRESH FRUIT SALAD

>   2 medium unpared apples, quartered and cut into
>   ¼-inch slices
>   1 pound seedless green grapes
>   2 oranges, pared and sliced
>   8 lettuce cups
> ½ cup fresh or frozen (thawed) blueberries
>   Limeade Dressing (below)

Arrange apple slices, grapes and orange slices in lettuce cups; sprinkle with blueberries. Pass Limeade Dressing to pour over fruit cups. *8 servings.*

Limeade Dressing

With rotary beater mix ⅓ cup frozen limeade concentrate (thawed), ⅓ cup honey and ⅓ cup salad oil.

NOTE—If you wish to make salads ahead of time, dip apple slices into Limeade Dressing; refrigerate.

SUMMER MACARONI SALAD

> 1 package (6 or 7 ounces) elbow or shell macaroni
> 1 cup cubed Cheddar cheese
> 1 cup sliced sweet pickles
> ½ cup minced onion
> ¾ cup mayonnaise or salad dressing
> 1 package (10 ounces) frozen green peas,
>   cooked and drained
>   Salt and pepper
>   Lettuce leaves

Cook macaroni as directed on package. Toss all ingredients except seasonings and lettuce. Season with salt and pepper to taste. Chill thoroughly. Serve in lettuce-lined bowl. *6 to 8 servings.*

RANCH-STYLE POTATO SALAD

> 2 teaspoons celery seed
> 2 tablespoons vinegar
> 7 cooked large potatoes, cooled, peeled and cubed
> 1 cup salad dressing
> 2 tablespoons salt
> 1 teaspoon dry mustard
> ½ teaspoon seasoned pepper
> 2 cups chopped celery
> 1 cup chopped green onions (with tops)
> 1 cup sliced radishes
> 6 hard-cooked eggs, diced
> 1 large cucumber, diced
>   Tomato slices
>   Cucumber slices
>   Parsley sprigs

Soak celery seed in vinegar 30 minutes. Place potatoes in large bowl. Mix salad dressing, salt, seed-vinegar mixture, mustard and pepper. Toss gently with potatoes. Cover bowl with plastic wrap; chill thoroughly. Add remaining ingredients except tomato and cucumber slices and parsley; toss gently. Spoon mixture into serving bowl; completely cover top with tomato and cucumber slices and parsley. *8 to 10 servings.*

FAMILY-STYLE POTATO SALAD

Garnish idea: reserve one hard-cooked egg; slice thinly and use to ring top of salad.

>   4 cups diced cooked pared potatoes
>   1 teaspoon salt
>   1 teaspoon celery seed
>   ¼ teaspoon pepper
>   ½ cup sliced green onions (with tops)
>   ⅔ cup finely chopped celery
>   ⅔ cup sliced radishes
>   ½ cup sweet pickle relish
>   1 cup salad dressing or mayonnaise
>   1 tablespoon prepared mustard
>   4 hard-cooked eggs, chopped

Combine first 8 ingredients in large bowl. Stir together salad dressing and mustard. Pour over potato mixture and toss lightly. Carefully stir in eggs. Cover; chill thoroughly. *8 servings.*

GRILLED GERMAN POTATO SALAD

>   5 unpared medium potatoes (about 1½ pounds)
>   8 slices bacon, crisply fried and crumbled
>   1 cup finely chopped celery
>   3 green onions (with tops), finely chopped
>   (about ⅓ cup)
>   ½ cup mayonnaise or salad dressing
>   ¼ cup white vinegar
>   2 teaspoons sugar
>   1 teaspoon salt
>   1 teaspoon dry mustard
>   ¼ teaspoon coarsely ground pepper

Cook potatoes in boiling salted water just until tender. Peel and cut into cubes (about 4 cups). In large bowl combine potatoes, bacon, celery and onions. Mix remaining ingredients and pour over potatoes; toss thoroughly. Place mixture on 18x13-inch piece of double thickness heavy-duty aluminum foil; wrap securely. Place packet on grill 4 inches from medium coals; cook 20 minutes, turning once. *4 to 6 servings.*

GOURMET POTATO SALAD

¾ cup dairy sour cream
½ cup salad dressing
¼ cup chopped dill pickle
2 teaspoons seasoned salt
½ teaspoon coarsely ground pepper
5 cups diced cooked pared potatoes

Stir together sour cream, salad dressing, dill pickle, seasoned salt and pepper. Pour over potatoes; toss to mix thoroughly. Chill several hours. *6 servings.*

POTATO SALAD À LA RUSSE—Follow recipe above except—increase salad dressing to 1 cup. Just before serving, add 1 can (8 ounces) sliced beets, drained and cut into strips. Toss mixture until beets are coated. *6 servings.*

GOOD 'N EASY POTATO SALAD

1 package (5.5 ounces) scalloped potatoes
3 cups water
2 tablespoons salad oil
½ cup water
2 tablespoons white wine tarragon vinegar
¼ cup mayonnaise or salad dressing
1 teaspoon prepared mustard
½ cup chopped celery
2 hard-cooked eggs, chopped

Empty potatoes into saucepan. Add 3 cups water. Heat to boiling. Reduce heat and simmer until tender, about 15 minutes. Rinse with cold water; drain thoroughly. Place in bowl, cover and chill. Blend seasoned sauce mix with oil in small saucepan; stir in ½ cup water and the vinegar. Heat to boiling over medium heat, stirring constantly. Cover and chill. When ingredients are cold, blend mayonnaise and mustard into sauce. Fold into potatoes, celery and eggs. *4 servings.*

Relishes

FOUR-DAY WATERMELON PICKLES

> 6 cups water
> 9 cups pared watermelon rind, cut into ¾-inch
> squares (for color, leave a thin layer of red pulp on
> rind)
> 4 cups sugar
> 1 cup white vinegar
> ¼ teaspoon oil of cinnamon
> ¼ teaspoon oil of cloves

FIRST DAY—Heat water to boiling in large saucepan. Add rind and simmer 10 to 15 minutes, or until rind is tender when pierced with fork. Drain thoroughly and place in glass bowl or crock. Combine remaining ingredients in saucepan; heat to boiling, stirring until sugar is dissolved. Pour syrup over rind. Cool; cover and let stand overnight.

SECOND DAY—Drain rind, reserving syrup. Heat syrup to boiling; pour over rind. Cool; cover and let stand overnight.

THIRD DAY—Repeat as directed for second day.

FOURTH DAY—Heat rind and syrup to boiling. If desired, tint with 1 to 2 drops red or green food coloring. Immediately pack pickles in sterilized jars and seal tightly. *Makes about 3 pints.*

CANTALOUPE GRILLE

Pare cantaloupe and cut into 1-inch rings. Grill 4 inches from medium coals 3 minutes on each side, brushing with lemon juice. *6 servings.*

PICKLED CARROTS

> 2 cans (1 pound each) tiny whole carrots
> 2 medium green peppers, cut into thin rings
> 2 medium onions, sliced and separated into rings
> ½ cup bottled garlic salad dressing
> ¼ cup vinegar
> ¼ cup salad oil
> ¼ cup sugar
> 1 teaspoon salt
> ½ teaspoon pepper
> 1 clove garlic, crushed

Combine carrots (with liquid), peppers and onions in large juice container. Stir together remaining ingredients; pour over vegetables. Cover; refrigerate several hours or overnight. Tip container occasionally to distribute vegetables. Drain before serving. *Makes about 5 cups.*

OLD-FASHIONED CORN RELISH

> ½ cup sugar
> ½ teaspoon salt
> ½ teaspoon celery seed
> ¼ teaspoon mustard seed
> ½ cup vinegar
> ¼ teaspoon red pepper sauce
> 1 can (12 ounces) whole kernel corn
> 2 tablespoons chopped green pepper
> 1 tablespoon chopped pimiento
> 1 tablespoon instant minced onion

In small saucepan heat sugar, salt, celery seed, mustard seed, vinegar and pepper sauce to boiling; boil 2 minutes. Remove from heat; stir in remaining ingredients. Cool; cover and chill. For better flavor, let stand several days. *Makes 2 cups.*

PICKLED MUSHROOMS

Also excellent served as an appetizer.

> 1 package (.63 ounce) Italian salad dressing mix
> ⅓ cup tarragon vinegar
> 2 tablespoons water
> ⅔ cup salad oil
> 1 tablespoon sugar
> 4 cloves garlic, crushed
> 6 drops red pepper sauce
> 1 medium onion, sliced and separated into rings
> 2 cans (4 ounces each) whole mushrooms, drained

Shake dressing mix, vinegar and water in tightly covered jar. Add salad oil, sugar, garlic and pepper sauce; shake to mix. Stir in onion rings and mushrooms; cover and refrigerate overnight. Drain; serve onion rings with mushrooms. *Makes 2 cups.*

Desserts

APPLES ALFRESCO

For each serving, wash 1 baking apple; core to within ½ inch of bottom. Score skin ⅛ inch deep in petal design. Fill cavity with 1 tablespoon brown sugar, 2 teaspoons red cinnamon candies, 2 teaspoons lemon juice and 1 pineapple spear. Wrap apple securely in 8-inch square of double thickness heavy-duty aluminum foil. Place on grill 4 inches from medium coals; cook 30 to 40 minutes or until soft. Serve with Cinnamon Whipped Cream (below).

Cinnamon Whipped Cream

Beat ½ cup whipping cream, 1 tablespoon granulated sugar and ½ teaspoon cinnamon until stiff. *Makes 1 cup.*

CARAMEL APPLES

For each serving, wash 1 large baking apple; core to within ½ inch of bottom. Place on 8-inch square of double thickness heavy-duty aluminum foil. Fill center of each apple with 1 teaspoon butter, 2 tablespoons brown sugar and another teaspoon butter. Wrap securely in foil. Cook directly on low-medium coals 25 to 30 minutes or until soft. Cook apples upright (if turned, the filling runs out). Serve with whipped or pressurized cream and chopped nuts.

SPICED APPLES—Follow recipe above except—fill center of each apple with mixture of 2 tablespoons granulated sugar and ¼ teaspoon cinnamon; dot with butter.

CRUNCHY BANANAS

    1 egg, beaten
    2 tablespoons brown sugar
    ½ teaspoon salt
    4 green-tipped bananas
    2 cups cornflakes cereal, crushed
    ¼ cup butter or margarine, melted

Mix egg, sugar and salt. Peel bananas; dip into egg mixture and roll in cornflakes. Place on 18x12-inch piece of heavy-duty aluminum foil. Place on grill 2 to 3 inches from hot coals. Cook 10 to 12 minutes, turning once and basting frequently with butter. *4 servings*.

HOT 'N SWEET GRAPEFRUIT

For each serving, seed, section and remove center from a grapefruit half. Place on 12-inch square of heavy-duty aluminum foil. Mix 1 teaspoon honey and, if desired, 1 teaspoon sherry; pour over fruit. Sprinkle with ¼ teaspoon nutmeg. Wrap securely in foil. Cook on medium coals 5 to 8 minutes or on grill 3 inches from hot coals 12 to 15 minutes until heated through.

BLUSHING PEACH DESSERT

For each serving, fill cavity of a well-drained canned peach half with 2 teaspoons red cinnamon candies and 1 teaspoon *each* chopped nuts and lemon juice. Place another peach half cavity side down on top. Wrap whole peach securely in 8-inch square of heavy-duty aluminum foil. Place on grill 4 inches from medium coals. Cook about 7 minutes on each side or until heated through. Top peach halves with scoop of ice cream, if desired.

GRILLED PEACHES 'N BERRIES

Select ripe medium peaches. Wash and halve; remove pit. For each serving, place a peach half on square of double thickness heavy-duty aluminum foil. Fill cavity with fresh or frozen blueberries; sprinkle with 2 teaspoons brown sugar and 1 teaspoon lemon juice. Wrap securely in foil. Cook on grill 3 inches from hot coals 18 to 20 minutes or on medium coals 10 to 15 minutes, turning once.

CHERRIES ON THE HALF-PEACH

        1 can (1 pound) cling peach halves
        1 cup uncooked instant rice
    ½ cup water
    ¼ teaspoon salt
    ¼ teaspoon allspice
    ½ cup diced dates
      6 maraschino cherries

Drain peaches, reserving ½ cup syrup. In 8-inch foil pan, thoroughly mix reserved syrup, rice, water, salt and allspice. Sprinkle dates over mixture. Top with peach halves cavity side up; place a cherry in each cavity. Cover pan with heavy-duty aluminum foil; seal securely. Place on grill 4 inches from medium coals; cook 30 minutes. Serve with cream, if desired. *4 servings.*

MELON CASCADE

>2 large bunches seedless green grapes,
>   washed and dried
>1 egg white
>   Sugar
>1 honeydew melon
>   Lemon wedges

Snip grapes into small bunches. Beat egg white until frothy; dip grapes into egg white. Let stand until almost dry; sprinkle with sugar. Refrigerate uncovered 4 hours or until dry. Fill deep platter or serving bowl with crushed ice. Cut melon into 6 or 8 wedges, not cutting through to bottom; remove seeds. Place melon in center of platter; heap ice around to hold melon upright. Fill center of melon with frosted grapes; hang a few grape clusters over top. Garnish with lemon wedges and, if desired, with lemon leaves. *6 or 8 servings.*

WATERMELON SUPREME

Cut a large watermelon in half lengthwise. Store one half in refrigerator. Cut melon balls from second half; scoop out melon to form a bowl for fruit. Fill this shell with watermelon and cantaloupe balls, pineapple chunks, sliced bananas, pitted sweet cherries, fresh strawberries and blueberries or any other small fruits in season. Pour Aloha Sauce (below) over fruits. Mix well. If desired, serve from a metal wheelbarrow lined with aluminum foil and filled with cracked ice.

Aloha Sauce

Mix thoroughly 2 tablespoons *each* strained lemon juice, orange juice and lime juice, ⅓ cup water and ⅔ cup sugar.

FRUIT COMPOTE IN FOIL

For each serving, place a slice of pineapple on a square of heavy-duty aluminum foil. Mound fresh blueberries or strawberries (or a combination) on top. Sprinkle with a little confectioners' sugar. Wrap fruit securely in foil. Grill 4 inches from medium coals 10 to 15 minutes. To serve, fold back foil and top with whipped cream or dairy sour cream.

CURRIED FRUIT—Follow recipe for Fruit Compote (above) except—omit confectioners' sugar and add 2 tablespoons butter or margarine and 1 teaspoon curry powder. Serve as an accompaniment with lamb or chicken.

FRUIT KABOBS

Guests may want to assemble their choice of fruits and grill their own kabobs.

Cut a variety of fresh or canned fruit into uniform pieces. Try pineapple chunks, firm pitted cooked prunes, dates stuffed with whole nuts, peach halves, pear halves, green and red maraschino cherries . . . anything in season. Thread fruit on long skewers. Blend 1 cup honey and 1½ tablespoons lemon juice; brush over fruit. Grease grill to prevent sticking. Grill kabobs over medium coals until hot, brushing occasionally with butter. Watch kabobs carefully to prevent scorching. Heat remaining honey mixture and serve with kabobs.

ISLAND PINEAPPLE

Select a fully ripe pineapple. Remove top, but do not pare. Cut pineapple lengthwise into 8 wedges. Place in oblong pan, 13x9x2 inches. Drizzle 3 tablespoons honey over fruit. Let stand 1 hour, turning occasionally so pineapple is thoroughly coated with honey. Place peel side down on grill 3 inches from medium coals. Cook 15 to 20 minutes, or until pineapple is steaming hot. For easiest eating, use a knife and fork. *8 servings.*

WAFFLE STRAWBERRY SUNDAES

Wonderful on-the-spot dessert! Guests toast frozen waffles on the grill, top them with ice cream and fresh strawberries.

    6 small frozen waffles, about 8 inches square
    1 quart vanilla ice cream
    1 quart fresh strawberries, hulled, sliced and
      sweetened

Place frozen waffles on grill 4 inches from low coals. Grill 3 to 4 minutes on each side or until crisp. Top each waffle with scoop of ice cream. Spoon berries over ice cream. *6 servings.*

MOCK ANGEL FOOD

Cut crusts from day-old unsliced bread; cut into 2-inch cubes. Place bread securely on skewers. If on a picnic or camp-out, a pointed green stick may be used instead of a skewer. Dip bread in sweetened condensed milk, then in coconut, coating evenly. Toast over medium coals until coconut is brown and bread is heated through.

TOASTED ENGLISH TRIFLES

    1 loaf angel food cake, 10x3x2½ inches
    6 tablespoons cherry preserves
    1 tablespoon sherry
    ¼ cup sherry
    6 tablespoons sliced Brazil nuts
    ⅓ cup butter or margarine, melted
    Custard Sauce (below)

Cut cake into 12 slices. Stir together preserves and
1 tablespoon sherry. Dip one side of each cake slice
quickly into the ¼ cup sherry. Spread 1 tablespoon
preserve mixture on each sherried side of 6 slices;
sprinkle each with 1 tablespoon nuts. Place remaining
cake slices sherried side down on top. Brush both sides
of sandwiches with melted butter. Grill 5 inches from
medium coals 3 to 4 minutes on each side or until
browned. Serve with Custard Sauce. *6 servings.*

Custard Sauce

Prepare 1 package (about 3½ ounces) vanilla pud-
ding and pie filling as directed except—increase milk
to 2½ cups. Stir in ½ cup sour cream; serve warm.

PEANUT BUTTER CRUMB CAKE

Bake Velvet Crumb Cake as directed on package of
buttermilk baking mix. While warm, spread cake with
Peanut Butter Topping (below). Set oven control at
broil and/or 550°. Place cake about 3 inches from
heat; broil about 3 minutes or until nicely browned.

Peanut Butter Topping

    2 tablespoons soft butter
    ⅓ cup brown sugar (packed)
    2 tablespoons milk or light cream
    ½ cup chopped peanuts
    2 tablespoons peanut butter

In small bowl, mix all ingredients thoroughly.

APRICOT JAM CAKE

Bake Velvet Crumb Cake as directed on package of buttermilk baking mix. While warm, spread with ½ cup apricot or peach jam.

BROWNIE FUDGE CAKE

1 package (15.5 ounces) fudge brownie mix
½ cup water
2 eggs
½ cup chopped nuts
    Quick Fudge Icing (below)

Heat oven to 350°. Grease square pan, 9x9x2 inches. Empty brownie mix into small mixer bowl. Blend in ¼ cup of the water and the eggs. Beat 1 minute medium speed on mixer or 150 vigorous strokes by hand. Scrape sides and bottom of bowl frequently. Blend in remaining ¼ cup water. Beat 1 minute longer, scraping bowl frequently. Fold in nuts. Pour into prepared pan. Bake about 30 minutes. Frost with Quick Fudge Icing.

Quick Fudge Icing

½ cup sugar
2 tablespoons cocoa
2 tablespoons butter or margarine
¼ cup milk
1 tablespoon light corn syrup
    Dash salt
½ to ¾ cup confectioners' sugar
½ teaspoon vanilla

Mix sugar and cocoa in saucepan. Stir in butter, milk, corn syrup and salt; heat to boiling. Boil vigorously 3 minutes, stirring occasionally. Cool. Beat in confectioners' sugar and vanilla. Spread icing on warm cake.

CHOCOLATE BUTTER-MALLOW CAKE

⅓ cup shortening
1 cup granulated sugar
½ cup brown sugar (packed)
2 eggs (⅓ to ½ cup)
1 teaspoon vanilla
2 squares (2 ounces) unsweetened chocolate,
  melted and cooled
1¾ cups cake flour
1½ teaspoons soda
¾ teaspoon salt
1 cup buttermilk
¼ cup water
  Butterscotch Filling (right)
½ cup chopped nuts
  Marshmallow Frosting (right)
½ square (½ ounce) unsweetened chocolate, melted

Heat oven to 350°. Grease and flour oblong pan,
13x9x2 inches, or two round layer pans, 9x1½ inches.
Cream shortening, sugars, eggs, vanilla and 2 squares
chocolate until fluffy. (Beat 5 minutes high speed on
mixer or by hand.) Stir together flour, soda and salt.
Add alternately in three additions with buttermilk.
Blend in water. Pour into prepared pan(s). Bake
oblong 35 to 40 minutes, layers 30 to 35 minutes, or
until top springs back when touched lightly with
finger. Let stand 10 minutes; remove from pan. Cool.
For oblong cake, spread Butterscotch Filling over top
to within ½ inch of edge; sprinkle with nuts. For
layer cake, fill with Butterscotch Filling and sprinkle
nuts over filling. Frost sides and top of cake with
Marshmallow Frosting. Drizzle ½ square melted
chocolate from spoon in straight lines, 1½ inches
apart, lengthwise across cake. Run knife edge crosswise over chocolate lines, alternating direction of knife
edge on each line.

Butterscotch Filling

1 cup brown sugar (packed)
4 tablespoons flour
1 cup milk
2 egg yolks, slightly beaten
2 tablespoons butter or margarine
1 teaspoon vanilla

Combine sugar and flour in saucepan. Stir in milk. Heat to boiling, stirring constantly; boil 1 minute. Remove from heat. Slowly blend at least half of hot mixture into egg yolks. Stir into remaining hot mixture in saucepan. Heat just to boiling, stirring constantly. Remove from heat and blend in butter and vanilla. Chill 2 hours.

Marshmallow Frosting

2 egg whites
1½ cups sugar
¼ teaspoon cream of tartar
1 tablespoon light corn syrup
⅓ cup water
1½ cups miniature marshmallows *or*
    10 large marshmallows, quartered

In top of double boiler, combine egg whites, sugar, cream of tartar, syrup and water. Place over boiling water and beat with mixer or rotary beater until mixture holds stiff peaks. Scrape bottom and sides of pan occasionally. Remove pan from heat and add marshmallows. Continue beating until of spreading consistency.

JOHNNY APPLESEED CAKE

> 1 package (18.5 ounces) spice with sour cream
> cake mix
> 1 can (1 pound) applesauce (1¾ cups)
> 2 eggs
> Apple Butter Frosting or Browned Butter Frosting
> (below)

Heat oven to 350°. Grease and flour oblong pan, 13x9x2 inches. Combine cake mix (dry), applesauce and eggs in large mixer bowl. Blend 30 seconds low speed on mixer, scraping sides and bottom of bowl constantly. Beat 4 minutes on medium speed. Scrape bowl often. Pour into prepared pan. Bake 30 to 35 minutes, or until cake tests done. Cool. Spread choice of frosting over top of cake.

Apple Butter Frosting

Prepare 1 package (7.2 ounces) fluffy white frosting mix as directed except—while beating, add ½ cup apple butter.

Browned Butter Frosting

Prepare 1 package (15.4 ounces) creamy white frosting mix as directed except—lightly brown the butter over low heat before adding to frosting mix.

HAWAIIAN DATE CAKE

> 1 package (14 ounces) date bar mix
> ½ cup hot water
> 2 eggs
> 1 teaspoon baking powder
> ½ cup chopped walnuts
> 1 can (8¾ ounces) crushed pineapple, drained
> Pineapple-Butter Frosting (below)

Heat oven to 375°. Lightly grease square pan, 8x8x2 inches. Mix date filling and hot water. Blend in crumb mixture, eggs, baking powder, walnuts and ½ cup pineapple. Spread in prepared pan. Bake about 35 minutes or until deep golden brown. Frost with Pineapple-Butter Frosting.

Pineapple-Butter Frosting

Blend 3 tablespoons soft butter or margarine and 1½ cups confectioners' sugar. Stir in remaining pineapple (about 3 tablespoons) until of spreading consistency.

HONEY-GLAZED PEACH PIE

> 1 package pie crust mix
> 1 cup sugar
> ¼ cup all-purpose flour
> 4 cups sliced fresh peaches
> 2 tablespoons butter or margarine
> ¼ teaspoon cinnamon
> ¼ cup honey

Heat oven to 425°. Prepare pastry for 9-inch Two-crust Pie as directed on package. Stir sugar and flour together. Sprinkle over the peaches and mix lightly. Pour into pastry-lined pie pan. Dot with butter. Cover with top crust; seal and flute. Stir cinnamon into honey; spread over top of pie to fluted edge. Cover edge with 2- to 3-inch strip of aluminum foil to prevent excessive browning. (Remove foil 15 minutes before end of baking time so edge will brown slightly.) Bake 35 to 40 minutes, or until crust is nicely browned and juice begins to bubble through slits in crust. Serve warm.

BLUEBERRY PIE

For 8-inch Pie
    3 cups fresh blueberries*
    ⅓ cup sugar
    ¼ cup all-purpose flour
    ½ teaspoon cinnamon
        Pastry for 8-inch Two-crust Pie (right)
    1 tablespoon butter or margarine

For 9-inch Pie
    4 cups fresh blueberries*
    ½ cup sugar
    ⅓ cup all-purpose flour
    ½ teaspoon cinnamon
        Pastry for 9-inch Two-crust Pie (right)
    2 tablespoons butter or margarine

Heat oven to 425°. Wash and sort fresh berries. Stir together sugar, flour and cinnamon. Mix lightly with berries. Prepare pastry as directed. Pour fruit into pastry-lined pie pan. Dot fruit with butter. Trim overhanging edges of pastry ½ inch from edge of pie pan. Cover with top crust; trim 1 inch from edge of pie pan. Fold edge under, seal and flute. Cover edge with 2- to 3-inch strip of aluminum foil to prevent excessive browning. (Remove foil about 15 minutes before end of baking time so edge will brown slightly.) Bake 35 to 45 minutes, or until crust is nicely browned and juice begins to bubble through slits in crust. Serve slightly warm.

* *Unsweetened frozen blueberries, partially thawed, may be substituted for the fresh blueberries.*

Pastry for 8-inch Two-crust Pie
   1½ cups all-purpose flour°
    ¾ teaspoon salt
    ½ cup plus 2 tablespoons shortening *or*
      ½ cup lard
     3 tablespoons cold water

Pastry for 9-inch Two-crust Pie
    2 cups all-purpose flour°
    1 teaspoon salt
   ⅔ cup plus 2 tablespoons shortening *or*
      ⅔ cup lard
    ¼ cup cold water

Stir flour and salt together. With pastry blender, cut
in shortening thoroughly. (Crumbs should be size of
tiny peas.) Sprinkle water over mixture, 1 tablespoon
at a time, mixing with fork until flour is moistened (1
to 2 teaspoons water may be added, if necessary).
Mix thoroughly until dough almost cleans sides of
bowl. Press dough into ball.

Divide dough in half. Shape each half into a flat-
tened circle. Roll out one part on lightly floured cloth-
covered board 1½ inches larger than inverted pie pan.
Fold pastry in half; transfer to pie pan. Unfold and
ease pastry into pan, being careful not to stretch. Roll
out other part of pastry 2 inches larger than pie pan.
Fold into fourths; make several slits near center of
folded edges.

° *If using self-rising flour, omit salt.*

FRESH RHUBARB PIE

For 8-inch Pie
   1 to 1¼ cups sugar
   ¼ cup all-purpose flour
   ¼ teaspoon grated orange peel, if desired
      Pastry for 8-inch Two-crust Pie (page 165)
   3 cups ½-inch pieces rhubarb (1½ pounds)
   1 tablespoon butter or margarine

For 9-inch Pie
   1⅓ to 1⅔ cups sugar
   ⅓ cup all-purpose flour
   ½ teaspoon grated orange peel, if desired
      Pastry for 9-inch Two-crust Pie (page 165)
   4 cups ½-inch pieces rhubarb (2 pounds)
   2 tablespoons butter or margarine

Heat oven to 425°. Mix sugar (amount depends on tartness of rhubarb), flour and orange peel. Prepare pastry as directed. Spread half of rhubarb into pastry-lined pie pan; sprinkle with half of sugar mixture. Repeat with remaining rhubarb and sugar. Dot with butter. Cover with top crust; seal and flute. Sprinkle crust with sugar. Cover edge with 2- to 3-inch strip of aluminum foil to prevent excessive browning. (Remove foil about 15 minutes before end of baking time.) Bake 40 to 50 minutes, or until crust is nicely browned and juice begins to bubble through slits. Serve warm.

HOMEMADE VANILLA ICE CREAM

   ½ cup sugar
   ¼ teaspoon salt
   1 cup milk
   3 egg yolks, beaten
   1 tablespoon vanilla
   2 cups whipping cream

For crank-type freezer—In a saucepan mix sugar, salt, milk and egg yolks. Cook over medium heat, stirring constantly, just until bubbles appear around edge of mixture in pan. Cool. Stir in vanilla and whipping cream. Place mixture in freezer can; put dasher in place. Cover can and adjust crank. Place can in freezer tub. Fill freezer tub ⅓ full of ice; add remaining ice alternately with layers of rock salt (6 parts ice to 1 part rock salt). Turn crank until it turns with difficulty. Draw off water. Remove lid; take out dasher. Pack mixture down. Repack in ice and rock salt. Let ripen several hours. *Makes 1 quart.*

For refrigerator—In saucepan mix sugar, salt, milk and egg yolks. Cook over medium heat, stirring constantly, just until bubbles appear around edge of mixture in pan. Cool. Stir in vanilla; pour into refrigerator tray. Freeze until mixture is mushy and partially frozen, ½ to 1 hour. Whip cream until soft peaks form. Spoon partially frozen mixture into chilled bowl; beat until smooth. Fold in whipped cream. Pour cream mixture into two refrigerator trays; freeze 3 to 4 hours until firm, stirring frequently and thoroughly during first hours. Keep trays covered with waxed paper to help prevent crystals from forming. *Makes 1 quart.*

FROZEN STRAWBERRY ICE CREAM—Follow recipe for Homemade Vanilla Ice Cream (left) except—decrease vanilla to 1 teaspoon. Thaw 1 package (16 ounces) frozen strawberry halves. After adding cream, stir in thawed strawberries. Add few drops red food coloring, if desired.

FRESH STRAWBERRY ICE CREAM—Follow recipe for Homemade Vanilla Ice Cream (left) except—decrease vanilla to 1 teaspoon. Mash 1 pint fresh strawberries with ½ cup sugar. After adding cream, stir in berries. Add few drops red food coloring, if desired.

WINTERGREEN OR PEPPERMINT ICE CREAM—Follow recipe for Homemade Vanilla Ice Cream (left) except—decrease vanilla to 1 teaspoon. After adding cream, stir in ½ cup crushed wintergreen or peppermint candy sticks. Add few drops green or red food coloring, if desired.

CHOCOLATE ICE CREAM—Follow recipe for Homemade Vanilla Ice Cream (page 166) except—decrease vanilla to 1 teaspoon and increase sugar to 1 cup. Melt 2 squares (2 ounces) unsweetened chocolate; stir into hot milk mixture in saucepan.

NUT BRITTLE ICE CREAM—Follow recipe for Homemade Vanilla Ice Cream (page 166) except—after adding cream, stir in 1 cup crushed almond, pecan or peanut brittle.

RHUMBA CHOCOLATE SAUCE

To serve with rich Homemade Vanilla Ice Cream.

> 1 package (14.3 ounces) dark chocolate fudge
>   flavor frosting mix
> 2 tablespoons light corn syrup
> 3 tablespoons soft butter or margarine
> ½ cup milk
> 2 tablespoons dark rum*

In top of double boiler combine frosting mix, syrup and butter. Gradually stir in milk. Heat over rapidly boiling water 5 minutes, stirring occasionally. Remove from heat; stir in rum. Cool. Serve warm or slightly chilled. *Makes 1 pint.*

* *If desired, omit rum and increase milk to ⅔ cup.*

ROCKY ROAD CHOCOLATE SAUCE—Follow recipe above except—omit rum and increase milk to ⅔ cup. When sauce is almost cool, stir in 1 cup miniature marshmallows and 1 teaspoon vanilla.

Patio Parties—
with a Cross-Country Flair

One of the prime advantages of moving a party outside the confines of the house is the opportunity it
offers you to entertain a large number of people at
one time—lots more than you'd be able to serve com-
fortably indoors. And this is where the patio party
comes into its own. Although service may be informal,
it may also be rather grand—a real outdoor counter-
part of your most sophisticated indoor dinner. The
mood is what you choose to make it.

Such a party calls for the same kind of planning that
goes into any party—but on a bigger scale. (See page
31 for more information about planning and presenting a meal outdoors.) Since you'll have more guests,
you'll need more food, more help and probably more
cooking gear. One of the most efficient ways to feed a
crowd is by pooling equipment. Ask some of your
guests to bring along their own grills and let each of
these auxiliary chefs concentrate on one task. Then
while some are grilling meats or basting roasts, others
are tending the potatoes, corn and other supplement-
ary dishes.

It's particular fun to theme a barbecue party, and
really carry it out—in food, table setting and dress.
With this idea in mind, on the following pages we
offer you five party-tested barbecue menus, starring
five very different sections of these United States. What
about treating your guests to the Hawaiian Luau?
Have the man of the hour wear his splashiest sport-
shirt and say "Aloha" to each guest with a paper lei.
Perhaps you'll even ask all the women to wear muu-
muu-style dresses. For the "Down-East" Special,
spread blankets on the grass and eat just as if you were
on a beach. To play up the Midwest Splurge, arrange

169

fresh or dried flowers, ears of corn and paper wheat stalks in a big breadbasket and center it on your table. Make blue jeans and slacks the preferred garb for the Texas Beef Bake and gift each feaster with a big red-and-white bandana to tie under his chin. Hail the sun and fun country and splash your California Patio Party table with bright citrus colors.

Try these ideas or your own variations on any theme. You'll be surprised how much they can add to the fresh-air fun.

Party Pointers

• *Have plenty of everything—fire and food alike. Fresh air sharpens appetites. Leftovers can be used another day, but nothing will save a meal that is too little and too late.*

• *Adopt a stern method of kibitzer control. Friends who would not dream of walking into your kitchen and adjusting the oven control seem unable to resist "helping" the barbecuer by stirring up his fire. They mean well, but discourage them.*

• *Expect the unexpected. Have some plan worked out in case a sudden summer storm blows up. Move the guests to the porch or house. If your grill's portable, find a safe, well-ventilated place where you can move it. In the yard, a huge sun umbrella or makeshift canvas covering will protect the fire in a stationary fireplace—and the cook.*

• *Develop a definite plan for cleanup. Scrape and stack plates in an orderly fashion, then carry them into the kitchen. You'll want to spend what's left of the evening in a pleasant atmosphere.*

• *Make some arrangements for throwing a bit of light on the situation. Dusk quickly turns to dark.*

• *Be prepared to cope with summer cookout enemies —mosquitoes, ants and flies. There are many safe pest-deterrents on the market. And if your party is for midday, have sunburn lotion ready.*

"Down-East" Special

Beef Bouillon on the Rocks

Broiled Lobster or
Lobster Tails on the Grill (page 69)

Steamed Clams and Vegetables

Melted Butter

French Bread

Blueberry Pie (page 161)

Hot Coffee

Invite a few friends or a crowd to this "clambake" party, an ideal cookout for beach or backyard. Plan on one lobster and one packet of steamed clams for each person. Then line up enough grills —or improvised bricks and grids—to do the job.

BROILED LOBSTER

Purchase one 1- to 2-pound live lobster for each serving. Parboil lobster in boiling water to cover, 5 to 10 minutes.

Split lobster lengthwise. Remove the stomach, which is just back of the head, and the intestinal vein, which runs from the stomach to the tip of the tail. Leave in the green liver and coral roe—they are delicious. Brush meat liberally with butter. Grill 4 inches from low coals 10 to 15 minutes, or until meat loses its transparent look. Do not turn or you will lose the luscious juice collected in the shell. Serve with melted butter, lemon wedges and plenty of paper napkins.

VARIATION—Place live lobster on its back; insert a sharp knife between body shell and tail segment, severing the spinal cord. Clean and grill lobster as in recipe above except—do not parboil. Grill 15 to 20 minutes. (If you can't face splitting a live lobster, ask your fish man to hold the lobsters until you call him. Have him kill the lobsters no more than an hour before you expect to grill them.)

How to Eat a Lobster

First, protect yourself with a napkin-bib. Then dig in.

1. Begin with the tail meat; twist out pieces with seafood fork. Dip in butter.

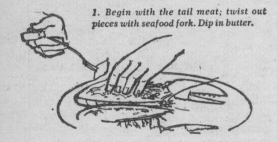

2. Twist off large claws; crack with nut-cracker. The delicious meat is inside.

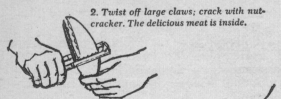

3. Pull off small claws; suck out the meat.

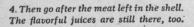

4. Then go after the meat left in the shell. The flavorful juices are still there, too.

STEAMED CLAMS AND VEGETABLES

For each serving, use an 18-inch square of heavy-duty aluminum foil. Place several corn husks, lettuce leaves or a strand of seaweed on foil. Top with 4 small new potatoes or 1 medium potato, cut into fourths; 1 small onion, peeled and sliced; 1 ear of corn, cut into fourths; 1 tablespoon butter or margarine and 4 fresh clams in shells, scrubbed. Sprinkle ½ teaspoon salt over mixture. Place additional corn husks, lettuce leaves or seaweed on top. Wrap in foil, leaving one side open; pour ½ cup water into packet. Seal securely. Place on grill 4 inches from hot coals. Cook 30 minutes.

Clambakes at the Shore

If you live within hailing distance of the seashore, you certainly won't want to let a summer go by without what the song describes as "a real nice clambake." Of course, a bake for fifty or more people is better left to a professional bakemaster who can provide the necessary special equipment and helpers, but a clambake for a dozen or so can be handled easily enough by amateurs.

There are several ways to set up a clambake, and all work well if the basic principle is understood and followed. Here are two procedures for this justly famous steam-cooked feast:

A TRADITIONAL NEW ENGLAND CLAMBAKE

1. Choose a location well above the high-tide line. Dig a circular hole about 1½ feet deep. The diameter of the hole depends on the size of the crowd—2 feet will do for a party of ten.

2. Line the hole with rocks packed as closely as possible. Choose hard dry rocks, at least 6 inches thick.

Wet porous rocks can explode when heated. Build a roaring wood fire on the rocks and keep it going *strong* for about 2 hours. It will take that long to bring the rocks to the high temperature required.

3. Rake off the fire and coals. Brush off the ashes with a damp broom or a branch of leafy twigs. Working fast so that the rocks will not lose their heat, cover them completely—and beyond their edges—with a 6-inch layer of wet seaweed (rockweed is the best). As fast as you can, add a layer of small scrubbed white potatoes or sweet potatoes, then a layer of split chickens, a layer of partially husked corn, a layer of plugged live lobsters (each about 1-1¼ pounds) and last a layer of clams. With clams on top, the clam juice seeps down, flavoring all the food. It's a good idea to put small items like clams, perhaps shrimp and mussels, in a cheesecloth net. Cover the heap with a big piece of dampened canvas. (Many people add another layer of wet rockweed before covering with the canvas, but this is not necessary.) The canvas must be large enough so that its edges can be firmly weighted into the sand with rocks, sealing the steam in the bake.

4. Relax for an hour or so—you've earned it. Then serve forth your steaming feast. And don't forget the melted butter for the corn and lobster.

A Traditional Clambake on the Grill

A clambake in the backyard is impressive, and you don't have to be near the ocean to enjoy it. Clams and live Maine lobsters can be ordered from several companies that make a specialty of mailing choice ones by fast freight. They are packed in seaweed in a cooking container which, in turn, is packed in ice for shipping hundreds of miles from their New England waters. All you do is put the cooking container on the grill and follow the enclosed cooking instructions.

THE CAN CLAMBAKE

1. Use a new galvanized iron garbage can with a tight-fitting lid. Dig a firepit deep enough to accommodate two thirds of the can.

2. Line the pit with dry stones and get a hot fire going in it. Keep it going for a couple of hours.

3. Meanwhile, place 6 inches of seaweed (or well-soaked corn husks) in the bottom of the can. Add in order: the plugged live lobsters, scrubbed potatoes, sweet corn ears and the washed clams. If desired, chicken quarters may be added after the lobsters. Top with a shallow layer of seaweed (or soaked husks). Put the lid on tightly. Lower the can into the firepit, amid the hot coals. Place a piece of canvas over top of can and shovel on sand.

4. Allow the bake to steam an hour or longer. It takes experience to gauge the cooking time.

Midwest Splurge

Barbecued Turkey Dinner

Cucumber Salad

Strawberry Shortcake

Lemonade (page 121)

This hearty feast cooks in a covered barbecue kettle. The vegetable rack, fitted neatly around kettle, is a handy space-saving accessory. (If such a rack is not available, simply arrange potatoes and corn on grill top with turkey. Serve the tomatoes chilled as salad.) This meal can be flavor duplicated—sans kettle—with Turnabout Turkey (page 88) on your rotisserie, Potatoes Roasted in Foil (page 134) and Roast Corn (page 131) grilled on a separate brazier.

BARBECUED TURKEY DINNER

    8- to 10-pound turkey
    2 tablespoons salt
 ¼ teaspoon red pepper sauce
    1 tablespoon salt
 ⅛ teaspoon red pepper sauce
    2 apples, cored and quartered
    2 onions, quartered
      Salad oil
      Thyme Butter (right)
      Roasted Potatoes (right)
      Roasted Corn (right)
      Grilled Tomatoes (right)

In covered barbecue kettle, heat coals about 30 minutes (with dampers on kettle and lid open). Wash the turkey and pat dry with paper towels. Rub body cavity of turkey with 2 tablespoons salt and ¼ teaspoon pepper sauce; rub neck cavity with 1 tablespoon salt and ⅛ teaspoon pepper sauce. Place apples and onions in body cavity. Close body cavity with skewers; lace. Fasten neck skin to back with skewer. Flatten wings over breast; tie with string to hold wings securely. Tie drumsticks securely to tail. Brush turkey with salad oil. Insert meat thermometer in turkey, making sure it does not touch bone. Arrange hot coals at the sides of charcoal grill of barbecue kettle; place foil drip pan under roasting area. Place cooking grill and vegetable rack (empty) in place. Place turkey breast side up on grill about 4 inches from coals; cover grill. Cook 2 to 2½ hours, or until leg bone moves easily, brushing frequently with Thyme Butter. (Meat thermometer should read 185°.) Approximately 1½ hours before turkey is done, add Roasted Potatoes; later add Roasted Corn and Grilled Tomatoes as directed below. At 30-minute intervals add hot coals, if necessary, to maintain even heat. *8 servings.*

Thyme Butter

Mix ½ cup butter or margarine, melted, and 1 teaspoon ground thyme.

Roasted Potatoes

For each serving, scrub 1 baking potato; rub with butter. Place in vegetable rack on grill. Cook 1½ hours, or until potatoes are tender.

Roasted Corn

For each serving, remove husk and silk from tender young sweet corn; place in vegetable rack on grill. Cook 20 to 30 minutes or until tender.

Grilled Tomatoes

For each serving, sprinkle ½ tomato with grated Parmesan cheese. Place on grill; cook 10 to 15 minutes, or until tomatoes are heated through.

CUCUMBER SALAD

    4 thinly sliced pared cucumbers
1½ cups dairy sour cream
    1 small clove garlic, crushed
    2 tablespoons salad oil
    2 teaspoons sugar
    1 teaspoon salt
    1 teaspoon white wine vinegar
    ½ teaspoon dill weed

Place cucumber slices in large bowl. Mix remaining ingredients except dill weed. Pour over cucumbers and toss lightly. Sprinkle with dill weed. Chill thoroughly. *8 servings.*

STRAWBERRY SHORTCAKE

    1 quart fresh strawberries
    1 cup sugar
    2 cups all-purpose flour*
    2 tablespoons sugar
    3 teaspoons baking powder
    1 teaspoon salt
    ⅓ cup shortening
    1 cup milk
      Soft butter
      Light cream or sweetened whipped cream

Wash, hull and slice strawberries. Sprinkle with 1 cup sugar and let stand 1 hour. Heat oven to 450°. Grease a round layer pan, 8x1½ inches. Stir together flour, 2 tablespoons sugar, the baking powder and salt. Cut in shortening. Stir in milk just until blended. Spread dough in prepared pan. Bake 15 to 20 minutes or until golden brown. Split layer crosswise while hot. Spread with butter; fill and top with sweetened berries. Serve warm with light cream or sweetened whipped cream. *8 servings.*

* *If using self-rising flour, omit baking powder and salt.*

Texas Beef Bake

Chips 'n Beans

Beef Brisket Bar-B-Q

Smokehouse Spareribs

Ranch-style Potato Salad (page 147)

Branded Slaw

Wagon Wheel Watermelon

Iced Coffee

For this meal you will need two grills, and one of them must have a cover. Serve Chips 'n Beans for your appetizer. For the Wagon Wheel Watermelon, arrange half-slices of melon spoke-fashion on a large platter.

CHIPS 'N BEANS

  2 cans (1 pound each) kidney beans
  1 can (1 pound) stewed tomatoes
  1 can (15 ounces) chili without beans
  1 cup shredded natural Cheddar cheese (4 ounces)
  ½ cup milk
  1 package (11 ounces) corn chips

Combine beans, tomatoes and chili in large skillet. Place on grill 5 inches from medium heat or on range top; heat to simmering. Stir in cheese and milk. Simmer uncovered 1 hour, or until mixture is consistency of thickened spaghetti sauce. Stir occasionally. To serve, spoon over chips. *8 servings.*

BEEF BRISKET BAR-B-Q

4- to 5-pound well-trimmed boneless beef brisket
1½ teaspoons salt
½ cup catsup
¼ cup vinegar
½ medium onion, finely chopped (about ½ cup)
1 tablespoon Worcestershire sauce
1½ teaspoons liquid smoke
1 bay leaf, crushed
¼ teaspoon coarsely ground black pepper

Wipe beef dry. Rub with salt. Place on 20x15-inch piece of double thickness heavy-duty aluminum foil. Combine remaining ingredients; pour over brisket. Wrap securely in foil. Place on grill 5 inches from medium coals. Cook 1½ hours or until tender, turning once. Cut diagonally across the grain into thin slices. If desired, serve in heated individual French rolls or toasted hamburger buns. *10 to 12 servings.*

SMOKEHOUSE SPARERIBS

½ cup Worcestershire sauce
½ cup vinegar
½ cup butter or margarine, melted
½ teaspoon salt
¼ teaspoon red pepper sauce
2 racks spareribs (about 6 pounds)

Soak wood chips in water about 30 minutes. Combine all ingredients except spareribs. Brush ribs with vinegar mixture. Arrange hot coals around edge of firebox; place foil drip pan under cooking area. Drain half of chips; add to hot coals. Place meat bone side down on grill 4 inches from coals; cover grill. Cook 1½ to 2 hours, or until meat is done. At 30-minute intervals, add drained wood chips and, if necessary, hot coals to maintain smoke and even heat. During last 40 minutes of cooking, turn and baste the spareribs every 10 minutes with vinegar mixture. *8 to 10 servings as second meat; 6 main-dish servings.*

BRANDED SLAW

12 cups shredded cabbage
2 green peppers, shredded (about 1¼ cups)
¼ cup sugar
2 teaspoons salt
1 teaspoon dry mustard
⅛ teaspoon pepper
⅔ cup vinegar
⅓ cup salad oil
Green pepper or pimiento strips

Combine cabbage and shredded green pepper in large mixing bowl. Stir together remaining ingredients except green pepper strips. Pour mixture over cabbage and green pepper; toss to mix thoroughly. Place salad in bowl lined with cabbage leaves; garnish with green pepper strips in shape of a favorite cattle brand. Or, shape your initial under a bar of green pepper or pimiento. *8 to 10 servings.*

California Patio Party

Guacamole

Grilled Stuffed Leg of Lamb

Buttered Asparagus   *Caesar Salad*

Sourdough on the Grill

Minted Pears Hélène

For this patio party you will need one barbecue grill and a foil-lined pan or bucket in which to heat a few additional pieces of charcoal. When the leg of lamb is done, remove it to a serving platter and allow it to "firm up"; this will make it easier to slice. Add a few hot coals to raise the grill temperature to hot for cooking the asparagus and toasting the bread. Start the pears before your guests finish the main course.

GUACAMOLE

    2 avocados, peeled and pitted
    1 medium onion, finely chopped
    2 green chili peppers, finely chopped
    1 tablespoon lemon juice
    1 teaspoon salt
    ½ teaspoon coarsely ground pepper
    1 medium tomato, peeled and finely chopped
      Mayonnaise

Beat avocados, onion, peppers, lemon juice, salt and pepper until creamy. Gently fold in tomato. Spoon into serving dish; spread top with a thin layer of mayonnaise. Stir gently just before serving. *6 to 8 servings.*

GRILLED STUFFED LEG OF LAMB

7-pound leg of lamb
½ pound ground uncooked veal
½ pound ground cooked ham
½ pound fresh mushrooms, washed, trimmed and
  finely chopped
½ cup fine soft bread crumbs
1 egg
1 clove garlic, crushed
1 tablespoon lemon juice
1 tablespoon Worcestershire sauce
¼ to ½ teaspoon oregano
¼ teaspoon pepper

Ask meatman to bone lamb without breaking surface and without tying it. Mix remaining ingredients thoroughly with hands or spoon. Pack mixture firmly into pocket of lamb. Sew opening with heavy string. Wrap in heavy-duty aluminum foil. Grill 6 to 8 inches from medium coals. Cook 20 to 30 minutes per pound, turning occasionally. Thirty minutes before end of cooking time, remove lamb from foil; place directly on grill, turning to brown all sides. Remove from grill; slice. (There will be stuffing in each slice.) *6 to 8 servings.*

BUTTERED ASPARAGUS

Tear three pieces heavy-duty aluminum foil, each 18x12 inches. Wrap 1 package (10 ounces) frozen asparagus spears securely in each piece of foil. Place directly on hot coals; grill 20 minutes, turning packets once. *6 to 8 servings.*

SOURDOUGH ON THE GRILL

Diagonally slice 1 loaf (1 pound) sourdough French bread into 1-inch slices. Place on grill 2 inches from hot coals. Toast 4 minutes on each side until brown. Butter lightly before serving. *18 to 20 slices.*

CAESAR SALAD

        1 clove garlic
     ⅓ cup olive oil
        8 anchovy fillets, cut up
        1 teaspoon Worcestershire sauce
     ½ teaspoon salt
     ¼ teaspoon dry mustard
        Freshly ground black pepper
     12 cups bite-size pieces romaine (about 1 large or
        2 small heads)
        1 egg, coddled*
        1 lemon
        Garlic Croutons (below)
     ⅓ cup grated Parmesan cheese

Rub large wooden salad bowl with cut edge of garlic.
If desired, allow a few small pieces of garlic to remain in bowl. Add oil, anchovy fillets, Worcestershire
sauce, salt, mustard and pepper; mix thoroughly. Add
romaine; toss lightly until leaves glisten. Break egg
onto salad greens; squeeze juice from lemon over
greens. Toss very gently until leaves are well coated.
Sprinkle croutons and cheese over salad; toss. Serve
immediately. *6 servings.*

* To coddle egg, place cold egg in warm water. Rapidly heat to boiling
enough water to completely cover egg. Transfer egg to boiling water with
spoon. Remove pan from heat. Cover and let stand 30 seconds. Immediately cool egg in cold water to prevent further cooking.

Garlic Croutons

Heat oven to 400°. Trim crusts from 4 slices white
bread; generously butter both sides of bread. Sprinkle
with ¼ teaspoon garlic powder. Cut into ½-inch
cubes; place on baking sheet. Bake 10 to 15 minutes,
or until cubes are golden brown and crisp, stirring
occasionally.

MINTED PEARS HÉLÈNE

For each serving, core an unpared fresh pear to within ½ inch of bottom. Fill cavity with 1 tablespoon sugar, 1 tablespoon semisweet chocolate pieces and ¼ teaspoon mint extract. Wrap each pear in 10-inch square of double thickness heavy-duty aluminum foil. Place on grill 4 inches from medium coals. (Pear must stand upright.) Cook 20 minutes, or until pear is soft. Serve with chilled Custard Sauce (page 158) or softened ice cream.

PUERTO RICAN PEARS—Follow recipe for Minted Pears Hélène (above) except—substitute ½ teaspoon rum flavoring for the mint extract.

Hawaiian Luau

Oysters Rumaki

"Pig" Roast on the Turnspit

Teriyaki Steak

Sweet Potatoes with Coconut

Baked Bananas   *Chinese Peas*

Tahitian Salad

Aloha Baked Pineapple

Blossom Tea

Have a potluck party, Hawaiian style. Invite your friends or neighbors to bring their barbecue grills and cook alongside you for a real feast. To prepare this luau, you will need two brazier-type grills and one grill with a rotisserie attachment. Aloha Baked Pineapple can be cooked while the main course is being enjoyed.

OYSTERS RUMAKI

12 slices bacon, cut in half
24 large oysters, fresh or frozen
½ teaspoon salt
¼ teaspoon pepper

Fry bacon 2 minutes on each side. Drain oysters; dry on paper towels. Sprinkle oysters with salt and pepper. Wrap each with bacon slice; secure with wooden pick. Grill on hibachi or in hinged grill 2 inches from hot coals 12 minutes, or until bacon is crisp, turning once. *24 appetizers.*

"PIG" ROAST ON THE TURNSPIT

4-pound boned pork shoulder
½ cup pineapple juice
½ cup salad oil
½ cup dark corn syrup
¼ cup lime juice
1 small clove garlic, crushed
2 tablespoons brown sugar
1 tablespoon prepared mustard
1 tablespoon soy sauce
2 teaspoons salt
1 teaspoon ground coriander
½ teaspoon ginger

Trim excess fat from roast. Place roast in plastic bag or shallow glass dish. Mix remaining ingredients; pour over meat. Fasten bag securely or cover dish with plastic wrap. Refrigerate at least 8 hours or overnight, turning meat occasionally. Remove roast from marinade; roll and tie securely with cord. Insert spit rod lengthwise through center of roast. Secure meat on spit with holding forks. Check balance by rotating spit in palms of hands. Insert meat thermometer in center of meat, making sure it doesn't touch fat or spit. Arrange medium-hot coals at back of firebox; place foil drip pan under spit area. Cook roast on rotisserie about 3 hours or until well done. (Meat thermometer should register 185°.) Add coals, if necessary, to maintain even heat. *10 servings.*

TERIYAKI STEAK

½ cup water
½ cup soy sauce
1 tablespoon brown sugar
1½ teaspoons ginger
2-pound sirloin steak, 1½ inches thick

Combine all ingredients except steak. Heat to boiling. Cool. Score both sides of steak in diamond pattern ¼ inch deep; slash fat around edge of steak. Place meat in shallow glass dish; pour soy mixture over meat. Cover dish with plastic wrap. Refrigerate 2 hours, turning 4 times. Grill steak 2 to 3 inches from hot coals 7 to 8 minutes on each side. (Meat should be brown and crusty on outside, rare and juicy on inside.) To serve, cut diagonally across the grain into ¼-inch slices. *8 servings.*

SWEET POTATOES WITH COCONUT

Pare and diagonally slice 3 pounds sweet potatoes into ½-inch slices. Boil 10 minutes. Stir 1 teaspoon salt into ½ cup melted butter. Grill potato slices 4 inches from medium coals 10 minutes on each side, basting frequently with butter mixture. Sprinkle potatoes with toasted coconut. *8 to 10 servings.*

BAKED BANANAS

For each serving, wash and dry 1 green banana. Do not peel. Place on grill 4 inches from medium coals. Cook 20 minutes, turning once, or until peel is black and banana is soft. Split and serve in the peel. Garnish plate with lime wedges.

CHINESE PEAS

> 2 packages (7 ounces each) frozen Chinese pea pods, partially thawed and broken apart
> 1 tablespoon butter
> 1 tablespoon water
> 1 teaspoon sugar

Place pea pods on 18-inch square of heavy-duty aluminum foil. Add remaining ingredients; wrap securely in foil. Place on grill 2 inches from hot coals. Cook about 14 minutes, turning once. *8 to 10 servings.*

TAHITIAN SALAD

    8 cups fresh spinach
    4 cups lettuce
    2 cups watercress
    ¼ cup salad oil
        Island Dressing (below)
        Cherry tomatoes

Wash greens well and pat dry. Tear into bite-size
pieces, discarding stems and cores; refrigerate. Just
before serving, toss greens with salad oil until leaves
glisten; pour on dressing and toss again. Garnish with
cherry tomatoes. Serve immediately. *8 to 10 servings.*

Island Dressing

Combine 2 tablespoons red wine vinegar, 1 teaspoon
sugar, 1 teaspoon dry mustard, ¾ teaspoon salt and
⅛ teaspoon coarsely ground pepper.

ALOHA BAKED PINEAPPLE

    3 pineapples
    ¾ cup brown sugar (packed)
    ⅓ cup butter or margarine
        About ½ cup rum

Cut thick slice from side of each pineapple. Cut out
pulp; remove core and cut pulp into bite-size pieces.
Toss with sugar in bowl. Fill pineapple shells with
fruit mixture; dot each with butter and sprinkle with
about 1½ tablespoons rum. Replace slices on pine-
apples. Wrap each securely in 20x18-inch piece of
heavy-duty aluminum foil, fanning foil over leaves.
Grill 4 inches from medium coals 20 minutes on each
side. Just before serving, sprinkle about 1½ tablespoons rum into each pineapple; stir lightly. Serve hot.
8 servings.

BLOSSOM TEA

> ¼ cup black tea (½ ounce)
> ¼ cup jasmine tea (½ ounce)
> 4 cups boiling water
> 12 cups cold water
>   Tropical Spears (below)
>   Frosted Mint Sprigs (below)

Place tea leaves in 4 large tea balls or in 10-inch square of double thickness cheesecloth; tie securely with string. Place tea balls in boiling water; let stand 10 minutes. Remove balls from tea; refrigerate tea concentrate. At serving time, dilute tea concentrate with cold water. Pour into ice-filled glasses; garnish with a Tropical Spear and Frosted Mint Sprig. *8 to 10 servings.*

Tropical Spears

For each glass, thread 1 canned pineapple spear on bamboo skewer. Top skewer with mandarin orange segment.

Frosted Mint Sprigs

For each glass, brush a fresh mint sprig with beaten egg white; dip in sugar.

On-the-go Cooking—Near and Far

Breakfasts and Brunches

An early-morning cookout? Why not! Even confirmed non-breakfasters have returned from dude-ranch vacations singing the praises of the out-of-doors breakfast. Take a tip from their experiences. Entertain at a summer-holiday or Sunday brunch cooked outside. It's certainly a different idea—deliciously different. And what a way to let the man of the house take center stage.

Most of these menus were planned for the backyard, where the barbecue chef can easily supplement the grill with electric griddles, skillets and coffee makers. But there's no need to limit them to the patio. With careful planning and packing, all of these morning meals can be adapted to park picnics or camping trips. (Be sure to see pages 222 and 242 for camp-out breakfasts.)

Breakfast at the Park

Tomato Juice
(carried cold in vacuum bottle)

Beefy Scrambled Eggs

Blueberry-Orange Coffee Cake

Coffee   Milk

BEEFY SCRAMBLED EGGS

3 tablespoons butter or margarine
¼ cup finely chopped green onion tops or chives
9 eggs, beaten
4 ounces dried beef, cut into thin strips
1 cup creamed cottage cheese

Melt butter in large skillet on grill over hot coals. Add onion; cook and stir until onion is tender. Combine eggs, dried beef and cottage cheese; stir into onion mixture. As mixture thickens, lift with spatula from bottom and sides. Avoid constant stirring. Cook until eggs are thickened throughout but still moist. *6 servings.*

BLUEBERRY-ORANGE COFFEE CAKE

Bake the coffee cake at home the day before; reheat it on the grill while you scramble the eggs.

Heat oven to 400°. Grease square pan, 8x8x2 inches. Drain thoroughly 1 can (11 ounces) mandarin orange segments. Prepare 1 package (13.5 ounces) wild blueberry muffin mix as directed except—pour into prepared pan. Arrange orange segments over batter. Sprinkle with Streusel Mixture (below). Bake 25 to 30 minutes. When cool, wrap in double thickness heavy-duty aluminum foil. At the breakfast cookout, heat coffee cake on grill 4 inches from hot coals 15 minutes, turning every 5 minutes. *9 servings.*

Streusel Mixture

Mix ¼ cup brown sugar (packed), 3 tablespoons flour, 2 tablespoons firm butter or margarine and ¼ teaspoon cinnamon with fingers or fork.

Eye-opener Breakfast

Sparkling Orange Juice

Grilled Canadian Bacon Slices

Raised Flapjacks

Coffee   Milk

SPARKLING ORANGE JUICE

Just before serving, fill 6-ounce glasses with 2 parts orange juice and 1 part chilled lemon-lime carbonated beverage. Float a slice of orange or a fresh mint sprig in each glass.

GRILLED CANADIAN BACON SLICES

Cut ¾ pound Canadian bacon into ⅛-inch slices. Grill 3 inches from hot coals 3 to 4 minutes on each side. *6 servings.*

RAISED FLAPJACKS

       1 package active dry yeast
    ¼ cup warm water (105 to 115°)
       1 egg
    1⅓ cups milk
       2 cups buttermilk baking mix
       1 tablespoon butter or margarine
          Butter
          Warm syrup

In mixing bowl dissolve yeast in warm water. Add egg, milk and baking mix; beat with rotary beater until smooth. Cover; let stand at room temperature 1½ hours or refrigerate overnight.

Heat 1 tablespoon butter in skillet on grill until sizzling hot. For each flapjack, spoon 2 tablespoons batter into skillet. Turn when edges begin to dry. Serve with butter and syrup. *Makes 20 flapjacks.*

Strawberry Shortcake Brunch

Pineapple-Sausage Kabobs

Strawberry Shortcake in Foil

Coffee

PINEAPPLE-SAUSAGE KABOBS

5 slices bacon, cut in half
10 fresh mushrooms, washed and trimmed
1 package (8 ounces) brown 'n serve sausages
20 pineapple chunks

Wrap piece of bacon around each mushroom. Cut sausage links in half. Alternate pineapple chunks and sausage links around mushroom on each of 10 bamboo skewers. Grill 3 inches from hot coals 20 minutes, turning frequently, until bacon is crisp. *Makes 10 kabobs.*

STRAWBERRY SHORTCAKE IN FOIL

1 quart strawberries, cut up and sweetened
Shortcake dough
Butter
Whipped cream

Ahead of time—Prepare strawberries. Heat oven to 425°. Prepare Shortcake dough as directed on package of buttermilk baking mix. Knead 8 to 10 times on floured surface. Roll dough ½ inch thick. With floured 3-inch cutter, cut 6 shortcakes. Bake on ungreased baking sheet about 10 minutes. Cool. Split and butter lightly. Wrap individually in double thickness foil.

For brunch—Reheat shortcakes in foil on grill 3 inches from medium coals. Heat 4 minutes on each side. Serve immediately. Open foil and shape into a plate with an edge. Spoon strawberries between layers and over top. Serve with whipped cream. *6 servings.*

Company Brunch on the Patio

Melon Cascade (page 155)

Fluffy French Toast

Hearty Ham Slice

Coffee   Milk

FLUFFY FRENCH TOAST

> ½ cup all-purpose flour
> 1½ tablespoons sugar
> ¼ teaspoon salt
> 2 cups milk
> 6 eggs
> 18 slices day-old French bread, 1 inch thick
> 1 tablespoon butter or margarine

Combine flour, sugar, salt, milk and eggs; beat with rotary beater until smooth. Soak bread in batter until thoroughly saturated. Heat butter in skillet on grill until sizzling hot. Cook bread 10 to 12 minutes on each side or until golden brown. Serve with syrup, jam or confectioners' sugar. *6 servings.*

HEARTY HAM SLICE

Buy 1½- to 2-pound fully cooked ham slice, cut about 1 inch thick. Place on lightly greased grill 3 inches from medium coals. Cook 7 minutes on each side, basting frequently with heated Chef's Special Sauce (below). Serve remaining sauce with ham. *6 servings.*

Chef's Special Sauce

Mix ¼ cup prepared mustard, ¼ cup pineapple juice, 2 tablespoons brown sugar, ½ teaspoon horseradish and dash salt. Heat on grill.

For Picnic Time

A fine summer day with a fresh breeze stirring, a cloth spread in a patch of cool shade, a basketful of good, filling food—these are the time-tested ingredients for a first-class picnic.

Whether the picnic is carried to the neighborhood park in a simple knapsack or many miles away in an elaborate fitted hamper, much of its success depends on advance planning and proper packing. Go over your menu carefully and list your needs, from napkins and forks to mustard and catsup.

Although special picnic gear is not *always* necessary, it does come in handy. Every year brings new paper and plastic picnic products that are just right for toting the spread and for serving it. Insulated coolers and vacuum jugs are invaluable aids for carrying cold foods and beverages, and fitted baskets and portable grills can add a special plus.

Whatever your plans and equipment, there's but one cardinal rule for the picnic food: Serve hot foods hot and cold foods cold.

Any dish that is to be served cold should be well chilled before it is packed—no matter how good your cooler. Use plenty of ice or frozen cans of chemical refrigerant to keep insulated bags and portable coolers *really* cold. Prechilled insulated plastic containers in handy sizes for individual servings will safely keep food cold for hours—even potato and macaroni salads and gelatin desserts.

If you don't have a cooler, improvise. For a do-it-yourself cooler, line a metal case with dry ice, then cover the ice with layers of wet newspapers. Tightly covered, this box will keep your food chilled for several hours. Or chill foods in a heavy pottery casserole; carry the cold container directly to the site in a thick wrapping of wet newspapers.

Hot food? A casserole will hold its heat for several hours if wrapped, right from the oven, in aluminum foil and then in newspapers.

A picnic at the shore usually calls for extra thought in the menu department. The combination of sun, wind and water always sharpens appetites, and the *all*-made-at-home picnic is often not hearty enough. Hot dogs and hamburgers cooked over a campfire or grill are traditional extras. But perhaps you'll be lucky enough to catch some fish. Simply clean them and panfry them whole (see page 243).

And remember that no picnic, whatever its locale, is over until the site is as clean as you found it—and maybe cleaner.

Three picnic plans are outlined on the following pages: the Family Picnic, a classic menu to satisfy many tastes; the Hamper Picnic, an elegant out-of-doors repast for sophisticates; and the Paper Bag Picnic, an easy-to-carry compact for the bicycle brigade. Adjust them to fit your own plans.

Picnic Plusses

• *Plan on desserts that can be easily transported. Carry cakes and bar cookies in their baking pans. Pies travel well between paper or aluminum-foil plates taped together.*

• *Unless you have a dependable insulated cooler, avoid carrying food containing a mixture of milk or cream and eggs. Don't risk food poisoning.*

• *Bring drinking water if there is the slightest chance it will not be available.*

• *Pack wet washcloths in a plastic bag—they'll come in handy for cleaning sticky hands. Or tuck in commercially packaged moist towelettes.*

• *For the neatest, easiest picnic service, pack each complete lunch—from napkins and utensils to the dessert—in an individual box, basket or bag.*

• *Bring along preparations for coping with ants, flies, mosquitoes, sunburn and poison ivy.*

Family Picnic

Parmesan Fried Chicken

Potato Salad in Tomato Cups

Relish Tray with Sour Cream Dip

Rolls   Butter

Hawaiian Date Cake (page 163)

Iced Lemonade Tea

PARMESAN FRIED CHICKEN

Crusty oven-fried chicken is baked at home, then refrigerated. Tote the chicken in a cooler; serve cold at the picnic.

  2 broiler-fryer chickens (2½ pounds each),
     cut into pieces
     Salt
  1 cup all-purpose flour
  2 teaspoons salt
  ¼ teaspoon pepper
  2 teaspoons paprika
  2 eggs, slightly beaten
  3 tablespoons milk
1⅓ cups grated Parmesan cheese
  ⅔ cup dry bread crumbs
  2 tablespoons butter or margarine
  2 tablespoons shortening
  ¼ cup butter or margarine, melted

Heat oven to 400°. Do not use chicken wings; remove skin from remaining pieces. Salt chicken. Coat chicken with a mixture of flour, 2 teaspoons salt, the pepper and paprika. Combine eggs and milk; dip chicken into egg mixture. Roll in mixture of cheese and bread crumbs. In oven melt 2 tablespoons butter and the shortening in jelly roll pan, 15½x10½x1 inch. Place chicken bone side down in pan. Drizzle with melted butter. Bake 1 hour. Cool; cover and chill. *6 servings.*

POTATO SALAD IN TOMATO CUPS

Be sure to take your well-chilled potato salad to the picnic in a cooler—storage under 40° is best for such a creamy-type food.

>   2 cups diced cooked pared potatoes
> ⅓ cup finely chopped celery
> ⅓ cup chopped radishes
> ¼ cup chopped green onions (with tops)
> ¼ cup sweet pickle relish
> ½ teaspoon salt
> ½ teaspoon celery seed
> ⅛ teaspoon pepper
> ½ cup salad dressing
>   2 teaspoons prepared mustard
>   2 hard-cooked eggs, chopped
> Tomato Cups (below)

Combine first 8 ingredients in large bowl. Stir together salad dressing and mustard. Pour over potato mixture and toss lightly. Carefully stir in eggs. Cover; chill thoroughly. At serving time, divide salad among Tomato Cups. *6 servings.*

Tomato Cups

Cut out stems of 6 chilled medium tomatoes. Cut each tomato into sixths, cutting to within ½ inch of bottom. Carefully spread out sections, forming a cup. Sprinkle inside of each tomato with salt.

RELISH TRAY WITH SOUR CREAM DIP

Artichoke hearts
Carrot sticks
Mushroom caps
Cucumber spears
Pickled miniature corn on the cob
Green pepper sticks
Sour Cream Dip (below)

Wrap vegetables in plastic bags; place dip in covered container. Refrigerate. Just before serving, arrange vegetables and dip on tray. *6 servings.*

Sour Cream Dip

Stir together 1 cup dairy sour cream, ¼ teaspoon garlic salt and ¼ teaspoon seasoned salt.

ICED LEMONADE TEA

6 tea bags
1 quart boiling water
1 can (6 ounces) frozen lemonade concentrate
2 quarts cold water
¼ cup sugar

Steep tea bags in boiling water 15 minutes. Add lemonade concentrate; stir until melted. Stir in cold water and sugar until sugar is dissolved. Chill. Serve over ice. *Makes twelve 8-ounce servings.*

Hamper Picnic

Shrimp-Sesame Platter

Gourmet Beef Roast

Cold Asparagus

Marinated Olives 'n Tomatoes

Cheese Loaf (page 125)   *Butter*

Sparkling Fruit Compote

Sugar Cookies

Coffee

SHRIMP-SESAME PLATTER

Ahead of time, prepare Sesame Cheese Squares (below). Chill 2 cans (4½ ounces each) jumbo shrimp. To serve, slice off bottom of medium eggplant; stand eggplant upright on platter. Drain shrimp. With plastic picks, attach Sesame Cheese Squares and shrimp to eggplant, arranging them evenly over the surface. Serve with assorted crackers. *8 to 10 servings.*

Sesame Cheese Squares

Heat oven to 350°. Place ¼ cup sesame seed on baking sheet; toast in oven about 10 minutes or until golden. Cool. Cut 2 packages (3 ounces each) cream cheese into 12 squares each. Roll each cheese square in sesame seed; dip into soy sauce. Chill.

GOURMET BEEF ROAST

> 5- to 5½-pound boned and rolled rump roast
> 1 tablespoon cracked pepper
> ¼ cup shortening
> ½ cup water
> 1 beef bouillon cube

Heat oven to 325°. Rub the outside of roast with cracked pepper. (Do not rub into ends of roast.) Melt shortening in Dutch oven; brown roast on all sides. Drain fat from pan; pour water over roast and add bouillon cube. Cover; bake 3 to 3½ hours or until tender. Remove roast from pan; cool and refrigerate overnight. Slice thinly before serving. *8 to 10 servings.*

COLD ASPARAGUS

Prepare 2 packages (10 ounces each) frozen asparagus spears as directed on package. Sprinkle drained asparagus with ½ teaspoon seasoned salt and ⅛ teaspoon pepper. Cover and chill several hours. *8 to 10 servings.*

MARINATED OLIVES 'N TOMATOES

> 1 can (1 pound) ripe olives
> ¾ cup salad oil
> 3 tablespoons vinegar
> 1 tablespoon lemon juice
> 3 cloves garlic, crushed
> 10 peppercorns, crushed
> 1 carton (1 pint) cherry tomatoes, cut in half

Drain olives; transfer to large jar. Combine salad oil, vinegar, lemon juice, garlic and peppercorns, and pour over olives. Cover and chill overnight. Shake olives occasionally to coat evenly. Olives may be kept in refrigerator several days. About 5 hours before serving, add halved tomatoes to marinade; shake to mix. Drain well before serving. *Makes 1 quart.*

SPARKLING FRUIT COMPOTE

    3 medium peaches
    2 cups sliced strawberries
    2 cups blueberries
    2 cups melon balls
    3 medium bananas
    1 bottle (1 pint 9 ounces) pink sparkling catawba
       grape juice, chilled

Peel peaches and slice into container. Cover peach
slices with strawberries, blueberries and melon balls.
Cover container tightly and chill. Just before serving,
peel and slice bananas into fruit mixture. Pour grape
juice over fruit; serve in small dishes. *8 to 10 servings.*

Paper Bag Picnic

Mile-high Ham Sandwich

Baked Bean Cups

Potato Chips

Olives, Radishes and Carrot Sticks

Fresh Fruit

Oatmeal Spice Cake

Canned Soda Pop

A complete lunch in each sturdy paper bag. What could be easier to carry? Don't forget paper napkins and plastic spoons, one in each bag.

MILE-HIGH HAM SANDWICH

  1 package (3 ounces) cream cheese, softened
  2 teaspoons brown sugar
  ¼ teaspoon grated orange peel
  2 teaspoons orange juice
  6 individual loaves French bread *or*
    1 loaf (1 pound) French bread
  1 pound sliced boiled ham
  1 package (8 ounces) Swiss cheese slices

Blend cream cheese, sugar, orange peel and juice. Cut bread in half horizontally. (If using large loaf, cut into 6 sections and then in half horizontally.) Spread cut sides of bread with cream cheese mixture. Layer the ham and cheese slices between bread. Wrap each sandwich in aluminum foil. *Makes 6 sandwiches.*

NOTE—If desired, butter may be substituted for the cheese spread.

BAKED BEAN CUPS

Divide 2 cans (1 pound 3 ounces each) baked beans among 6 paper cups; cover. *6 servings.*

OLIVES, RADISHES AND CARROT STICKS

For each of 6 servings, place olives, radishes and carrot sticks on plastic wrap or foil; wrap securely.

OATMEAL SPICE CAKE

    1½ cups all-purpose flour*
      1 cup brown sugar (packed)
      ½ cup granulated sugar
      1 cup quick-cooking oats
    1½ teaspoons soda
      1 teaspoon cinnamon
      ½ teaspoon salt
      ½ teaspoon nutmeg
      ½ cup shortening
      1 cup water
      2 eggs (½ to ⅔ cup)
      2 tablespoons dark molasses
        Coconut Topping (below)

Heat oven to 350°. Grease and flour oblong pan, 13x9x2 inches. Measure all ingredients except Coconut Topping into large mixer bowl. Blend 30 seconds lowest speed on mixer. Beat 3 minutes on medium speed, scraping bowl often. Pour into prepared pan. Bake 35 to 40 minutes, or until wooden pick inserted in center comes out clean. Let cool slightly. Carefully spread Coconut Topping over top of cake. Set oven control at broil and/or 550°. Broil 2 to 3 minutes.

* *Do not use self-rising flour in this recipe.*

Coconut Topping

Melt ¼ cup butter; mix with ⅔ cup brown sugar (packed), ½ cup flaked coconut, ½ cup chopped pecans and 3 tablespoons light cream.

Cooking Afloat

If cooking with all outdoors as your kitchen is a challenge, certainly dishing up a delicious meal in the postage-stamp confines of the typical ship's galley is a test of heroic proportions. But with planning, the test can be met. And as any sailor will agree, the game is well worth the candle.

A restricted cooking area needn't mean a restricted or monotonous diet; it simply demands special techniques. You'll find life at sea easier if you clean up as you cook. Serve directly from pots and pans; wash them before the food hardens and return them to their storage space. If you can't wash pots immediately, wipe them out with paper towels.

Chart your menu course with cruising plans and cooking equipment in mind. Plan ahead; list your every need, and make sure you've packed it. For a cruise lasting several days, a galley with refrigeration is a boon; lacking this plus, a good supply of canned and convenience foods and dehydrated or freeze-dried foods will fill the bill. On a one-day outing, insulated bags or portable coolers are useful for carrying aboard ice, chilled beverages, salads and other foods prepared at home. One-dish meals, brought from home in a thermos or prepared right on board, are perennial favorites. Many of the suggestions and recipes for picnics (see pages 197-206) are practical for days on the water, and the recipes on the following pages were developed *especially* for such times.

Some small-boat cooks use hibachis and charcoal for the quick grilling of meats, but any such fire can be hazardous on a boat. Instead, use one of the many stoves designed specifically for use aboard ship and that operate on the safer bottled or canned fuels. Most of them maintain a steady balance in rough waters.

A small craft with any kind of cabin usually has sizable lockers. And basic foods for a week or more of cruising can be stored in a small space if you stock and stow away wisely. Let common sense be your guide. Keep cans and cartons off counter tops and open shelves. They'll fly off and slide around on the galley floor. Secure all glass jars in some way to guard against breakage. If you like, store canned foods in the bilges. But if you do this, be sure to remove the labels and mark the contents on each can with a grease or china marking pencil. The labels could soak off and clog the bilge pumps—and unidentified cans would certainly baffle the cook.

Dampness and rust are the enemies of food and equipment kept aboard ship. Dry staples are best not stored in their cardboard packages. Transfer the contents to plastic or tin containers with tight-fitting lids. Leave a film of oil or grease on all cast-iron utensils; otherwise they will produce a layer of rust quickly.

Don't leave litter floating in your wake. Keep refuse in a covered container; dispose of it at the end of the day, in port or at home.

Remember to bring sunburn ointment and motion-sickness pills. Without them no trip afloat can be a guaranteed success.

Moonlight Coffee Party

Fruit Dessert Platter

with Lemon Pound Cake
(brought from home)

Coffee Duo

FRUIT DESSERT PLATTER

Leaving a space in center for Lemon Pound Cake (below), arrange fruit on an oblong platter (aluminum or plastic would be ideal) of a size to fit your ice chest or refrigerated compartment. Use your choice of perfect peaches, apples, pears and/or apricots. Garnish these whole fruits here and there with strawberries and clusters of Bing cherries or bunches of green or Tokay grapes. Chill. To serve, complete the platter by placing cake on tray; center with a small bowl of raspberries, if desired.

LEMON POUND CAKE

Heat oven to 350°. Grease and flour tube pan, 10x4 inches, bundt pan or 2-quart anodized aluminum mold. Prepare 1 package (18.5 ounces) lemon cake mix as directed except—use 2 tablespoons less water. Add ½ cup chopped nuts, if desired. Pour into prepared pan. Bake 45 to 55 minutes, or until wooden pick inserted in center comes out clean. Cool 10 minutes; remove from pan. Dust with confectioners' sugar.

COFFEE DUO

2/3 cup instant cocoa mix
1/2 cup instant coffee
8 cups boiling water
Sweetened whipped cream or pressurized
whipped cream

Mix cocoa and coffee in a serving pot. Pour in boiling water; stir. Serve steaming hot and top with whipped cream. *8 to 10 servings.*

Vacuum Bottle Lunches

MANHATTAN CLAM CHOWDER

1/4 cup finely cut bacon
1/4 cup minced onion
2 cans (7 ounces each) minced or whole clams*
2 cups finely diced pared potatoes
1 cup water
1/3 cup diced celery
1 can (1 pound) tomatoes
2 teaspoons snipped parsley
1 teaspoon salt
1/4 teaspoon thyme
1/8 teaspoon pepper

Cook and stir bacon and onion in large kettle until bacon is crisp and onion is tender. Drain clams, reserving liquor. Add clam liquor, potatoes, water and celery to onion and bacon. Cook until potatoes are tender, about 10 minutes. Add clams, tomatoes and seasonings. Heat to boiling, stirring occasionally. Immediately pour into vacuum bottle; seal and carry along. Serve with assorted crackers, if desired. *6 servings.*

* *If available, substitute 1 pint shucked fresh clams with liquor for canned clams. Drain clams, reserving liquor. Chop clams and add with potatoes.*

CAPTAIN'S CHILI

        2 pounds ground beef
        2 cups chopped onions
        2 cans (1 pound 12 ounces each) tomatoes
        2 cans (1 pound each) kidney beans, drained
          (reserve liquid)
        1 can (8 ounces) tomato sauce
        1 tablespoon sugar
    1½ to 2 tablespoons chili powder
        2 teaspoons salt

Brown meat and onions in large kettle. Stir in tomatoes, liquid from kidney beans, tomato sauce, sugar and seasonings. Simmer uncovered 45 minutes, stirring occasionally. Stir in beans and simmer uncovered 15 minutes longer or until desired consistency. Spoon into wide-mouth vacuum bottle; seal. Serve hot from vacuum bottle. Or cool chili and pour into a plastic container; cover and chill thoroughly. When ready to serve, reheat. *6 to 8 servings.*

"SLOPPY" FRANKS

For a satisfying lunch, take along a bag of potato chips and a vacuum bottle of milk.

    ½ cup chopped green pepper
    ⅓ cup chopped onion
    2 tablespoons shortening
    ½ cup bottled hickory-flavored barbecue sauce
    1 can (8 ounces) tomato sauce
    1 pound frankfurters, cut into ¼-inch slices
      Hamburger buns

In large skillet cook and stir green pepper and onion in hot shortening until onion is tender. Stir in barbecue sauce, tomato sauce and frankfurter slices; simmer 10 minutes. Spoon into wide-mouth vacuum bottle; seal. To serve, spoon mixture into hamburger buns. *Makes 8 to 10 sandwiches.*

One-Dish Meals

TUNA NOODLES ROMANOFF

Carry-along meal-mate: a head of crisp lettuce to be cut into wedges and topped with French dressing.

> 1 package (5.5 ounces) noodles Romanoff
> 1 can (8 ounces) green peas, drained
> ¾ cup water
> ⅓ cup nonfat dry milk
> 2 tablespoons butter or margarine
> 1 can (6½ ounces) tuna, drained

Cook noodles as directed on package; drain. Stir in peas, water, dry milk, butter and sour cream-cheese sauce mix. Cook over medium heat just to boiling, stirring constantly. Stir in tuna; heat. *4 servings.*

CHEF'S SALAD

Round out your midday menu with hot tomato bouillon (from a vacuum bottle) and thick slices of French Bread (page 127).

> 2 heads lettuce
> 1 bunch romaine or endive
> 2 cans (2 ounces each) anchovy fillets, if desired
> 1 cup chopped green onions
> 1 cup sliced celery
> 2 cups julienne strips cooked meat (beef, ham)
> 2 cups julienne strips cooked chicken or turkey
> 2 cups julienne strips Swiss cheese
> 1 cup mayonnaise or salad dressing
> ½ cup bottled creamy French dressing
>   Ripe olives
> 4 hard-cooked eggs, sliced

Have all ingredients chilled. Tear head lettuce and romaine into bite-size pieces; drain anchovies. Toss with onion, celery, meat, chicken and cheese, reserving a few strips of meat and cheese. Just before serving, blend mayonnaise and French dressing; toss with salad. Top with reserved meat and cheese strips, ripe olives and egg slices. *8 servings.*

CHERRY-GLAZED HAM

For a festive dinner afloat, serve with mounds of hot buttered instant rice and chilled canned asparagus spears on greens.

In a large skillet, heat 1 can (1 pound 5 ounces) cherry pie filling and 1 to 2 teaspoons cut-up crystallized ginger until bubbly, stirring frequently. Cut 1½-pound sterilized canned ham (the non-refrigerated type) in half lengthwise; place in skillet. Spoon pie filling over ham. Cover; simmer 30 minutes, basting occasionally. To serve, spoon sauce over ham. *4 or 5 servings.*

DRIED BEEF-MACARONI MIX-UP

Serve-with suggestion: Cut plump tomatoes into four sections, cutting only to within ½ inch of bottom. Place a carrot stick and a green onion crisscross in cuts of each tomato. Fill center with a large olive. Wrap individually. Keep chilled.

   1 package (8 ounces) macaroni and Cheddar dinner
1½ cups hot water
   1 can (10½ ounces) condensed cream of celery or
      mushroom soup
   1 can or jar (4 ounces) dried beef, torn into
      bite-size pieces

Cook macaroni as directed on package for range-top method; drain. Add water, soup, dried beef and cheese sauce mix. Heat to boiling; simmer until thick, about 2 minutes. *4 servings.*

CORNED BEEF-POTATO SKILLET

Serve with chilled vegetable relishes brought from home.

In 10-inch skillet combine potato slices and seasoned sauce mix from 1 package (5.5 ounces) scalloped potatoes. Add the amount of liquid designated on package. Open 1 can (12 ounces) corned beef and break meat into pieces; stir into potato mixture. Heat to boiling. Reduce heat; cover and simmer 30 minutes, or until potatoes are tender. *4 servings.*

Family Camp-outs

When you take to the road for a car or trailer trip, a bit of camp-cooking equipment stowed in the back gives you a kind of gypsylike independence. You can stop at a restaurant when and if you feel like it, but you're completely free to pass up costly-looking establishments or second-rate snackstands in favor of a pleasant, inexpensive meal of your own making in a pretty setting of your own choosing. All it really takes to insure this nice option is a carton of staples, an ice chest, a camp stove or portable grill, and a bit of foresight.

Whether your gear is simple or elaborate, and whether you plan to stay in camp for the entire vacation, a night en route or just for lunchtime, you'll want to turn out tasty meals with a minimum of time and effort. Everyone is tired after hours of driving, sightseeing, hiking or just plain playing, and no camp meal is a pleasure if it takes hours to prepare.

Pack food and cooking utensils so that they can be easily reached and unloaded first. If possible, arrange the contents of the cooler and food box so the items you'll need first will be on top, right at hand. The cook can get the meal started while others in the party are collecting wood and setting up the camp.

Plan your menus around your camping scheme and the type of cooking gear you have. It goes without saying that you'll bring along as many condensed, canned and convenience foods as possible, but don't forget taken-for-granted foods like sugar, flour, buttermilk baking mix, salt, pepper and coffee. And tuck in some of the dehydrated foods specifically developed for packtrips . . . just in case. (In any of the recipes that follow you can substitute reconstituted dried eggs or dried milk.) Store perishables in a sturdy portable cooler.

One of the bonuses of car-based camping is the

214

chance it offers to travel light, carrying only the *basic* seasonings and staples. Fresh fruits, vegetables and meats can be purchased along almost any route. Make a point of sampling the foods for which each region is famous. Let a holiday be a change in every way. Look for a pot of sweet-salty beans when driving in New England. Buy fresh live or boiled lobsters from a lobster pound in Maine. (See page 171 for a delicious dinner featuring the food of the New England coastland.) Along the shores of Lake Superior, try the delicately smoked Ciscoes; on the east coast of Florida you'll find stands offering fresh-smoked shrimp; in the Southwest, sample tamales; in California, tuna and langouste. Wherever you travel, keep an eye out for the church bazaars and food sales so popular in small towns. Aid a good cause and help yourself to a superb homemade dessert.

Utensils from your own kitchen are unwieldy to pack, and chances are they'll be dented and sooted by the time you get home again. You'll be much happier if you use one of the complete, compact sets of nested camping utensils. And be sure to pack lightweight or disposable plates and cups.

Camp stoves that operate on bottled fuel are among the most practical items you can have for camp cooking. They can be set up quickly and are ready for use just as soon as you get the pots or skillets on them. No special skills are needed to operate a camp stove, for its principle is the same as that of the gas range. It is, however, strictly for pot, pan and skillet cooking. A tiny one-burner stove, perhaps the type that uses canned heat, is useful even for those who do not intend to turn out a whole dinner. It can make even a quick roadside lunch much more palatable by producing one hot item—soup, tea, coffee or hot sandwiches. Try buttering sandwiches on the outside and sautéing them—very good on a chilly day.

Most camp stoves can be fitted with a folding oven that has its own thermometer. This separate unit sits right on top of the camp stove and is perfect for baking hot breads and rolls.

Good-sized campgrounds have stationary fireplaces available, but it's best not to count on finding one ready and waiting just for you. Instead, rely on a compact portable grill and a good supply of easy-to-transport charcoal briquets. Some sites even offer electricity. If you know you'll be staying in such a spot bring any appliance your heart desires.

Many stalwarts like to prepare main dishes over a campfire, but they often supplement the fire with a reflector oven. Basically, this is a collapsible box of aluminum or other bright metal, with one side open—facing the fire—and the other sides set at angles that bounce the heat from the fire against the breads, biscuits or cookies baking on the level shelf.

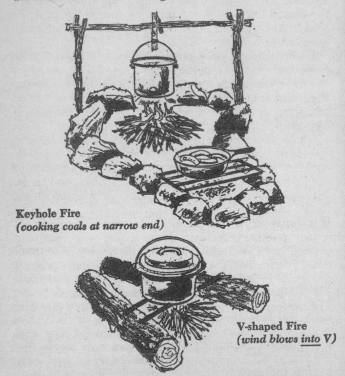

Keyhole Fire
(cooking coals at narrow end)

V-shaped Fire
(wind blows <u>into</u> V)

A roll of heavy-duty aluminum foil is one of the best friends a camp cook can have. In addition to its many uses on and around the barbecue grill (see page 26), aluminum foil can provide unique services in a camping-out situation. Here are some examples:

• Aluminum foil can be used for making a temporary reflector oven.

• Use foil for pot tops and drip pans of just the right size.

• Make a foil cup to hold a basting sauce.

• Bend a piece of wire into a circle; span it with foil and you have an emergency skillet.

• Nothing to roll biscuit dough or pastry on . . . or with? Think again. Spread foil on any fairly level surface (a large flat rock or the hood of your car, for example); for a rolling pin, wrap another piece of foil around a tent peg or a newspaper rolled into a tight rod.

• Need a strainer or colander? Punch holes in a piece of foil that has been molded into a bowl shape.

• Need a dishpan? Scoop a hole in the ground and line it with foil.

• Use foil to wrap all kinds of food. It's especially good for wrapping and transporting fresh-caught fish —to protect the car from that well-known lingering fish odor.

Often campers drive or hike to an altitude much higher than the one they live in, and camp chefs are bound to encounter problems if they forget that cooking times are affected by altitude. At sea level, water boils at 212°, but it boils at about one degree less with each 500 feet of altitude. For example, at 5,000 feet water will boil at about 202°. This means that anything cooked in water will need extra time on the fire. Baking at altitudes above sea level has its problems, too. In thinner atmosphere, baking powder acts more powerfully. Biscuits and muffins do bake satisfactorily at high altitudes, but above 5,000 feet you may find it necessary to decrease the amount of baking powder slightly. However, even experienced camp cooks find cake-baking under high-altitude camping conditions very tricky.

A favorite camp feast is beans cooked in a bean hole. Dig a hole about twice as deep and twice as wide as your Dutch oven (which should be cast iron with a heavy lid). Line the hole with rocks or bricks. Build a wood fire in the rock-lined hole and keep it burning for at least two hours. Remove most of the coals. Put in your hot Dutch oven (in which the beans have been boiling) and, if possible, reverse the lid. Heap the discarded coals on top. Cover with at least 8 inches of earth, and leave it all day or overnight.

If you're an avid camper, you're well aware of the wide variety of camping equipment now on the market. There's hardly a need that hasn't been met by some manufacturer. If you're a neophyte or would-be camper, keep an eye out for such gear in magazines, department stores and sporting-goods stores. And do examine the outfittings of other campers. Profit from the mistakes and advice of old pros; they'll be happy to help you.

Some fledgling campers automatically think of buying tents and trailers and other big, expensive furnishings. Don't even consider this type of purchase until you've taken an experimental trip or two, using borrowed sleeping bags or the cabins available in so many campgrounds. Concentrate instead on the day-to-day, and happily more inexpensive, needs of camping; for example, a portable charcoal grill, a lantern, a fitted camp cupboard, perhaps a heater. A table for food preparation is considered a necessity by many, and a compact folding table and camp chairs will be greatly appreciated at mealtime. Sitting on the ground for a picnic is fun . . . but not three times a day, every day. Another valuable and inexpensive item that will always be a useful supplement to whatever camping equipment you eventually acquire is a canvas awning that attaches to the roof of your car and stretches out to protect your stove and table from sun and rain. Some of these awnings have sides that can be dropped, forming a windbreak or a cabaña arrangement for changing clothes.

Whatever your plans, don't let a camp trip turn into a chore-trip. Camping out should be fun—and it is. Plan ahead, and plan carefully. If you forget something, laugh it off and work around the missing items. One of the joys of car- or trailer-based camping is that if you do overlook an important item, such as charcoal for the grill or fuel for the stove, you can always drive to a town. You may have to travel many miles, but at least you can get there. The same is not true of packtrip camping (see page 240).

(see page 240)

Following are recipes for the campfire or charcoal grill, for the camp stove and reflector oven that will help you produce quick, solid and well-balanced camp meals. Don't save all of them for the summer camping trip; some will be equally good for winter warm-ups by the skating pond and for those something-to-do cookouts for the youngsters.

Camp-keeping Tips

Whether camping for a day or a week, at a public campground or in a remote mountain pass, there are certain clean-up and safety rules that should be followed:

• *Clean up immediately after eating. (It's easier to clean utensils if you do it before food hardens in them.) Burn all paper wrappers and containers; bury cans and other tins that cannot be burned. The smallest trace of food is attractive to insects, mice, rats, chipmunks . . . and bears.*

• *Don't throw away dishwater near the campbase unless you want to draw a congress of ants and flies. They love it. Dump dishwater far away, or dig a small trench and bury it.*

• *Don't attempt to burn wet garbage. Bury it, or dry small quantities over the fire and then burn each batch completely.*

• *Carry insect repellent. Sprays are effective and can be used over the entire campsite. Stick-form repellents are practical, too—provide one for each member of the party. Mosquitoes, no-see-ums, black flies, mites, chiggers and ticks can make the camper wish he'd never left home. Wasps love meat, especially fish meat. If you have any fresh-caught fish, skin a small one and hang it a little distance from your eating area. Wasps will leave table meats for the raw fish.*

• *If mosquitoes are a nuisance, build smudge fires 30 to 50 feet upwind of your cooking fire to clear the area of them—without smoking out your party. (Don't depend on the smoke from a campfire to drive mosquitoes away.) Be careful of fire hazards. Build a smudge fire in a tin can with a small hole punched near the base for a draft door. A few brightly burning coals covered with evergreen branches, green ferns or grass will produce a dense smoke. Place smudge fires on rocks or other safe ground, clear of trees and bushes.*

• *Never leave a fire unwatched, and when leaving the campsite, make sure that all fires are out. Drown the fire with water; spread the ashes and make sure no coal is still smoldering. Douse again, just to make sure.*

• *Carry a flashlight and a first-aid kit.*

First Night Out Dinner

Camporee Cassoulet

Tossed Green Salad

Bacon Corn Bread (page 232)

Peach or Blueberry Pie (page 164)
(brought from home)

Milk or Coffee

CAMPOREE CASSOULET

1 pound ground beef
1 cup sliced celery
½ cup chopped onion
½ cup chopped green pepper
1 clove garlic, crushed
1 teaspoon salt
1 can (1 pound) pork and beans
1 can (1 pound) lima beans
1 can (6 ounces) tomato paste

In large heavy skillet, cook and stir ground beef, celery, onion, green pepper, garlic and salt until meat is brown and onion is tender; drain excess fat from skillet. Stir in pork and beans, lima beans (with liquid) and tomato paste; simmer 10 minutes. *4 to 6 servings.*

> # Chuck Wagon Breakfast
>
> *Grilled Canadian Bacon and Sausages*
>
> *Pancakes*
>
> *Hot Coffee*

GRILLED CANADIAN BACON AND SAUSAGES

1½ pounds unsliced Canadian bacon
¼ cup maple syrup
½ teaspoon hickory-smoked salt
⅛ teaspoon cloves
1 package (8 ounces) brown 'n serve sausages

With sharp knife make diagonal cuts, ½ inch deep, at ½-inch intervals in surface of bacon. Continue scoring entire surface in diamond pattern. Combine syrup, salt and cloves to make a basting sauce. Place bacon on grill 3 inches from medium coals. Cook, turning and basting frequently, 30 to 45 minutes. Just before serving, grill sausages about 6 minutes or until heated through. *8 servings.*

PANCAKES

Beat 2 cups buttermilk baking mix, 1 egg and 1⅓ cups milk with rotary beater or spoon until smooth. For thinner pancakes, add more milk; for thicker pancakes, add more baking mix. Bake on hot lightly greased griddle or skillet, turning when bubbles appear and before they break. Serve hot with syrup. *Makes about eighteen 4-inch pancakes.*

BLUEBERRY PANCAKES—Follow recipe for Pancakes (above) except—add 2 tablespoons sugar to batter; gently fold in 1 cup fresh or drained canned blueberries.

CHEESE PANCAKES—Follow recipe for Pancakes (left) except—add ½ to 1½ cups shredded sharp cheese to batter. For lunch or supper, serve with creamed meats or vegetables.

CORN PANCAKES—Follow recipe for Pancakes (left) except—stir 1 cup drained whole kernel corn and ½ teaspoon paprika into batter.

HAM PANCAKES—Follow recipe for Pancakes (left) except—add 1 to 1½ cups ground or chopped cooked ham to batter. For lunch or supper, serve with cranberry sauce or cheese sauce.

Quick Camp Dinner

Saucy Corned Beef with Dilled Potatoes

Skillet Biscuits

Fresh or Canned Fruit

Doughnut Sandwiches (page 237)

Coffee

SAUCY CORNED BEEF WITH DILLED POTATOES

1 can (12 ounces) corned beef, cubed
1 can (1 pound) peas and onions, drained
1 envelope (1¼ ounces) chicken gravy mix

Combine corned beef and peas and onions in 2-quart saucepan. Prepare gravy mix as directed on package; add to meat mixture. Heat on grill or camp stove until bubbly. Serve over Dilled Potatoes; sprinkle with shredded sharp process American cheese, if desired. *4 to 6 servings.*

DILLED POTATOES

Prepare instant mashed potato puffs as directed on package for 4 servings except—add ½ teaspoon dill weed to boiling water.

SKILLET BISCUITS

Melt ¼ cup butter or margarine in 9- or 10-inch skillet on grill. Sprinkle butter with onion salt, garlic salt and paprika. Prepare Biscuit dough as directed on package of buttermilk baking mix. Roll or pat ½ inch thick; cut 12 biscuits. Arrange in skillet, turning biscuits to coat both sides with seasoned butter. Cover skillet with heavy-duty aluminum foil. Place on grill 4 inches from hot coals. Bake 10 minutes; lift foil to be sure biscuits are not burning. Bake 5 minutes longer or until the biscuits are done. *Makes 12 biscuits.*

Main Dishes

CALICO COMBO

1 pound ground beef
2 tablespoons instant minced onion
1 teaspoon garlic powder
1 can (1 pound) French-cut green beans, drained
1 can (10½ ounces) condensed tomato soup
Instant mashed potato puffs
1 package (4 ounces) shredded Cheddar cheese

In large heavy skillet on grill, cook and stir ground beef, onion and garlic powder until meat is brown; drain off excess fat. Stir in green beans and soup; heat through. Prepare mashed potato puffs as directed on package for 4 servings; stir in shredded cheese. To serve, spoon beef over potatoes. *4 to 6 servings.*

DINNER-IN-A-CAN

1 pound ground beef
4 tomatoes, sliced
1 can (1 pound 1 ounce) whole kernel corn, drained
Butter or margarine
Salt and pepper
1 cup buttermilk baking mix
⅓ cup milk

Season meat as desired; shape into 4 patties. Grease four 2-pound coffee cans. Place a meat patty in each can. Top each patty with 3 tomato slices and ¼ of the corn. Dot with butter. Season with salt and pepper. Cover each can securely with heavy-duty aluminum foil. Place on grill 3 to 4 inches from hot coals; cook 20 to 30 minutes. Mix baking mix and milk thoroughly with fork for dumpling batter. Remove foil lids and drop small spoonfuls of batter into each can. Sprinkle with parsley, if desired, or with garlic or onion salt. Cook uncovered 10 minutes; cover and continue cooking 10 minutes longer. Eat dinner directly from the can. *4 servings.*

POCKET STEW

So named because hikers can carry all the ingredients in their pockets.

For each serving, make patty of ¼ pound ground beef. Place patty on 12-inch square of double thickness heavy-duty aluminum foil. Top with a slice of onion and a slice of potato. Add 2 carrot sticks. Sprinkle with salt and pepper. Seal foil securely. Cook directly on hot coals 25 minutes, turning once. Eat stew from foil packet. *4 servings.*

BURGER DOGS

>1 pound ground beef
>8 frankfurters, split lengthwise
>1 can (8 ounces) tomato sauce
>1 medium onion, finely chopped
>2 tablespoons water
>8 frankfurter buns, split

In heavy skillet cook and stir beef until meat is browned. Add franks, tomato sauce, onion and water; cook about 15 minutes. During the last 3 to 4 minutes, toast buns cut side down on grill. Serve meat mixture on warm buns. *8 servings.*

CORNED BEEF STIR-UP

>1 package (6 or 7 ounces) elbow macaroni
>1 can (12 ounces) corned beef, chopped
>1 cup shredded process American cheese (4 ounces)
>1 can (10½ ounces) condensed cream of celery soup
>1 cup milk
>2 tablespoons instant minced onion
>1 teaspoon onion salt

Cook macaroni as directed on package; drain. Stir together all ingredients in skillet or saucepan. Heat over medium heat on grill or camp stove until bubbly, stirring occasionally. *5 or 6 servings.*

CAN-OPENER CHICKEN COOKOUT

1 can (1 pound) French-style green beans
1 can (10½ ounces) condensed cream of
mushroom soup
2 cans (5 ounces each) boned chicken
1 package (8 ounces) chow mein noodles

Stir beans, soup and chicken together in saucepan.
Heat on grill or camp stove until bubbly. Serve over
noodles. *4 to 6 servings.*

CHEESY PUPS

Biscuit dough
½ cup shredded Cheddar cheese
1 pound frankfurters
10 slices bacon

Prepare Biscuit dough as directed on package of
buttermilk baking mix except—add cheese with the
baking mix. Divide into 10 portions. Pat one portion
of dough around each frankfurter, making a thin
covering. Wrap a bacon slice around dough, securing
ends with wooden picks. Place on grill 4 inches from
hot coals. Cook, turning frequently, 15 minutes, or
until bacon is crisp and biscuit done. *5 servings.*

SQUAW CORN

4 slices bacon
1 medium green pepper, chopped
1 small onion, chopped
1 can (1 pound) cream-style corn
1 teaspoon salt
⅛ teaspoon pepper
4 eggs, beaten

Fry bacon until crisp; drain on paper towels. Drain
all but about 3 tablespoons drippings from skillet.
Cook and stir green pepper and onion in drippings
until onion is tender. Add remaining ingredients. Cook
and stir until eggs are thickened throughout but still
moist. Crumble bacon over eggs. *4 to 6 servings.*

EGGS IN FOIL

For each serving, make a foil cup by molding 7-inch square of heavy-duty aluminum foil around bottom of 1-pound can. Crack an egg into each cup. Cook eggs in foil cups directly on coals 7 to 10 minutes or until of desired consistency.

POTATO-EGG SCRAMBLE

6 slices bacon, diced
5 cooked pared medium potatoes, diced
1 bunch green onions *or* 1 onion, finely chopped
Salt and pepper
4 eggs, beaten

Fry bacon until crisp; drain half of drippings from skillet. Add potatoes and onions; season with salt and pepper. Fry until lightly browned. Add eggs and, if desired, additional salt and pepper. Cook and stir until eggs are thickened throughout but still moist. *4 servings.*

CAMPER'S PIZZA

Biscuit dough
½ teaspoon salt
1 bottle (14 ounces) catsup
1 package (3½ ounces) sliced pepperoni
2 packages (4 ounces each) shredded mozzarella cheese
Oregano leaves

Prepare Biscuit dough as directed on package of buttermilk baking mix except—add salt with the baking mix. Divide dough into 4 equal parts. Pat each part into an 8-inch circle. Place circles on grill 5 inches from medium coals or campfire; cook 8 minutes. Turn grilled side up; spread catsup over. Top with pepperoni, cheese, oregano. Cook 12 to 15 minutes longer, or until sauce bubbles and edges of dough are browned. *4 servings.*

Vegetables

CANNED VEGETABLES, CAMPFIRE STYLE

A good way to deal with baby beets, boiled new potatoes or whole onions.

Remove the label from can of vegetables. Cut *almost* completely around can top, leaving it in place as a lid. Place can at back of grill; whatever heat is being used for cooking main dish is fine for vegetables. Cook 15 to 20 minutes or until steaming. Drain; add butter and seasonings.

SKILLET SCALLOPED OR AU GRATIN POTATOES

No potato peeling on your camping trip if you use scalloped or au gratin potatoes. Prepare as directed on 5.5-ounce package except—cook in covered 9- or 10-inch skillet over a slow fire. If packing space is at a premium, clip the directions off the package and slip into a plastic bag with the potato and sauce packets—no box to crush now and burn later.

Breads

ONION BUTTER BISCUITS

⅓ cup butter or margarine
¼ cup dry onion soup mix
   Biscuit dough

Melt butter in 8-inch foil pie pan on grill. Add 2 tablespoons of the dry onion soup mix; stir. Spoon half the butter mixture into another 8-inch foil pan. Prepare Biscuit dough as directed on package of buttermilk baking mix except—add remaining dry onion soup mix with the baking mix. Drop dough by spoonfuls into the hot pan. Drizzle with remaining half of butter mixture. Invert second pan over pan with dough. Secure rims together with spring-type clothespins. Place on grill 4 inches from hot coals. Bake 8 to 10 minutes. Remove pan from grill; turn each biscuit with spatula. Cover pan and bake 8 to 10 minutes longer. *Makes about twelve 2-inch biscuits.*

HUSH PUPPIES

1½ cups cornmeal
1½ cups water
⅓ cup milk
1 tablespoon salad oil
2 teaspoons grated onion
2 eggs, beaten
1 cup all-purpose flour°
3 teaspoons baking powder
2 teaspoons salt
1 teaspoon sugar

Cook and stir cornmeal and water until mixture becomes stiff and begins to form a ball (about 6 minutes). Remove from heat; add milk, 1 tablespoon oil and the onion. Stir until smooth. Gradually stir into beaten eggs in medium bowl. Stir dry ingredients together. Add to cornmeal mixture; blend thoroughly.

Heat fat (about 1 inch deep) to 375°. Drop batter by teaspoonfuls into hot fat. Fry 6 to 7 minutes or until golden brown. Drain on paper towels. *Makes 24 to 30 hush puppies.*

° *If using self-rising flour, omit baking powder and salt.*

ZEBRA BREAD

Prepare Biscuit dough as directed on package of buttermilk baking mix except—add ¼ cup sesame seed and ½ teaspoon salt with the baking mix. Divide dough in half. Pat each half into a rectangle, 12x8 inches; cut in half lengthwise. Grill strips 5 inches from medium coals 3 to 4 minutes on each side. Cut each into 4 pieces; serve hot with butter. *Makes 16 pieces.*

CHEESE-FILLED ZEBRA BREAD—Follow recipe above except—before grilling, place thin slice of Cheddar cheese on half of each strip; fold over and seal edges securely.

CAMPER'S BLUEBERRY COFFEE CAKE

Ingenious clothespinned pie pans turn your grill into an oven in which to bake quick breads from handy packaged mixes.

Lightly grease two 9-inch foil pie pans. Prepare the batter as directed on 1 package (13.5 ounces) wild blueberry muffin mix. Pour batter into a prepared pan. Invert second pan over pan with batter. Secure rims together with spring-type clothespins. Place on grill 4 inches from hot coals. Cook 15 minutes on each side, rotating pans occasionally for even baking. *6 to 8 servings.*

CAMPER'S CORN BREAD—Follow recipe above except—substitute 1 package (14 ounces) corn muffin mix for the blueberry muffin mix.

For the Camp Oven

BACON CORN BREAD
    6 slices bacon
 1¼ cups all-purpose flour*
    2 tablespoons sugar
    3 teaspoons baking powder
    1 teaspoon salt
    1 cup cornmeal
   ⅓ cup salad oil or melted shortening
    1 egg, beaten
 1½ cups milk

Heat camp oven to 425°. Fry bacon until crisp. Drain bacon on paper towels and crumble. Spoon 2 tablespoons bacon drippings into 9-inch round pan; sprinkle bacon over drippings. In mixing bowl stir together flour, sugar, baking powder, salt and cornmeal. Add remaining ingredients and mix well. Pour batter slowly over bacon and drippings in pan. Bake 25 to 30 minutes. To serve, invert on serving plate. *8 to 10 servings.*

* *If using self-rising flour, decrease baking powder to 1 teaspoon and salt to ½ teaspoon.*

CAMP OVEN GINGERBREAD

Heat camp oven to 350°. Prepare batter for 1 package (14.5 ounces) gingerbread mix as directed, beating by hand. Bake specified time or until done. Serve with fresh fruit or cream.

For the Reflector Oven

DROP BISCUITS

Prepare Biscuit dough as directed on package of buttermilk baking mix. Drop dough by spoonfuls onto greased shiny side of sheet of heavy-duty aluminum foil. Bake in hot reflector oven about 15 minutes or until brown. *Makes 16 small or 8 large biscuits.*

BLUEBERRY-TRAIL BISCUITS—Follow recipe for Drop Biscuits (left) except—add 2 tablespoons sugar and carefully fold in 1 cup blueberries.

PAN BISCUIT BREAD—Follow recipe for Drop Biscuits (left) except—spread dough into greased square pan, 9x9x2 inches; bake 25 to 30 minutes.

MAIN-DISH SHORTCAKES—Bake Drop Biscuits (left). Split biscuits and spread with butter or margarine. Serve with creamed meat or seafood.

SWEET CINNAMON ROLLS

Prepare Biscuit dough as directed on package of buttermilk baking mix. Drop dough by teaspoonfuls into a mixture of 2 tablespoons sugar and 1 teaspoon cinnamon. Roll each ball to coat entire surface. Place on greased shiny side of sheet of heavy-duty aluminum foil. Bake in hot reflector oven 8 to 10 minutes or until brown. *Makes 16 small or 8 large rolls.*

MEAT TURNOVERS

⅓ cup milk or water
¼ cup butter or margarine, melted
2 cups buttermilk baking mix
Eight ⅛-inch slices cooked or canned meat
Chili sauce or pickle relish

Mix milk, butter and baking mix with fork to a soft dough. Divide dough into 8 pieces. Place each piece of dough on sheet of waxed paper; pat into 5-inch square. Place slice of meat on half of each square; spread each with 2 teaspoons chili sauce or pickle relish. Fold dough over meat and press edges together with tines of fork. Make slit on top of each turnover. Place on greased dull side of sheet of heavy-duty aluminum foil. Bake turnovers in hot reflector oven 25 to 30 minutes or until golden brown. *4 servings.*

Desserts

FRUIT TURNOVERS

> 2 pie crust sticks, crumbled
> 1 tablespoon plus 1 teaspoon nonfat dry milk
> ¼ cup water
> 1 can (1 pound 5 ounces) cherry, blueberry or
>   apple pie filling

Mix pie crust sticks, dry milk and water until dough loses stickiness and cleans bowl. Remove label from unopened can of pie filling; lightly flour sides of can. Divide pastry into 6 parts; roll each part on aluminum foil into 6-inch circle, using floured can as rolling pin. Place scant 2 tablespoons pie filling on each pastry circle. Fold pastry over; seal edges with tines of fork. Place on grill over medium coals or campfire; cook 10 minutes on each side, or until pastry is delicately browned. *6 turnovers.*

CHOCOLATE DUMPLINGS

> 1 cup brown sugar (packed)
> ⅓ cup buttermilk baking mix
> 3 cups water
> 1 package (6 ounces) semisweet chocolate pieces
> 2 cups buttermilk baking mix
> ¼ cup granulated sugar
> 2 tablespoons nonfat dry milk
> ½ teaspoon cinnamon
> ½ cup water

Stir together brown sugar and ⅓ cup baking mix in large heavy skillet. Gradually stir in 3 cups water; add chocolate pieces. Cook over low heat, stirring constantly until chocolate melts and mixture thickens slightly. Mix remaining ingredients thoroughly. Drop batter by tablespoonfuls into simmering chocolate mixture. Cook 10 minutes uncovered and 10 minutes covered. To serve, spoon chocolate mixture over dumplings. *6 to 8 servings.*

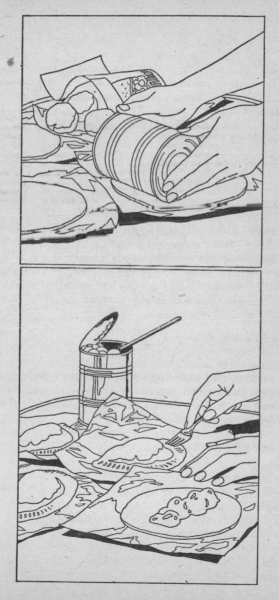

BANANA BOATS

For each serving, cut a V-shaped wedge lengthwise in a firm peeled banana. Place on 18x6-inch piece of double thickness heavy-duty aluminum foil. Fill groove with cut-up or miniature marshmallows and chocolate pieces. Wrap securely in foil. Cook directly on medium coals about 10 minutes.

Campfire Snacks

CAMPFIRE FONDUE

In small saucepan heat 1 can (11 ounces) condensed Cheddar cheese soup and 1 package (6 ounces) Swiss cheese, shredded, until cheese is melted; stir frequently to prevent sticking. To eat the fondue, place cubes of French bread or toast on peeled wooden sticks; dip into the hot cheese mixture. *4 servings.*

SURPRISE BISCUIT BALLS

Mix 1 cup buttermilk baking mix and ¼ cup water. Place dough on aluminum foil; pat into 6-inch square. Cut dough into 3x1-inch strips. Wrap each strip around a 1-inch cube of process American cheese, completely covering cheese. Insert pointed end of peeled green stick in cheese ball; rotate slowly over hot coals or campfire 5 minutes or until evenly browned. *12 biscuit balls.*

MAGIC MALLOW DROPS

   Cocoa Sauce (below)
16 marshmallows
   Coconut or chopped nuts

Prepare Cocoa Sauce. Secure marshmallows on pointed sticks or skewers; dip into warm sauce, then roll in coconut or nuts. Keep sauce over low heat while dipping marshmallows. Let drops cool before eating. *Makes 16 drops.*

Cocoa Sauce

Combine in small saucepan 1 cup sugar, 2 tablespoons cocoa and ½ cup milk. Cook over fire, stirring constantly, until small amount of mixture dropped into cold water forms a soft ball.

EGGHEADS

Cut day-old doughnuts into 1-inch pieces. Break 1 or 2 eggs into small covered container; cover and shake until eggs are well mixed. Place doughnut pieces on peeled ends of green sticks; dip into egg and toast over low coals or campfire.

CHOCOLATE-COVERED EGGHEADS—Follow recipe above except—after toasting Eggheads, dip them into warm Cocoa Sauce (above). Keep sauce warm while dipping Eggheads.

DOUGHNUT SANDWICHES

For each serving, cut 1 plain cake doughnut in half horizontally. Place a third of a 1.26-ounce milk chocolate candy bar on one half of doughnut; top with other half of doughnut. Grill 4 inches from low coals 4 minutes on each side. Serve as finger food or on serving plate topped with ice cream.

SHAGGY DOGS

Melt milk chocolate candy bars, adding milk to make a thin syrup (1 small candy bar plus 1 tablespoon milk makes enough syrup for 2 Shaggy Dogs). Place shredded or flaked coconut on flat dish. Toast marshmallows on fork or stick, dip into chocolate syrup and then roll in coconut.

ANGEL'S HALOS

For each serving, place a marshmallow in the hole of a glazed large doughnut. Run pointed green stick or picnic skewer through doughnut and marshmallow. Rotating stick slowly, toast Angel's Halo over campfire or low coals until doughnut is warm and marshmallow is soft.

S'MORES

For each serving, place 4 squares of a milk chocolate candy bar on a graham cracker. Toast a marshmallow over campfire; slip onto the chocolate and top with a second graham cracker. Eat S'more like a sandwich.

SUGAR HORNS

Mix 1 cup buttermilk baking mix and ¼ cup water. Place dough on sheet of aluminum foil; with fingers pat into 12-inch circle. Cut dough into 8 triangles. Wrap triangles around peeled ends of green sticks, making certain the top is sealed tightly. Rotating stick slowly, bake horns over coals 10 minutes or until evenly browned. Carefully remove from stick; fill horn with butter and brown sugar. *8 horns.*

SUGAR BALLS

 ¼ cup butter or margarine
 1 cup buttermilk baking mix
 ¼ cup water
 ⅓ cup sugar
 1 teaspoon cinnamon

Melt butter in small pan on grill. Mix baking mix and water to form a soft dough. Shape dough into 1-inch balls around peeled ends of green sticks; secure dough by pressing gently. Rotate slowly over campfire 5 minutes or until balls are evenly browned. Push balls off stick into melted butter; roll in cinnamon-sugar mixture. *12 balls.*

CHOCOLATE SUGAR BALLS—Follow recipe above except—substitute ⅓ cup instant cocoa mix for the cinnamon-sugar mixture.

Packtrips

If the pioneer spirit is strong in you and you want a real back-to-nature adventure, you'll probably plan a packtrip that will take you, for a day or a week, as far from civilization as time and endurance permit. And plan you'd better, because where you're going there are no shopping centers to pick up forgotten supplies. So take *everything* you will actually need but nothing else, and match the size and weight of your gear to the trip.

Because the packtripper's every need has to be met by the supplies in his pack, all equipment—for setting up camp, sleeping, cooking and eating—should be light and compact. A cast-iron skillet may be worth its poundage if you're traveling by horseback or canoe, but not if you're going it on foot. Choose pans that can be nested and with tops that can serve as extra pans. Depend on heavy-duty aluminum foil for additional cooking utensils and other camping aids (see page 217). A good packing trick is to take foil off its roll and fold it around a piece of flat cardboard.

Thanks to the great variety of condensed and dehydrated foods available, packtrip cooking is immeasurably easier today than it was in the past. Any supermarket offers dried milk and dried soups; handy gravy and sauce mixes; instant mashed, scalloped and au gratin potatoes; packaged macaroni and cheese; noodle-and-sauce dinners; ready-mixed pastry; buttermilk baking mix; and muffin mixes. Canned meats are available, and some markets carry canned bacon. Sporting-goods stores and mail-order houses that specialize in outfitting campers have an astonishing number of concentrated non-perishable delicacies as well as basic foods. These come in both individual packets and in complete meal units. Especially worth investigating are the freeze-dried items that come in

very small, lightweight packages and need no refrigeration. A little packet of stew meat, for example,
weighs only 7 ounces but will swell to feed four
hungry hikers. Such concentrated foods are not inexpensive, but they are a tremendous saving of strain
on the back of a packtripper.

Carry everything possible pre-mixed. Buy or make
your own pancake and bread mixes, leaving out only
the liquids. Pack small quantities in stout plastic bags,
roomy enough so that the batter can be mixed right in
the container. (Be sure to label the contents of each
bag.)

Another way to make packtrip meals neat and easy
to fix is to carry everything you'll need for an entire
meal in one plastic bag. Pack all the ingredients
needed for each course—in just the right amounts—in
separate small plastic bags or in compact tins; then
put them all in the large bag. Include recipe directions,
too. (See the easy-to-pack menus that follow.)

Don't underestimate the amount of food you'll need.
Be prepared if bad weather or a particularly beautiful
campsite keeps you out a day longer than planned.
And remember, packtrippers' appetites soar in the
fresh air.

If you are setting up a campsite for several days'
use, get ready for rain while the weather is still good.
Collect all the wood you will need for the entire period
and keep it in assorted piles—kindling, small pieces,
heavier sticks and logs. Cover the wood to keep it dry.

Carry spare matches in a waterproof tin. Make
doubly sure they will stay dry by dipping the heads
in paraffin. Candle stubs are one of the best, most
easily carried fire starters, especially useful when
tinder is damp. Or use solid canned fuel. It's an extremely fast and efficient fire starter.

Although packtrip camping and car-based camping
call for different gear and supplies, there are many
basic, overlapping rules and guides. So before you
set out, read over the Family Camp-outs section of
this book (pages 214-220). You'll find many helpful
suggestions on those pages, too.

Packtrip Breakfast

Crunchy French Toast

*Crisp Bacon
(canned prefried bacon)*

*Applesauce (dehydrated)
or
Grilled Apple Rings*

Coffee or Hot Chocolate

CRUNCHY FRENCH TOAST

In a small plastic bag, place 1 cup whole wheat flakes or cornflakes cereal; crush slightly and seal bag. In another small plastic bag, place enough dried egg for two eggs; seal. Place sealed plastic bags in a large plastic bag along with 6 slices bread which have had crusts removed and have been cut lengthwise into rectangles. Add a copy of the Cooking Instructions (below) and fasten bag securely. Also pack syrup.

Cooking Instructions

Reconstitute dried egg. Dip bread pieces into egg, then into crushed cereal. Fry until golden brown in lightly greased skillet or on griddle over campfire. Serve with syrup if desired. *4 to 6 servings.*

GRILLED APPLE RINGS

Also good at dinnertime with ham or chicken.

Place ¼ cup brown sugar (packed) and 1 teaspoon cinnamon in a small plastic bag; seal. Place sealed plastic bag in a larger plastic bag with 4 to 6 medium baking apples and a copy of the Cooking Instructions (below). Fasten bag securely. Also pack shortening or salad oil (or butter, if desired).

Cooking Instructions

Core apples. Cut crosswise into 1-inch slices. Brush both sides lightly with shortening (or butter). Grill 3 to 4 inches from medium coals or campfire 8 minutes. Turn; dust with sugar mixture (sugar melts while other side browns). Cook 5 to 10 minutes longer or until tender.

Fish Fry

Fried Fish

Hot Shoestring Potatoes
and/or
Hot Onion Rings

Fruit Dumplings

FRIED FISH

Place 1 cup all-purpose flour, buttermilk baking mix or cornmeal in a small plastic bag with a copy of the Cooking Instructions (below); seal securely. Also pack shortening, salt and pepper.

Cooking Instructions

Scale and clean small game fish, such as trout, perch, sunfish or crappies; remove heads, if you wish. Dip fish in water or milk. Sprinkle with salt and pepper. Dip in flour, baking mix or cornmeal. Melt shortening in heavy skillet to ⅛-inch depth. Fry fish over medium heat about 10 minutes or until golden brown, turning once. Do not crowd fish in the pan. Drain on paper towels. Serve the fish immediately.

HOT SHOESTRING POTATOES

Pack 1 can (4 ounces) shoestring potatoes and heavy-duty aluminum foil. Tape a copy of the Cooking Instructions (below) to side of can.

Cooking Instructions

Empty can of potatoes onto a piece of foil; wrap securely. Heat on grill about 4 inches from medium coals or campfire 20 minutes, turning once. *3 or 4 servings.*

HOT ONION RINGS—Follow directions above except—substitute 1 can (3½ ounces) French fried onion rings for the shoestring potatoes.

FRUIT DUMPLINGS

Remember the hot fruit mixture minus the dumplings for a camping breakfast.

In a small plastic bag combine 1 cup buttermilk baking mix and 3 teaspoons dry milk. Seal and place in large plastic bag with contents of 1 package (1 pound) assorted dried fruit, 1 cup raisins, ½ cup sugar, 1 tablespoon cornstarch, ½ teaspoon cinnamon, ½ teaspoon nutmeg and a copy of the Cooking Instructions (below). Fasten securely.

Cooking Instructions

Pour fruit mixture from large plastic bag into pan; add 4 cups water. Heat to boiling, stirring frequently. Simmer 30 minutes, stirring occasionally, until fruit is tender. Stir ⅓ cup water into baking mix mixture.

Drop dough by tablespoonfuls onto simmering fruit mixture. Cook uncovered 10 minutes, covered 10 minutes. To serve, spoon fruit mixture over dumplings. *6 to 8 servings.*

North Woods Dinner

Woodsman's Bean Soup

Camper's Corn Bread (page 231)

Grilled Sweet 'n Spice Oranges

Campfire Coffee

WOODSMAN'S BEAN SOUP

Select a 1½-pound sterilized canned ham (the non-refrigerated type); pack in a large heavy plastic bag. In small plastic bag, place contents of 2 boxes (10 ounces each) precooked beans, ¼ cup instant minced onion, 1 tablespoon sugar, 1½ teaspoons salt and 1 teaspoon *each* celery salt, onion powder and chili powder plus a copy of the Cooking Instructions (below). Fasten bag securely. Place in large bag with ham.

Cooking Instructions

Cut ham into cubes; place in large saucepan. Add contents of small plastic bag and 10 cups water. Heat to boiling, stirring occasionally. Simmer 30 minutes. *Makes 10 cups.*

GRILLED SWEET 'N SPICE ORANGES

Place ¼ cup brown sugar (packed) and 1 teaspoon cinnamon in small plastic bag; seal. Place sealed bag in a larger bag with 6 seedless oranges, a copy of the Cooking Instructions (below) and six 9-inch squares of double thickness heavy-duty aluminum foil. Fasten bag securely.

Cooking Instructions

Peel and section oranges. Place 1 orange on each square of foil; sprinkle with cinnamon-sugar mixture. Wrap each orange securely in foil. Cook, turning once, on medium coals 5 to 8 minutes or on grill 3 inches from hot coals 12 to 15 minutes. *About 6 servings*.

Home
Is the
Hunter

This chapter is meant for tyro or would-be sportsmen—and for those of you who one day are presented by a friend, a fellow camper or your boss with concrete evidence of his skill in hunting or fishing. Be it fish, fowl or animal, such a prize deserves proper handling, in the field *and* in the kitchen. Thus, the cook as well as the hunter should be acquainted with some basic guidelines concerning the care and preparation of fish and game. Although no number of printed words can possibly match firsthand observation and experience, you will be able to garner some necessary and important tips from the following.

Once caught, fish present few problems for either the angler or the cook. Any fish will keep better if cleaned right after it is caught. Besides, it may well be easier to perform this task in the field, where there is plenty of water, than at the campsite—and cleaned fish are certainly more welcome at home. Slit the fish from vent to gills; draw it, remove any blood along the spine, cut out the gills and, if you wish, cut off the head. Then rinse the fish quickly, scale it (if necessary) and wipe dry with paper towels—now it's ready for cooking.

Make every effort to keep fish cool until it reaches the campsite or kitchen. Never leave it lying in the sun, and in hot weather be sure to insulate it in some way. Don't keep fish cool by soaking in water. If carrying the catch in a creel or box, first line it with a layer of damp newspaper and then with ferns or other greenery. The ferns will prevent the fish from sticking to the paper. If carrying fish in an ice chest, keep them above the water line and away from direct contact with the ice. Here's a good way to do this: Dust fish lightly with cornmeal, then slip each one

Cleaning a Fish

Insert knife at vent.
Slit belly up to head.

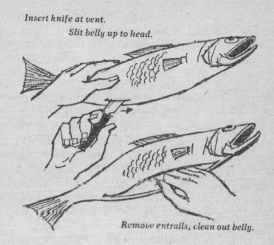

Remove entrails; clean out belly.

into a plastic bag. (The cornmeal will keep the fish from adhering to the plastic.) But seal the bags securely to keep out the water.

The sooner fish is cooked, the better it will be. Whether grilled, fried, planked, baked or broiled, all fish are best when cooked only until the flesh loses its transparent color and is flaky. In addition to the fish recipes in this chapter, refer to those for quick campfire cooking on page 243 and for grilling on pages 63-69.

Because the meat of game is leaner, tougher and has a stronger flavor than that of domestic animals, it calls for special techniques in handling and cooking. For any game to be served at its best, preparation of the meat should start in the field. The animal should be bled and drawn right after it is killed, allowed to cool as rapidly as possible, and kept cool until it can be cooked or stored in a refrigerator or freezer. Quick cleaning is important for two reasons: If the body cavity is emptied, the meat will cool faster, and so will keep better; and cleaning will prevent undesirable juices from contaminating portions of the edible meat.

Small game animals, like rabbits and squirrels, are generally skinned before cleaning; for this reason, some hunters wait until the end of the day to perform this dual operation. But skinning, which is an easy process with warm game, is somewhat more difficult if the animal is thoroughly chilled.

Even experienced hunters prefer to have a butcher or packing plant take care of the processing of big game, such as deer and elk. In this case, the game should be kept as cool as possible until it can be processed and refrigerated. Thus, game should be transported under well-ventilated conditions, on a cartop carrier or in the partially open trunk, not draped over the hot hood. And special care should be taken during the early part of the deer season, when the weather may be quite warm.

Big game and mature small game, like most mature domestic animals, need some aging. Few hunters agree on just how much. Even then, certain cuts may call for additional tenderizing or long, slow cooking, or both. The standard aging process is "hanging," which means holding the game under refrigeration at about 40 degrees for a time, just as beef is aged. For big game, this process usually calls for the facilities of a butcher or packing plant (except for campers who are spending weeks in the woods in cold weather). And since the time needed for hanging depends on the type and age of the animal, professional advice should be welcomed. Hanging game does not mean stringing it up in the backyard or elsewhere in the open in temperatures above 40 degrees to "ripen." This method of aging, used before the day of the refrigerator, can only produce "high meat" with some degree of spoilage and an undesirable flavor.

A very young animal will be succulent and tender without aging, particularly if it is grilled, broiled or panfried briefly at high heat. And it is equally good when roasted or stewed. A steak from a young deer is especially tender when brushed with fat and cooked just like a rare beef steak, but it will be tough if exposed to high heat until well done.

Mature game and tougher cuts of young game can be prepared for cooking either before or after aging by the use of a marinade. A commercial tenderizer can be used or, as in the classic preparation of hare for hasenpfeffer, the meat can be soaked for several days under refrigeration in a seasoned brine of water and wine or vinegar. If the meat has a strong flavor, throw away the marinade. Otherwise, use it during the cooking.

Grinding is another good way of dealing with tougher cuts. Gameburgers are a great treat if properly prepared. Remove all fat from the meat, then have your butcher grind the meat with beef fat, bacon or fresh pork (without this the patties will be too dry); add onion, sage and other seasoning and brush with molted fat or oil.

The distinctive flavor of game is much prized, but remember that too much of a "gamy" taste—like too much of any flavor—is distinctly unappetizing. The strongest taste is lodged in the fat, and so it should be removed before cooking. But since much game is extremely lean, a substitute fat must be added. A roast of venison, for example, may be larded with strips of salt pork or bacon. (Use a larding needle to draw strips of fat through the meat or place the fat over the roast.) Smaller cuts of meat will need a brushing of butter, bacon fat or salad oil.

Game birds, like game animals, will have a much less gamy taste if they are drawn soon after being shot. Small game birds, such as quail, need not be field dressed but they should be drawn and plucked on the day they are bagged. (And usually small birds are not drawn until after they are plucked.) Regardless of its size, if a bird is badly shot up, it is best to clean it *immediately* rather than risk contamination of the meat.

It's always best, and easier, to pluck a bird before it is completely chilled. When a bird grows cold, the feathers stiffen into the skin and are troublesome to remove; in fact, they will probably tear the skin if jerked out. A good way to speed the plucking process of an *undrawn* bird is to dip it briefly into a pot of hot, but not boiling, water covered with a layer of hot paraffin. Let the paraffin harden on the feathers. Then the feathers, all stuck together, can be stripped off in handfuls. In either case, always singe off the fuzz and remove pin feathers with tweezers. Another fast way to defeather a bird is simply to skin it. This is especially good if the bird is to be fricasseed or stewed—which, by the way, are the best methods of preparing a mature bird.

A young bird can be grilled, broiled, fried or cooked any other way the very day it is shot. A mature bird will need some tenderizing. Many hunters will hang a bird for up to four days, but this too is a matter of controversy. When in doubt about the age of the bird, cook it long and slowly, just as you would a mature domestic fowl.

The meat of wild birds is especially lean, so fat must be used in the cooking. The bird may be larded with salt pork or bacon, or basted with butter during the cooking period.

It is to be fervently hoped for, then, that the hunter or fisherman has taken care of cleaning the fish or game before it reaches the home kitchen. But if it has not been dressed, do so immediately—or ask your butcher to do it for you.

On the following pages you will find an array of recipes for fish and game that are sure to delight you, if the meat has been properly handled in the field. And once the sportsman knows you can do right by him, and by his offering, you can be sure that he will be gifting you again and again.

RAINBOW TROUT WITH CRABMEAT STUFFING

    6 rainbow trout, 8 ounces each (dressed weight)
    Salt
    1 can (7¾ ounces) crabmeat, drained and cartilage
        removed
    1 can (5 ounces) water chestnuts, drained and
        chopped
    ¼ cup dry bread crumbs
    ¼ cup mayonnaise or salad dressing
    ½ teaspoon crushed tarragon leaves
    ¼ cup butter or margarine, melted
    1 tablespoon lemon juice

Wash trout and pat dry with paper towels. Sprinkle
cavities of fish lightly with salt. Combine crabmeat,
water chestnuts, crumbs, mayonnaise and tarragon;
toss lightly to mix. Spoon stuffing into fish cavities;
secure with skewers, if necessary. Mix butter and
lemon juice. Place fish in well-greased hinged grill or
basket. Grill 4 inches from medium coals 8 to 10 minutes on each side, basting frequently with butter mixture. Fish is done when it flakes easily. *6 servings.*

PIKE IN A PACKAGE

    1 pound fresh or frozen walleye pike fillets
    1½ teaspoons salt
    ¼ teaspoon pepper
    1 small onion, thinly sliced
    1 tomato, peeled and cut into ½-inch slices
    1 tablespoon lime juice
    1 tablespoon salad oil
    1 tablespoon snipped parsley
    8 pitted ripe olives

If fillets are frozen, thaw before using. Sprinkle fillets
with salt and pepper. Place on 18x15-inch piece of
double thickness heavy-duty aluminum foil. Cover fish
with onion and tomato slices; sprinkle with lime juice,
salad oil and parsley. Top with olives. Wrap securely
in foil. Cook 4 inches from hot coals 20 to 30 minutes.
2 or 3 servings.

PHEASANT EN CRÈME

    1 pheasant, cleaned and quartered
    1 can (10½ ounces) condensed cream of chicken soup
  ½ cup apple cider
    1 tablespoon plus 1 teaspoon Worcestershire sauce
  ¾ teaspoon salt
  ⅓ cup chopped onion
    1 clove garlic, crushed
    1 can (3 ounces) sliced mushrooms, drained
    Paprika

Heat oven to 350°. Place pheasant in square pan, 9x9x2 inches. Mix soup, cider, Worcestershire sauce, salt, onion, garlic and mushrooms; pour over pheasant. Sprinkle generously with paprika. Bake 1½ to 2 hours or until tender, basting with sauce during baking. After baking 1 hour, sprinkle with ½ teaspoon paprika. *2 or 3 servings.*

PARTY PHEASANT—Follow recipe above, using 2 pheasants and doubling all ingredients except paprika. Place pheasants in oblong pan, 13x9x2 inches. *4 to 6 servings.*

BAKED PHEASANT BOURGUIGNON

    2 pheasants, cleaned
    1 teaspoon salt
  ¼ teaspoon *each* cloves, nutmeg, pepper and ground
      thyme
    4 slices bacon
    1 chicken bouillon cube
  ½ cup boiling water
    1 cup Burgundy
    2 tablespoons minced onion
    2 tablespoons snipped parsley
  ⅓ cup currant jelly

Heat oven to 350°. Wash pheasants and pat dry with paper towels. Combine salt, cloves, nutmeg, pepper and thyme; rub cavity and outside of each pheasant. Tie legs of each bird securely. Place breast side up on rack in jelly roll pan, 15½x10½x1 inch; place bacon slices over breasts. Dissolve bouillon cube in boiling water; mix with remaining ingredients except currant jelly; pour into jelly roll pan. Bake 1 to 1½ hours, or until pheasant is tender. Place pheasant on warm platter; strain hot juices into saucepan. Add currant jelly; heat until jelly is melted, stirring constantly. To serve, cut pheasants into serving pieces and top with sauce. *4 to 6 servings.*

DUCK CERISE

   2 wild mallard ducks, cleaned and quartered
   2 tablespoons sugar
   1 tablespoon finely cut-up crystallized ginger
     Dash salt
   1 tablespoon finely shredded orange peel
   ¼ cup orange juice
   2 cans (1 pound each) pitted Bing cherries, drained
     (reserve syrup)
   2 tablespoons cornstarch
   ¼ cup cherry-flavored brandy or orange juice

Heat oven to 350°. Wash ducks and pat dry with paper towels. Brown ducks in small amount hot fat in skillet. Place pieces skin side up in oblong baking dish, 13½x9x2 inches. In small saucepan, combine sugar, ginger, salt, orange peel, orange juice and ¾ cup reserved cherry syrup. Heat to boiling; pour over ducks. Bake, basting occasionally with sauce, 45 to 60 minutes, or until meat is done. Duck is done when juices are no longer pink when meat is pricked with fork, and meat is no longer pink when cut with knife between leg and body. Remove meat to warm platter. In small saucepan, combine remaining cherry syrup with cornstarch. Cook, stirring constantly, until mixture thickens and boils. Boil and stir 1 minute. Skim excess fat from pan juices and drippings. Add drippings, cherries and brandy to sauce. Heat through. Serve over ducks. *6 to 8 servings.*

ROAST WILD DUCK

> 2 wild mallard ducks, cleaned
> 1 teaspoon salt
> ½ teaspoon pepper
> ¼ teaspoon crushed rosemary leaves
> 1 medium onion, cut into eighths
> 1 apple, cut into eighths
> 2 stalks celery, cut up
> ½ cup butter, melted
> ¼ teaspoon pepper
> ¼ teaspoon crushed rosemary leaves

Heat oven to 350°. Wash ducks and pat dry with paper towels. Stir together salt, ½ teaspoon pepper and ¼ teaspoon rosemary; sprinkle cavities and outsides of ducks. Place half of onion, apple and celery in cavity of each duck. Place ducks breast side down on rack in shallow roasting pan. Roast 40 minutes. Combine butter, ¼ teaspoon pepper and ¼ teaspoon rosemary; baste ducks frequently during roasting. Turn ducks and roast 50 minutes longer or until done. Ducks are done when juices are no longer pink when meat is pricked with fork, and the meat is no longer pink when cut with knife between leg and body. Remove ducks from pan; split in half lengthwise. Remove and discard stuffing. *4 servings.*

ORANGE-BRAISED DUCK—Follow recipe above except— place ducks breast side up on rack in roasting pan. Omit basting mixture of butter, pepper and rosemary; instead pour 1½ cups orange juice into pan. Cover and bake 1½ hours, or until ducks are done. Uncover and bake 20 minutes longer to brown.

GLACÉ GOOSE

    1 wild goose, 5 to 6 pounds (dressed weight)
    ⅓ cup minced onion
    ¾ cup chopped celery (stalks and leaves)
    ½ cup butter or margarine
    4 cups bread cubes
 1½ teaspoons salt
    ¾ teaspoon ground sage
    ½ teaspoon ground thyme
    ¼ teaspoon pepper
 1½ cups finely chopped apple
    ⅓ cup raisins
    1 cup apple cider
    ¼ cup butter or margarine
    ¼ cup grape jelly
    1 cup apple cider

Heat oven to 325°. Wash goose and pat dry with paper towels. In large skillet cook and stir onion and celery in ½ cup butter until onion is tender. Stir in about a third of the bread cubes. Turn into deep bowl; add remaining bread cubes, the salt, sage, thyme, pepper, apple and raisins. Toss; stuff the body cavity lightly. Close the opening with skewers; lace. Place goose breast side up on rack in shallow roasting pan; pour 1 cup apple cider over goose. Cover; roast 30 minutes. In saucepan cook and stir ¼ cup butter, the jelly and 1 cup apple cider over low heat until jelly is melted. Uncover goose; roast 2 to 2½ hours longer or until done, basting frequently with jelly mixture. Goose is done when juices are no longer pink when meat is pricked with fork, and meat is no longer pink when cut between leg and body. *6 servings.*

ROAST WILD GOOSE

    1 wild goose, 5 to 6 pounds (dressed weight)
    ½ cup minced onion
    ¾ cup chopped celery (stalks and leaves)
    ½ cup butter or margarine
    4 cups bread cubes
    1 teaspoon salt
    ¾ teaspoon ground sage
    ½ teaspoon ground thyme
    ¼ teaspoon pepper
    2 to 3 tablespoons lemon juice
 1½ teaspoons salt
    ¼ teaspoon pepper

Heat oven to 325°. Wash goose and pat dry with paper towels. In large skillet cook and stir onion and celery in butter until onion is tender. Stir in about a third of the bread cubes. Turn into deep bowl; add remaining bread cubes, 1 teaspoon salt, the sage, thyme and ¼ teaspoon pepper. Toss; stuff the body cavity lightly. Close the opening with skewers; lace. Brush goose with lemon juice; sprinkle with 1½ teaspoons salt and ¼ teaspoon pepper. Place goose breast side up on rack in shallow roasting pan. Roast about 2 hours or until done, basting goose frequently with melted butter or pan drippings. Goose is done when juices are no longer pink when meat is pricked with fork, and meat is no longer pink when cut with knife between leg and body. *6 servings.*

QUAIL À L'ORANGE

    6 quail, cleaned
     Hot oil
    3 tablespoons minced onion
    ½ teaspoon tarragon leaves, crushed
    3 tablespoons butter or margarine
    1 cup orange juice
    ¼ teaspoon salt
    ¼ teaspoon dry mustard
    ½ cup currant jelly
    3 tablespoons shredded orange peel
    ¼ cup port wine or cranberry cocktail
    1 orange, pared and sectioned
    4 cups hot cooked rice

Tie legs of quail together, if desired. In large skillet brown quail in hot oil. Remove quail; discard oil. Cook and stir onion and tarragon in butter until onion is tender. Add orange juice, salt, mustard, jelly and orange peel. Cook over medium heat, stirring until jelly melts. Reduce heat; stir in wine and orange sections. Add quail; cover and simmer gently 20 to 25 minutes, or until meat is done. Turn quail occasionally. Serve quail with sauce on rice. *6 servings.*

VENISON STROGANOFF

    1½ pounds venison round steak
    ⅓ cup all-purpose flour
    ½ cup butter or margarine
    1 cup chopped onion
    1 can (6 ounces) sliced mushrooms, drained
    1 can (10½ ounces) beef bouillon
    1 teaspoon salt
    1 teaspoon Worcestershire sauce
    1 teaspoon soy sauce
    1 cup dairy sour cream
    4 to 6 cups hot cooked noodles

Cut meat diagonally into very thin slices; dip in flour until well coated. In large skillet brown meat lightly in butter. Remove meat from skillet; cook and stir onion and mushrooms in butter until onion is tender. Stir in meat and remaining ingredients except sour cream and noodles; cover and simmer 45 to 60 minutes, or until meat is tender. Stir in sour cream; heat through. Serve over noodles. *4 to 6 servings.*

VENISON SCALLOPINI

The meat of the deer is readily adaptable to recipes typically used for veal, like this Italian classic. Serve with buttered vermicelli and a tossed salad.

  1½ pounds venison round steak, cut into serving pieces
      about ½ inch thick
  ½ cup all-purpose flour
  1 teaspoon salt
  ½ teaspoon pepper
  1 egg, slightly beaten
  ⅓ cup light cream
  ¾ cup fine cracker crumbs
  ¾ cup grated Parmesan cheese
  ¼ cup snipped parsley
  ½ cup butter or margarine
  1 clove garlic, crushed
  1 cup Marsala or pineapple juice

Heat oven to 375°. Pound venison pieces ¼ inch thick with edge of saucer or meat pounder. Stir together flour, salt and pepper. Dip venison in flour mixture until well coated. Stir together egg and cream. Mix cracker crumbs, cheese and parsley. Dip venison into egg mixture; roll in crumb mixture. In large skillet heat butter and garlic until golden. Brown meat on both sides. Place browned meat in square baking dish, 8x8x2 inches; pour wine over top and cover. Bake 45 to 60 minutes, or until meat is tender. *4 to 6 servings.*

VENISON SAUERBRATEN

    3- to 3½-pound venison chuck roast
    2 onions, sliced
    2 bay leaves
  12 peppercorns
  12 juniper berries, if desired
    6 whole cloves
    2 teaspoons salt
 1½ cups red wine vinegar
    1 cup boiling water
    2 tablespoons shortening
  12 gingersnaps, crushed (about ¾ cup)
    2 teaspoons sugar

Place roast in an earthenware bowl or glass baking dish with onions, bay leaves, peppercorns, berries, cloves, salt, vinegar and boiling water. Cover bowl with plastic wrap; marinate 3 days or longer in refrigerator, turning meat twice a day with 2 wooden spoons. (Never pierce meat with a fork.) Drain meat, reserving marinade; brown meat on all sides in hot shortening in heavy skillet. Add marinade mixture; cover skillet; simmer slowly 3 to 3½ hours, or until meat is tender. Remove meat and onions from skillet and keep warm. Strain and measure liquid in skillet; add water, if necessary, to measure 2½ cups liquid. Pour liquid into skillet; cover and simmer 10 minutes. Stir gingersnaps and sugar into liquid. Cover and simmer gently 3 minutes. Serve meat and onions on a platter; accompany with gingersnap gravy. *6 servings.*

RABBIT À LA MARYLAND

    1 rabbit, cleaned, skinned and cut into serving pieces
  ½ cup shortening
  ½ teaspoon salt
  ¼ teaspoon pepper
  ¾ cup all-purpose flour
    2 eggs, slightly beaten
  ¾ cup fine cracker or bread crumbs
    1 small onion, minced
    1 bay leaf

Heat oven to 350°. Wash rabbit and pat dry with paper towels. Melt shortening in oblong baking dish, 11½x7½x1½ inches. Sprinkle rabbit with salt and pepper. Roll each piece in flour, then in beaten eggs and cracker crumbs. Place in hot shortening in baking dish; add onion and bay leaf. Roast until tender, about 1½ hours, basting frequently. *4 to 6 servings.*

Subject Index

Names of menus are listed in italicized type

Aluminum foil, 26-28
  cooking in, 26-28
  drip pan, 27
  grill liner, 4
  in camp, 216
  packing, 240
  windbreak, 13
Ash, 7, 10, 13

Baking
  at high altitudes, 217
  in camp ovens, 216, 232
  in reflector ovens, 216, 232-233
Barbecue
  equipment, 16-30
  fires. *See* Fire(s)
  parties, 31, 169-190
Basket grills, 25
Basting, 103
  brushes, 25
Bean holes, 218
Boats, cooking on, 207-213
Braziers, 17
Breakfast at the Park, 192
Breakfasts and brunches, 192-196,
  222-223, 242
Briquets. *See* Charcoal
Bucket grills, 18

California Patio Party, 182-185
Camp
  ovens, 216, 232
  stoves, 215
Camping, 214-246
  equipment, 214-220
  grills, 16
  packtrip, 240
"Cape Cod logs," 9
Charcoal, 4. *See also* Fire(s)
  adding, 3, 13
  arrangement for cooking, 10, 14,
    34, 75, 93
  cooking temperatures, 10, 34, 75
  lighting, 6-9
Chinese smoke ovens, 22, 93, 101
Chuck Wagon Breakfast, 222
Clambakes, 173
Company Brunch on the Patio, 196

Cooking
  at high altitudes, 217
  distance, of food from fire, 12
  equipment. *See* Equipment
  in foil, 26
  kettles, 19
  temperatures, 10, 11, 12, 34, 75
  wagons, 20
Coolers and insulated containers,
  197, 207

"Down-East" Special, 171-173
Draft control, 13, 94
Drip pan, 27, 76
Drippings, 14, 34, 71, 76

Electric
  appliances, 29
  fire starters, 8
Equipment
  barbecue, 16-30
  boating, 207
  camping, 214-220, 240
  picnic, 197
Eye-opener Breakfast, 194

Family Picnic, 199-201
Fire(s), 2-15
  base for, 3-4
  controlling heat of, 12
  extinguishing, 15, 220
  for bean holes, 218
  for clambake, 173-174
  for grilling, 10, 14, 34
  for rotisserie cooking, 14, 75
  for smoke cooking, 10, 11, 93,
    101
  fuel for, 4
  locating, 3
  shape, 6, 7, 8, 9, 10, 11, 12, 13
  smudge, 220
  starting, 6, 241
  wood, 5, 9, 93, 220, 241
Fireplaces, stationary, 20
First Night Out Dinner, 221
Fish, cleaning and handling,
  248-249
Fish Fry, 243-245
Flare-ups, controlling, 14, 34, 71

Folding grills, 19
Fuels, 4-6. *See also* Charcoal;
    Fire(s)

Game, care and handling, 248-252
Garbage disposal, 208, 220
Gas grills, 21
Grill(s), 16-25
    accessories and tools, 21-32
    care of, 4, 14, 15
    clambakes on, 174
    lining, 4
    thermometers, 10, 26, 34
Grilling, 34-74

Hamper Picnic, 202-203
Hawaiian Luau, 186-190
Heat control, 12-13
Herbs in smoke cooking, 94
Hibachis, 18
Hickory chips, 93
Hinged grills, 25, 34

Insects and repellents, 170, 198,
    220

Kabobs, 70
    coals for grilling, 14
Kindling, 9, 241

Liquid starters, 6-7

Marinating, 103
Menus
    boating, 209
    breakfast, 192, 193, 194, 222,
        242
    brunch, 195, 196
    camping, 221, 222, 223
    packtrip, 242, 243, 245
    party, 171, 176, 179, 182, 186
    picnic, 199, 202, 205
Midwest Splurge, 176-178
Moonlight Coffee Party, 209

North Woods Dinner, 245

Packtrip Breakfast, 242
Packtrips, 240-246
Paper Bag Picnic, 205-206
Patio parties
    cross-country, 169-190
    presenting, 31
Picnic(s), 197-206
    breakfast, 192
    equipment, 17, 197

Quick Camp Dinner, 223

Reflector ovens, 216, 232
Refrigeration, 197, 207
Rotisserie cooking, 10, 75-92

Sandwiches, 215
Sauces, use of, 103
Serving, 31, 169
Skewer racks, 24
Skewers, 24
    cooking on, 14, 70
Smoke
    cooking, 10, 93-102
    ovens, 22, 93, 102
Starting the fire, 6-9
Strawberry Shortcake Brunch, 195

Tables and settings, 31, 169
Temperatures. *See* Cooking
    temperatures
Texas Beef Bake, 179-181
Thermometers, 10, 26, 34, 78
Tongs, 24
Tools, 30
Trussing, 77

Weather problems, 170, 241
Wheelbarrow serving cart, 28
Windbreaks, 13, 17, 27
Woods. *See also* Fire(s), wood
    for smoke cooking, 93

Recipe Index

Accompaniments for meats. *See also*
    Relish(es); Sauce(s)
  apple(s)
    caramel, 153
    chutney, 61
    rings, grilled, 242
    spiced, 153
  baked bananas, 188
  cantaloupe grille, 150
  curried fruit, 156
  four-day watermelon pickles, 150
  pickled
    carrots, 151
    mushrooms, 152
Acorn squash
  halves, roasted, 137
  stuffed, 137
  with honey-chili sauce, 137
Alfresco apples, 152
Aloha
  baked pineapple, 189
  sauce, 155
Angel food, mock, 157
Angel's halos, 238
Appetizers, 114–119. *See also*
    Dip(s)
  cheese pastry squares, 115
  chicken bites, 119
  chips 'n beans, 179
  easy pizza, 116
  fruited salami kabobs, 116
  gazpacho, 114
  glazed pork tenderloin, 44
  guacamole, 182
  oysters rumaki, 186
  Paul Bunyan frank, 98
  pickled mushrooms, 152
  "rare 'n" to go steak, 115
  rumaki on the hibachi, 117
  sesame cheese squares, 202
  shrimp
    en brochette, 118
    Louisiana boiled, 118
    sesame platter, 202
  smoked. *See also* Smoke-flavored,
    appetizers
    cereal mix, 96
    trout, 96
  smoky snacks, 97
  surprise meatballs, 115
  sweetbread hors d'oeuvres, 117
  tenderloin Orientale, 95

Apple(s)
  alfresco, 152
  butter frosting, 162
  caramel, 153
  chutney, 61
  cranberry cooler, 122
  rings, grilled, 242
  spiced, 153
    marinade, 110
Apricot
  glazed lamb shoulder, 86
  jam cake, 160
Asparagus
  buttered, 183
  cold, 203
Au gratin potatoes, skillet, 229
Autumn supper en brochette, 72
Avocado
  guacamole, 182
  sauce, 65

Bacon. *See also* Canadian bacon
  corn bread, 232
Baked
  bananas, 188
  bean(s)
    cups, 206
    speedy, 129
  pheasant Bourguignon, 254
  pineapple, aloha, 189
  potatoes, hickory, 100
Banana(s)
  baked, 188
  boats, 235
  crunchy, 153
Barbecued. *See specific food*
Bar-b-q
  beef brisket, 180
  franks and kraut, 55
  sauce, 51
Bastes, 103–108. *See also* Sauce(s)
Bean(s)
  and egg salad, marinated, 144
  baked
    cups, 206
    speedy, 129
  bonanza, 145
  chips 'n, 179
  green
    Rio, 129
    with mushrooms and onions,
      129

Bean(s) (*cont.*)
  salad, creamy, 145
  soup, woodsman's, 245
Beef. *See also* Corned beef; Dried
      beef; Hamburger(s)
  brisket bar-b-q, 180
  chuck roast, barbecued, 39
  grilled, 36–40, 49–53, 180
  ground. *See also* Hamburger(s)
    burger dogs, 226
    calico combo, 225
    camporee cassoulet, 221
    dinner-in-a-can, 225
    pocket stew, 226
    "rare 'n" to go steak
        appetizers, 115
    surprise meatballs, 115
  kabobs, 73
  liver with snippets of green
      onion, 58
  marinades for
    California, 39
    herb, 109
    Riviera, 109
    soy-garlic, 111
    sweet 'n pungent, 108
    teriyaki sauce, 111
  on a skewer, 73
  roast
    chuck, barbecued, 39
    gourmet, 203
    rolled rib on the turnspit, 80
    rump, Californian, 79
    tenderloin, 37
  rotisserie-cooked, 80
  rump roast Californian, 79
  sauces for
    bar-b-q, 51
    blue cheese topping, 36
    easy horseradish, 80
    Laffite, steak with, 38
    New Orleans tomato, 104
    pantry-shelf barbecue, 103
    rancho-red, 104
    sesame butter, 36
    smoky, 105
    sparkle 'n spice barbecue, 105
    steak, Eastern style, 104
  short ribs, tangy, 81
  smoked, 97
  steak(s)
    Border style, 38
    charcoal-grilled, 36
    cube, grilled, 39
    London broil with onions, 40
    marinade (Riviera), 109
    minute, on onion rolls, 40
    startling, 37
    teriyaki, 187
    with sauce Laffite, 38
Beefburger specials, 49
Beefy scrambled eggs, 193

Beets, nippy, 130
Bermuda onions, roasted, 133
Berries 'n peaches, grilled, 154
Best tossed salad, 140
Beverages, 119–122
  blossom tea, 190
  citrus cider, 120
  coffee
    à la mode, 122
    duo, 210
  cranberry-apple cooler, 122
  frosty mocha, 122
  grape crush, 119
  iced lemonade tea, 201
  lemonade, 121
  limeade, 121
  melonade, 120
  minted lemonade, 121
  Persian tea punch, 121
  pink
    fruit punch, 121
    lemonade, 121
  sparkling
    orange juice, 194
    punch, 120
    tomato juice, 119
Biscuit(s). *See also* Bread(s)
  balls, surprise, 236
  blueberry-trail, 233
  bread, pan, 233
  drop, 232
  onion butter, 229
  skillet, 224
Blossom tea, 190
Blue cheese
  bread, 123
  topping, 36
Blueberry
  coffee cake
    camper's, 231
    orange, 193
  pancakes, 222
  pie, 164
  trail biscuits, 233
Blushing peach dessert, 154
Bologna
  barbecued, 92
  cuts, orange-glazed, 91
  Paul Bunyan frank, 98
Border-style steak, 38
Bourguignon, baked pheasant, 254
Branded slaw, 181
Bread(s), 123–128. *See also*
      Biscuit(s); Buns; Corn
      bread; Muffin Rolls
  blue cheese, 123
  butter spreads for, 124
  camp, 229–231, 232
  caraway-cheese twists, 126
  cheese
    loaf, 125
    twists, 126

crunchy French toast, 242
fluffy French toast, 196
French, 127
garlic croutons, 184
glaze, egg white, 127
hickory-cheese loaf, 128
hush puppies, 230
in foil, hot, 124
Indienne, hot, 125
Italian breadsticks, 126
pan biscuit, 233
Parmesan slices, 123
sourdough on the grill, 183
zebra, 231
cheese-filled, 231
Breadsticks, Italian, 126
Broiled lobster, 171
Browned butter frosting, 162
Brownie fudge cake, 159
Brussels sprouts salad, 141
Buns. *See also* Bread(s)
herbed, franks 'n, 55
smoked, 97
Burger(s). *See also* Hamburger(s)
Capri, 50
dogs, 226
smoke-flavored, 97
Butter(s)
frosting
apple, 162
browned, 162
pineapple, 163
lemon-parsley, 65
mallow cake, chocolate, 160
mushrooms in, 133
mustard, 65
onion, biscuits, 229
sesame, 36
spreads, for bread, 124
thyme, 177
Butterscotch filling, 161

Cabbage
Heidelberg dinner, 57
outdoor creamy, 131
slaws. *See* Slaw(s)
Caesar salad, 184
Cajun fried yams, 136
Cake(s). *See also* Coffee cake
apricot jam, 159
brownie fudge, 159
camp oven gingerbread, 232
chocolate butter-mallow, 160
Hawaiian date, 163
Johnny Appleseed, 162
lemon pound, 209
oatmeal spice, 206
peanut butter crumb, 158
toasted English trifles, 158
Calico combo, 225

California marinade, 39
Californian rump roast, 79
Camp oven gingerbread, 232
Camper's
blueberry coffee cake, 231
corn bread, 231
pizza, 228
Campfire
fondue, 236
snacks, 236-239
style canned vegetables, 229
Camporee cassoulet, 221
Can clambake, 175
Canadian bacon, grilled
and sausages, 222
slices, 194
Canned vegetables, campfire style,
229
Can-opener chicken cookout, 227
Cantaloupe grille, 150
Capri burgers, 50
Captain's chili, 211
Caraway-cheese twists, 126
Carmel shrimp, 69
Carrot(s)
herb-seasoned grilled, 130
pickled, 151
sticks
grilled sweet, 130
olives and radishes, 200
Catsup-curry marinade, 110
Cauliflowerets, tossed salad with,
140
Cereal mix, smoked, 96
Charcoal-grilled. *See specific food*
Cheese. *See also* Blue cheese;
Parmesan
filled zebra bread, 231
filling, peppy, 53
fondue, campfire, 236
grilled tomatoes, 138
herb butter spread, 124
loaf, 125
hickory, 128
'n fruit slaw, 143
pancakes, 223
pastry squares, 115
sesame squares, 202
surprise biscuit balls, 236
twists, 126
caraway, 126
Cheeseboats, 56
Cheeseburgers in foil, barbecued,
50
Cheesy pups, 227
Chef's
salad, 212
special sauce, 92, 196
Cherry(ies)
glazed ham, 213

Cherry(ies) (*cont.*)
  on the half-peach, 154
  orange sauce, 112
Chicken(s)
  and chutney apples, golden, 61
  barbecued, 60
  bites, 119
  Chinese smoked, 101
  cookout, can-opener, 227
  grilled, 59-60
  halves, charcoal-grilled, 59
  hickory smoked, 98
  island-in-the-sun, 60
  Italian, 62
  livers (rumaki on the hibachi),
    117
  marinades for
    catsup-curry, 110
    Oriental, 111
    soy-garlic, 111
    teriyaki sauce, 111
  Mexican, 59
  on the rotisserie, 87
  Parmesan fried, 199
  rotisserie-cooked, 87
  sauces for
    lemon, 107
    Parisian, 108
    sparkle 'n spice barbecue, 105
    tropical, 113
  smoked, 98, 101
  teriyaki, 61
  with pâté dressing, 87
Chili
  captain's, 211
  honey sauce, squash with, 137
  stuffing, 134
Chinese
  peas, 188
  smoked
    chicken, 101
    potatoes, 102
    ribs, 101
Chips 'n beans, 179
Chocolate. *See also* Cocoa
  butter-mallow cake, 160
  covered eggheads, 237
  dumplings, 234
  ice cream, 168
  sauce
    rhumba, 168
    rocky road, 168
    sugar balls, 239
Chops. *See* Lamb chops; Pork
    chops; Veal chops
Chuck roast, barbecued, 39
Chutney apples, 61
Cinnamon
  glazed ham, 45
  rolls, sweet, 233
  whipped cream, 152

Citrus cider, 120
Clam(s)
  and vegetables, steamed, 173
  chowder, Manhattan, 210
Clambakes, 173
Classic French dressing, 140
Cocoa. *See also* Chocolate
  coffee duo, 210
  sauce, 237
Coconut
  sweet potatoes with, 188
  topping, 206
Coffee
  à la mode, 122
  duo, 210
  frosty mocha, 122
Coffee cake
  blueberry-orange, 193
  camper's blueberry, 231
Coleslaw, 144. *See also* Slaw(s)
Coney Islands, 55
Corn
  bread
    bacon, 232
    camper's, 231
  full o' smoke ears, 100
  pancakes, 223
  relish, old-fashioned, 151
  roast(ed), 131, 177
  skewered lamb, tomatoes and,
    71
  squaw, 227
Corned beef
  potato skillet, 213
  saucy, with dilled potatoes, 223
  stir-up, 226
Cornish game hens, 89
Cosmopolitan lamb roast, 86
Country-style halibut fillets, 63
Cranberry-apple cooler, 122
Creamy
  bean salad, 145
  cabbage, outdoor, 131
  cucumber sauce, 113
Croutons, garlic, 184
Crunchy
  bananas, 153
  French toast, 242
Cube steaks, grilled, 39
Cucumber
  salad, 178
  sauce, creamy, 113
Curry(ied)
  catsup marinade, 110
  fruit, 156
  golden chicken and chutney
    apples, 61
  hot bread Indienne, 125
  lamb chops Bharati, 48
Custard sauce, 158

Date cake, Hawaiian, 163
Dessert(s), 152-168. *See also*
    Cake(s); Ice cream;
    Pie(s)
  angels' halos, 238
  apples
    alfresco, 152
    caramel, 153
    spiced, 153
  banana(s)
    baked, 188
    boats, 236
    crunchy, 153
  cantaloupe grille, 150
  cherries on the half-peach, 154
  chocolate
    covered eggheads, 237
    dumplings, 234
    sugar balls, 239
  doughnut sandwiches, 237
  eggheads, 237
  fruit. *See also specific fruits*
    compote in foil, 156
    compote, sparkling, 204
    dumplings, 244
    kabobs, 156
    platter, 209
    turnovers, 234
  gingerbread, camp oven, 232
  grapefruit, hot 'n sweet, 153
  magic mallow drops, 237
  melon cascade, 155
  mock angel food, 157
  oranges, sweet 'n spice grilled,
    240
  peach(es)
    blushing, 154
    cherries on the half, 154
    'n berries, grilled, 154
  pears
    Hélène, minted, 185
    Puerto Rican, 185
  pineapple
    aloha baked, 189
    island, 157
  sauce(s)
    aloha, 155
    cinnamon whipped cream, 152
    cocoa, 237
    custard, 158
    rhumba chocolate, 168
    rocky road chocolate, 168
  shaggy dogs, 238
  s'mores, 238
  strawberry shortcake, 178
    in foil, 195
  sugar
    balls, 239
    horns, 238
  toasted English trifles, 158
  watermelon supreme, 155

Deviled dip with vegetable relishes,
  145
Dilled potatoes, 224
Dinner-in-a-can, 225
Dip(s)
  avocado sauce, 65
  deviled, with vegetable relishes,
    145
  guacamole, 182
  sour cream, relish tray with, 201
Double-decker hamburgers, 53
Doughnut(s)
  angels' halos, 238
  eggheads, 237
  sandwiches, 237
Dried beef
  beefy scrambled eggs, 193
  macaroni mix-up, 213
Drop biscuits, 232
Duck, wild
  cerise, 255
  orange-braised, 256
  roast, 256
Duckling, savory, 90
Dumplings
  chocolate, 234
  fruit, 244

Easy
  horseradish sauce, 80
  pizza appetizers, 115
Egg(s)
  and marinated bean salad, 144
  in foil, 228
  scramble(d)
    beefy, 193
    potato, 228
    squaw corn, 227
    white glaze, 127
Eggheads, 237
Eggplant "combo," 132
English
  muffins, spicy, 123
  trifles, toasted, 158

Family-style potato salad, 148
Fiesta salad, 142
Filling(s). *See also* Stuffed;
    stuffing(s)
  butterscotch, 161
  for frankfurters, 54
  for hamburgers, 53
Fish. *See also specific fish or*
    seafood
  fillets, barbecued, 63
  fried, 243
  grilled, 63-70
  marinade (princess), 112
  sauces for
    avocado, 65
    creamy cucumber, 113

Fish (*cont.*)
  lemon, 107
    lemon-parsley butter, 65
    mustard butter, 65
  smoked, 96, 100
  steaks, 65
  stuffed whole, barbecued, 67
Flapjacks, raised, 194
Fluffy French toast, 196
Foil-grilled. *See specific food*
Fondue, campfire, 236
Four-day watermelon pickles, 150
Frank(s). *See also* Frankfurter(s)
  Paul Bunyan, 98
Frank-a-bobs, 73
Frankfurter(s), 54–56
  and kraut, bar-b-q, 55
  bastes for, 54
  burger dogs, 226
  cheeseboats, 56
  cheesy pups, 227
  Coney Islands, 55
  filled, 54
  kabobs, 73
  'n herbed buns, 55
  plum good, 56
  "sloppy," 211
  whirling, 91
French
  bread, 127
    sourdough on the grill, 183
  dressing, classic, 140
  rolls, 127
  toast
    crunchy, 242
    fluffy, 196
Fresh
  fruit salad, 146
  rhubarb pie, 166
  strawberry ice cream, 167
Fried
  chicken, Parmesan, 199
  fish, 243
  yams, Cajun, 136
'Frisco-style turkey roast, 88
Frosted mint sprigs, 190
Frosting(s)
  apple butter, 162
  browned butter, 162
  coconut topping, 206
  marshmallow, 161
  peanut butter topping, 158
  pineapple-butter, 163
  quick fudge icing, 159
Frosty mocha, 122
Frozen potato products, grilled, 136
Fruit. *See also specific fruits*
  compote
    in foil, 156
    sparkling, 204
  curried, 156

  dessert platter, 209
  dumplings, 244
  full spareribs, 82
  kabobs, 156
  'n cheese slaw, 143
  punch, pink, 121
  salad, fresh, 146
  turnovers, 234
Fruited salami kabobs, 116
Fudge
  cake, brownie, 159
  icing, quick, 159
Full o' smoke ears, 100

Game, 248–262. *See also specific type*
  duck, 255–256
  goose, 257–258
  pheasant, 254
  quail, 259
  rabbit, 262
  venison, 259–261
Game hens, 89
Garden vegetable stuffing, 67
Garlic
  butter spread, 124
  croutons, 184
  soy marinade, 111
Gazpacho, 114
German potato salad, grilled, 148
Gingerbread, camp oven, 232
Glacé goose, 257
Glaze. *See also* Glazed; Marinade(s); Sauce(s)
  egg white, for bread, 127
  rainbow, 106
Glazed. *See also* Glaze
  bologna cuts, orange, 91
  goose, glacé, 257
  ham
    cherry, 213
    cinnamon, 45
  lamb shoulder, apricot, 86
  luncheon meat grill, 58
  peach pie, honey, 163
  pork tenderloin, 44
Golden chicken and chutney apples, 61
Good 'n easy potato salad, 149
Goose, wild
  glacé, 257
  roast, 258
Gourmet
  beef roast, 203
  potato salad, 149
Grape crush, 119
Grapefruit, hot 'n sweet, 153
Green beans. *See* Bean(s), green
Grilled. *See specific food*
Guacamole, 182

Halibut
  fillets, country style, 63
  fish steaks, 65
Ham
  cherry-glazed, 213
  cinnamon-glazed, 45
  grilled, 45, 196
  Hawaiian, 45
  marinade (Oriental), 111
  on the spit, barbecued, 84
  pancakes, 223
  rotisserie-cooked, 84
  sandwich, mile-high, 205
  sauces for
    chef's special, 196
    cherry-orange, 112
    o' gold, 106
    orange, 106
    rancho-red, 104
    sugar-sweet basting, 107
  slice(s)
    Hawaiian, 45
    hearty, 196
    sugar-crusted, 46
  sugar crusted, 40
Hamburger(s), 49-53. *See also*
        Beef, ground
  beefburger specials, 49
  Capri burgers, 50
  cheeseburgers in foil, barbecued,
        50
  double-decker, 53
  fillings, 53
  sauces for
    bar-b-q, 51
    pantry-shelf barbecue, 103
    sparkle 'n spice barbecue, 105
  smoke flavored burgers, 97
  steaks
    grilled, 51
    Oriental, 51
  zesty, on rye, 52
Hawaiian
  date cake, 163
  ham, 45
Hearty ham slice, 196
Heidelberg dinner, 57
Herb(ed)
  buns, franks 'n, 55
  cheese butter spread, 124
  lemon butter spread, 124
  marinade, 109
  seasoned grilled carrots, 130
  slaw, 144
  zucchini, 139
Hickory. *See also* Smoke-flavored
  baked potatoes, 100
  cheese loaf, 128
  smoked chicken, 98
Homemade vanilla ice cream, 166

Honey
  chili sauce, squash with, 137
  glazed peach pie, 163
Hors d'oeuvres. *See* Appetizers
Horseradish sauce, easy, 80
Hush puppies, 230

Ice cream, 166
  coffee à la mode, 122
  frosty mocha, 122
  sauces, 168
  sundaes, waffle strawberry, 157
Iced lemonade tea, 201
Icing, quick fudge, 159
Internationale, shrimp, 68
Island
  dressing, 189
  in-the-sun chicken, 60
  pineapple, 93
Italian
  breadsticks, 126
  chicken, 62

Jam apricot cake, 159
Johnny Appleseed cake, 162

Kabobs, 70-74
  autumn supper en brochette, 72
  beef on a skewer, 73
  frank-a-bobs, 73
  fruit, 156
  fruited salami, 116
  lamb, 72
    skewered, tomatoes and corn,
        71
  pineapple-sausage, 195
  scallop, 74
  shrimp en brochette, 118
King Arthur lamb shanks, 49

Lamb
  chops
    Bharati, 48
    grilled, 47
  grilled, 47-48, 183
  kabobs, 71, 72
  leg
    barbecue, 48
    grilled stuffed, 183
    minted, 99
    roast cosmopolitan, 86
  marinades for
    catsup-curry, 110
    tomato-soy, 112
  roast cosmopolitan, 86
  rotisserie-cooked, 86-87
  sauces for
    New Orleans tomato, 104
    o' gold, 106
    orange, 106
    mint, 113

Lamb (*cont.*)
    rainbow glaze, 106
    rancho-red, 104
    shanks, King Arthur, 49
    shish kabobs, 72
    shoulder
        apricot-glazed, 86
        rolled stuffed, 85
    skewered, tomatoes and corn, 71
    smoked, 99
Lemon
    herb butter spread, 124
    parsley butter, 65
    pound cake, 209
    sauce, 107
    tart potatoes, 135
Lemonade, 121
    minted, 121
    pink, 121
    tea, iced, 201
Limeade, 121
    dressing, 146
Limed veal roast, 84
Liver(s)
    chicken (rumaki on the
            hibachi), 117
    with snippets of green onion, 58
Lobster
    broiled, 171
    sauce (creamy cucumber), 113
    tails on the grill, 69
London broil with onions, 40
Louisiana boiled shrimp, 118
Luncheon meat grill, glazed, 58

Macaroni
    corned beef stir-up, 226
    dried beef mix-up, 213
    salad, summer, 147
Magic mallow drops, 237
Main-dish shortcakes, 233
Manhattan clam chowder, 210
Marinade(s), 108–112. See also
            specific food; Sauce(s)
    California, 39
    catsup-curry, 110
    herb, 109
    Oriental, 111
    princess, 112
    Riviera, 109
    soy-garlic, 111
    spiced apple, 110
    sweet 'n pungent, 108
    teriyaki sauce, 111
    tomato-soy, 112
Marinated
    bean and egg salad, 143
    olives and tomatoes, 203
Marshmallow(s)
    angels' halos, 238
    frosting, 161

magic mallow drops, 237
    shaggy dogs, 238
    s'mores, 238
Meat(s). See also *specific type*
    turnovers, 233
Meatballs, surprise, 115
Mediterranean salad, 141
Melon cascade, 155
Melonade, 120
Meloned franks, 54
Mexican chicken, 59
Mile-high ham sandwich, 205
Mint(ed)
    leg of lamb, 99
    lemonade, 121
    orange sauce, 113
    pears Hélène, 185
    sprigs, frosted, 190
Minute steaks on onion rolls, 40
Mix-and-match fillings for
            hamburgers, 53
Mocha, frosty, 122
Mock
    angel food, 157
    slaw, 143
Monterey broiled swordfish, 64
Muffins. See also Bread(s)
    en brochette, 124
    spicy English, 123
Mushroom(s)
    green beans with onions and, 128
    in butter, 133
    Lyonnaise, 132
    'n franks, 54
    pickled, 152
Mustard butter, 65

New Orleans tomato sauce, 104
Nippy beets, 130
Nut brittle ice cream, 168

Oatmeal spice cake, 206
Old-fashioned corn relish, 151
Olives
    and tomatoes, marinated, 203
    radishes and carrot sticks, 206
Onion(s)
    and potatoes, roast, 136
    butter, 124
        biscuits, 229
    filling, 53
    green beans with mushrooms
            and, 128
    London broil with, 40
    'n franks, 54
    rings, hot, 244
    roasted, 133
    rolls, minute steaks on, 40
Orange(s)
    blueberry coffee cake, 193
    braised duck, 256

glazed bologna cuts, 91
juice, sparkling, 194
quail à l'orange, 259
sauce, 106
　cherry, 112
　mint, 113
　roast pork with, 83
sweet 'n spice, grilled, 246
Oriental
franks, 54
hamburger steaks, 51
marinade, 111
Outdoor
creamy cabbage, 131
pilaf, 138
Oysters rumaki, 186

Pan biscuit bread, 233
Pancakes, 222
raised flapjacks, 194
Pantry-shelf barbecue sauce, 103
Parisian sauce, 108
Parmesan
fried chicken, 199
olives, 183
Parsley-lemon butter, 65
Party pheasant, 254
Pastry. See also Dessert(s);
　　　　Pie(s); Turnovers
for pies, 165
squares, cheese, 115
Paul Bunyan frank, 98
Peach(es)
cherries on the half, 154
dessert, blushing, 154
'n berries, grilled, 154
pie, honey-glazed, 163
Peanut butter
crumb cake, 158
topping, 158
Peanutty pork chops, 41
Pears
Hélène, minted, 185
Puerto Rican, 185
Peas
almondine in foil, 134
Chinese, 188
Peppermint ice cream, 167
Peppers, foil-grilled, 134
Peppy cheese filling, 53
Persian tea punch, 121
Pheasant
Bourguignon, baked, 254
en crème, 254
party, 254
Pickled
carrots, 151
mushrooms, 152
Pickles
four-day watermelon, 150
'n franks, 54

Pie(s)
blueberry, 164
fresh rhubarb, 166
honey-glazed peach, 164
pastry for, 165
"Pig" roast on the turnspit, 187
Pike
fish fillets, barbecued, 63
in a package, 253
stuffed whole fish, barbecued, 67
Pilaf, outdoor, 138
Pineapple
aloha baked, 189
butter frosting, 163
island, 157
sausage kabobs, 195
tropical spears, 190
Pink
fruit punch, 121
lemonade, 121
Pizza
appetizers, easy, 110
camper's, 228
Plum good franks, 56
Pocket stew, 220
Polynesian veal cutlets, 47
Pork. See also Ham
chops
　grilled, 41
　peanutty, 41
grilled, 41-46
marinades for
　catsup-curry, 110
　Oriental, 111
　soy-garlic, 111
　spiced apple, 110
　sweet 'n pungent, 108
　teriyaki sauce, 111
ribs, split-barbecued, 81
roast
　"pig" on the turnspit, 187
　with orange sauce, 83
rotisserie-cooked, 81-84, 187
sauces for
　cherry-orange, 112
　New Orleans tomato, 104
　o' gold, 106
　orange
　　mint, 113
　　roast pork with, 83
　rainbow glaze, 106
　rancho-red, 104
　spunky spice, 43
　sugar-sweet basting, 107
　sweet and sour, 42
　Texas barbecue, 43
shoulder slices, spunky, 43
smoked, 99, 101, 180
spareribs
　barbecued, 42
　Chinese smoked, 101

Pork (*cont.*)
  fruit-full, 82
  smokehouse, 180
  tenderloin
    charcoal-grilled, 44
    glazed, 44
    Orientale, 95
  teriyaki, 44
Potato(es)
  au gratin, skillet, 229
  Chinese smoked, 102
  corned beef skillet, 213
  dilled, with saucy corned beef,
    223
  egg scramble, 228
  hickory baked, 100
  lemon-tart, 135
  products, grilled frozen, 136
  roast(ed), 135, 177
    and onions, 136
  salad
    à la Russe, 149
    family-style, 148
    good 'n easy, 149
    gourmet, 149
    grilled German, 148
    in tomato cups, 200
    ranch-style, 147
  scalloped, skillet, 229
  shoestring, hot, 244
  sweet, with coconut, 188
  yams, Cajun fried, 136
  zesty grilled, 135
Poultry. *See specific type*
Pound cake, lemon, 209
Princess marinade, 112
Puerto Rican pears, 185
Puget Sound smoked salmon, 100
Punch
  Persian tea, 121
  pink fruit, 121
  sparkling, 120

Quail à l'orange, 259
Quick fudge icing, 159

Rabbit à la Maryland, 262
Radishes, olives and carrot sticks,
  206
Rainbow
  glaze, 106
  trout with crabmeat stuffing, 253
Raised flapjacks, 194
Rancho-red sauce, 104
Ranch-style potato salad, 147
"Rare 'n" to go steak appetizers,
  115
Relish(es), 150. *See also* Accom-
    paniments for meat

corn, old-fashioned, 151
marinated olives and tomatoes,
  203
olives, radishes and carrot sticks,
  206
tray with sour cream dip, 201
vegetable, with deviled dip, 145
Rhubarb pie, fresh, 166
Rhumba chocolate sauce, 168
Rice (outdoor pilaf), 138
Riviera marinade, 109
Roast(ed). *See specific food*
Rocky road chocolate sauce, 168
Rolled stuffed lamb shoulder, 85
Rolls. *See also* Bread(s)
  French, 127
  onion, minute steaks on, 40
  sweet cinnamon, 233
Roman zucchini, 139
Romanoff, tuna noodles, 212
Rotisserie-cooked. *See specific food*
Rumaki
  on the hibachi, 117
  oysters, 186
Rump roast Californian, 79

Salad(s), 140-150. *See also*
    Slaw(s)
  bean
    bonanza, 145
    creamy, 145
    marinated, and egg, 143
  Brussels sprouts, 141
  Caesar, 184
  chef's, 212
  cucumber, 178
  fiesta, 142
  fruit
    fresh, 146
    'n cheese slaw, 143
  gazpacho, 114
  macaroni, summer, 147
  Mediterranean, 141
  potato. *See* Potato salad
  sensational, 142
  Tahitian, 189
  tomatoes vinaigrette, 146
  tossed
    best, 140
    with cauliflowerets, 140
    zucchini, 143
Salad dressings
  classic French, 140
  island, 189
  limeade, 146
Salami kabobs, fruited, 116
Salmon
  fish steaks, 65
  smoked, Puget Sound, 100
  stuffed whole fish, barbecued, 67

Sandwich(es)
  doughnut, 237
  mile-high ham, 205
Sauce(s). *See also specific food;*
       Dessert(s), sauce(s);
       Marinade(s)
  avocado, 65
  bar-b-q, 51
  blue cheese topping, 36
  chef's special, 92, 196
  cherry-orange, 112
  creamy cucumber, 113
  easy horseradish, 80
  Laffite, steak with, 38
  lemon, 107
    parsley butter, 65
  mustard butter, 65
  New Orleans tomato, 104
  o' gold, 106
  orange, 106
    mint, 113
    roast pork with, 83
  pantry-shelf barbecue, 103
  Parisian, 108
  rainbow glaze, 106
  rancho-red, 104
  sesame butter, 36
  smoky, 105
  sparkle 'n spice barbecue, 105
  spunky spice, 43
  steak, Eastern style, 104
  sugar-sweet, 51, 107
  sweet and sour, 42
  teriyaki, 111
  Texas barbecue, 43
  thyme butter, 177
  tropical, 113
  Waikiki baste, 54
Saucy corned beef with dilled
    potatoes, 223
Sauerbraten, venison, 261
Sauerkraut
  bar-b-q franks and, 55
  mock slaw, 143
Sausage(s)
  and Canadian bacon, grilled, 222
  Heidelberg dinner, 57
  pineapple kabobs, 195
Savory duckling, 90
Scallop kabobs, 74
Scalloped potatoes, skillet, 229
Scallopini, venison, 260
Seeded butter spread, 124
Sesame
  butter, 36
  cheese squares, 202
  shrimp platter, 202
Shaggy dogs, 238
Shellfish. *See specific type*
Shish kabob. *See* Kabobs
Shoestring potatoes, hot, 244

Short ribs, tangy, 81
Shortcake(s)
  main-dish, 233
  strawberry, 178
  in foil, 195
Shrimp
  Carmel, 69
  en brochette, 118
  fillet of sole en papillote, 66
  internationale, 68
  Louisiana boiled, 118
  sauce (creamy cucumber), 113
  sesame platter, 202
Skewered lamb, tomatoes and
    corn, 71
Skillet
  biscuits, 224
  scalloped or au gratin potatoes,
    229
Slaw(s)
  branded, 181
  co'eslaw, 144
  fruit 'n cheese, 143
  herbed, 144
  mock, 143
"Sloppy" franks, 211
Smoke-flavored
  appetizers
    cereal mix, 96
    cheese pastry squares, 115
    Paul Bunyan frank, 98
    snacks, 97
    tenderloin Orientale, 95
    trout, 96
  beef
    burgers, 97
    steak with sauce Laffite, 38
  breads
    buns, 97
    hickory-cheese loaf, 128
  chicken
    Chinese smoked, 101
    hickory smoked, 98
  corn (full o' smoke ears), 100
  fish
    salmon, Puget Sound, 100
    trout appetizers, 96
  frank(s)
    cheeseboats, 56
    Paul Bunyan, 98
    "sloppy," 211
  lamb, minted leg of, 99
  pork
    Chinese smoked ribs, 101
    smokehouse spareribs, 180
    tenderloin Orientale, 95
  potatoes
    Chinese smoked, 102
    hickory baked, 100
  sauce, 105
Smokehouse spareribs, 180

Smoky
  sauce, 105
  snacks, 97
S'mores, 238
Snacks
  campfire, 236-239
  smoky, 97
Sole, fillet of, en papillote, 66
Soup(s)
  gazpacho, 114
  Manhattan clam chowder, 210
  woodsman's bean, 245
Sour cream dip, relish tray with, 201
Sourdough on the grill, 183
Soy
  garlic marinade, 111
  tomato marinade, 112
Sparkle 'n spice barbecue sauce, 105
Sparkling
  fruit compote, 204
  orange juice, 194
  punch, 120
  tomato juice, 119
Speedy baked beans, 129
Spice sauce, spunky, 43
Spiced apple(s), 153
  marinade, 110
Spicy English muffins, 123
Spit-barbecued ribs, 81
Spit-cooked. *See specific food*
Spunky shoulder slices, 43
Squash. *See* Acorn squash
Squaw corn, 227
Startling steak, 37
Steak. *See* Beef; Fish; Veal
Steamed clams and vegetables, 173
Stew, pocket, 226
Strawberry
  ice cream, 167
  shortcake, 178
    in foil, 195
  sundaes, waffle, 157
Streusel mixture, 193
Stroganoff, venison, 259
Stuffed. *See also* Stuffing(s)
  acorn squash, 137
  goose, wild
    glacé, 257
    roast, 258
  lamb
    leg, grilled, 183
    shoulder, rolled, 85
  peppers, foil-grilled, 134
  pork chops, peanutty, 41
  veal cutlets, Polynesian, 47
  whole fish, barbecued, 67
Stuffing(s). *See also* Stuffed
  chili, 134

crabmeat, rainbow trout with, 253
  garden vegetable, 67
  pâté dressing, chicken with, 87
  whitefish with, 64
Sugar
  balls, 239
    chocolate, 239
  crusted ham, 46
  horns, 238
  sweet
    baste, 54
    basting sauce, 107
Summer macaroni salad, 147
Sundaes, waffle strawberry, 157
Surprise
  biscuit balls, 236
  meatballs, 115
Sweet
  and sour sauce, 42
  carrot sticks, grilled, 130
  cinnamon rolls, 233
  'n hot grapefruit, 153
  'n pungent marinade, 108
  'n spice oranges, grilled, 246
  potatoes with coconut, 188
Sweetbread hors d'oeuvres, 117
Swordfish
  fish steaks, 65
  Monterey broiled, 64

Tahitian
  franks, 54
  salad, 189
Tangy short ribs, 81
Tarragon butter spread, 124
Tea
  blossom, 190
  iced lemonade, 201
  punch, Persian, 121
Tenderloin
  beef roast, 37
  pork
    charcoal-grilled, 44
    glazed, 44
    Orientale, 95
Teriyaki
  chicken, 61
  pork, 44
  sauce, 111
  steak, 187
Texas barbecue sauce, 43
Thyme butter, 177
Toasted English trifles, 158
Tomato(es)
  and olives, marinated, 203
  cups, potato salad in, 200
  grilled, 177
    cheese, 138
  juice, sparkling, 119

salad(s)
  fiesta, 142
  Mediterranean, 141
  vinaigrette, 146
  sauce, New Orleans, 104
  skewered lamb, corn and, 71
  soy marinade, 112
  vinaigrette, 146
Toppings. *See* Frosting(s);
    Sauce(s)
Tossed salads. *See* Salad(s),
    tossed
Trifles, toasted English, 158
Tropical
  sauce, 113
  spears, 190
Trout
  appetizers, smoked, 96
  fish fillets, barbecued, 63
  fried fish, 243
  rainbow, with crabmeat stuffing,
    253
  stuffed whole fish, barbecued, 67
Tuna
  fish steaks, 65
  noodles Romanoff, 212
  stuffed whole fish, barbecued, 67
Turkey
  dinner, barbecued, 176
  roast, 'Frisco style, 88
  turnabout, 88
Turnabout turkey, 88
Turnovers
  fruit, 234
  meat, 233

Vanilla ice cream, homemade, 166
Veal
  autumn supper en brochette, 72
  chops, grilled, 46

  cutlets, Polynesian, 47
  roast, limed, 84
  steaks, grilled, 46
Vegetable(s), 128-139. *See also*
    specific vegetables
  and clams, steamed, 173
  canned, campfire style, 229
  relishes, deviled dip with, 145
  stuffing, garden, 67
Venison
  sauerbraten, 261
  scallopini, 260
  Stroganoff, 259
Vinaigrette, tomatoes, 146

Waffle strawberry sundaes, 157
Waikiki baste, 54
Watermelon
  melonade, 120
  pickles, four-day, 150
  supreme, 155
Whipped cream, cinnamon, 152
Whirling franks, 91
Whitefish with stuffing, 61
Wintergreen ice cream, 167
Woodsman's bean soup, 245

Yams, Cajun fried, 136

Zebra bread, 231
  cheese-filled, 231
Zesty
  grilled potatoes, 135
  hamburgers on rye, 52
Zucchini
  foil-grilled, 139
  herbed, 139
  Roman, 139
  tossed salad, 143

KITCHEN POWER!

- [ ] PUTTING FOOD BY—Hertzberg, Vaughan & Green   2030 • $2.50
- [ ] BETTER HOMES & GARDENS HOME CANNING COOKBOOK 2150 • $1.50
- [ ] AMERICAN HERITAGE COOKBOOK   2220 • $1.95
- [ ] THE ART OF FRENCH COOKING—Fernande Garvin   2285 • $1.25
- [ ] CROCKERY COOKERY—Mable Hoffman   2400 • $1.95
- [ ] AMERICA'S FAVORITE RECIPES FROM
  BETTER HOMES & GARDENS   6368 • $1.25
- [ ] ORIENTAL COOKING—Myra Waldo   8482 • $1.25
- [ ] THE ART OF JEWISH COOKING—Jennie Grossinger   7033 • $1.25
- [ ] COMPLETE BOOK OF WINE COOKERY—Waldo   7080 • $1.25
- [ ] THE GRAHAM KERR COOKBOOK—Galloping Gourmet   7424 • $1.95
- [ ] BETTER HOMES & GARDENS CASSEROLE COOKBOOK   7854 • $1.25
- [ ] FANNIE FARMER BOSTON COOKING SCHOOL COOKBOOK
  —Wilma Perkins   7934 • $1.95
- [ ] BETTY CROCKER'S DO AHEAD COOKBOOK   7944 • $1.25
- [ ] THE COMPLETE BOOK OF PASTA—Jack Denton Scott   8064 • $1.25
- [ ] BETTY CROCKER'S COOKBOOK   8108 • $1.95
- [ ] THE ART OF ITALIAN COOKING—Mario LoPinto   8298 • $1.25
- [ ] MADAME WU'S ART OF CHINESE COOKING   8642 • $1.50

Buy them wherever Bantam Bestsellers are sold or use this handy coupon:

How's Your Health?

Bantam publishes a line of informative books, written by top experts to help you toward a healthier and happier life.

☐	FASTING: The Ultimate Diet, Cott, M.D.	2111	$1.75
☐	A DICTIONARY OF SYMPTOMS, Gomez	5754	$1.95
☐	THE BRAND NAME NUTRITION COUNTER, Carper	6417	$1.95
☐	HONEY AND YOUR HEALTH, Bodog Beck and Doree Smedley	6522	95¢
☐	WEIGHT CONTROL THROUGH YOGA, Richard Hittleman	6864	$1.25
☐	THE DOCTOR'S QUICK WEIGHT LOSS DIET COOKBOOK, Stillman, M.D. and Baker	7381	$1.50
☐	WHOLE EARTH COOKBOOK, Cadwallader and Ohr	7555	$1.50
☐	SWEET AND DANGEROUS, John Yudkin, M.D.	7602	$1.95
☐	NUTRITION AGAINST DISEASE, Roger J. Williams	7709	$1.95
☐	DR. ATKINS DIET REVOLUTION, Robert Atkins, M.D.	7731	$1.95
☐	THE FAMILY GUIDE TO BETTER FOOD AND BETTER HEALTH, Ron Deutsch	7750	$1.95
☐	NUTRITION AND YOUR MIND, George Watson	7793	$1.95
☐	THE NEW AEROBICS, Kenneth Cooper, M.D.	7907	$1.75
☐	THE ALL-IN-ONE CALORIE COUNTER, Jean Carper	8313	$1.50
☐	THE ALL-IN-ONE CARBOHYDRATE GRAM COUNTER, Jean Carper	8314	$1.50
☐	THE PRUDENT DIET, Bennett & Simon	8328	$1.95
☐	WHICH VITAMINS DO YOU NEED? Martin Ebon	8371	$1.50

Buy them at your local bookstore or use this handy coupon for ordering:

Facts at Your Fingertips!

- ☐ THE BANTAM BOOK OF CORRECT LETTER WRITING — 8852 — $1.50
- ☐ AMY VANDERBILT'S EVERYDAY ETIQUETTE — 8092 — $1.95
- ☐ DICTIONARY OF CLASSICAL MYTHOLOGY — 8004 — $1.25
- ☐ HOUSE PLANTS — 7994 — $1.95
- ☐ SOULE'S DICTIONARY OF ENGLISH SYNONYMS — 7883 — $1.25
- ☐ IT PAYS TO INCREASE YOUR WORD POWER — 6856 — $1.25
- ☐ THE BETTER HOMES AND GARDENS HANDYMAN BOOK — 4613 — $1.25
- ☐ THE MOTHER EARTH NEWS ALMANAC — 2927 — $2.25
- ☐ THE BANTAM NEW COLLEGE FRENCH & ENGLISH DICTIONARY — 2704 — $1.50
- ☐ THE GUINNESS BOOK OF WORLD RECORDS — 2777 — $1.95
- ☐ THE BANTAM NEW COLLEGE SPANISH & ENGLISH DICTIONARY — 2751 — $1.50
- ☐ THE COMMON SENSE BOOK OF PUPPY AND DOG CARE — 2658 — $1.50
- ☐ THE COMMON SENSE BOOK OF KITTEN AND CAT CARE — 2659 — $1.50

Ask for them at your local bookseller or use this handy coupon:

Bantam Books, Inc., Dept. RB, 414 East Golf Road, Des Plaines, Ill. 60016

Please send me the books I have checked above. I am enclosing $_____
(please add 35¢ to cover postage and handling). Send check or money order
—no cash or C.O.D.'s please.

Mr/Mrs/Miss_____

Address_____

City_____State/Zip_____

RB—6/76

Please allow three weeks for delivery. This offer expires 6/77.

Bantam Book Catalog

It lists over a thousand money-saving bestsellers originally priced from $3.75 to $15.00 —bestsellers that are yours now for as little as 50¢ to $2.95!

The catalog gives you **a great** opportunity to build your own private library at huge savings!

So don't delay any longer—send us your name and address and 25¢ (to help defray postage and handling costs).